Decade of Iron

By

Richard L. Cañas

The Prequel to *Jaguars-A Tale of El Salvador*

ISBN: 1-4140-1281-0 (e-book)
ISBN: 1-4140-1282-9 (Paperback)

Library of Congress Control Number 2003097516

This book is printed on acid free paper.

Printed in the United States of America
Bloomington, IN

1stBooks — rev. 10/07/03

For my children, my grandchildren, and theirs…

Acknowledgements

First of all, a "tip of the hat" to all the intrepid folks who struggled through the early versions, and continued to encourage me with their suggestions and support.

Then, special recognition is bestowed on the following people for "above and beyond" contributions:
Elaine for the endless devotion, and understanding
David for the "ambassadorial" and gracious reaction
Max for the masterful tutorial and collegial reception
Marian for the provocative candor and encouragement
Edd for the patronage and invaluable memories

And finally, the inspiration awards go to:
Joey, Doug, Chepe, Ricardo, and the many "Hugcs" and "Andersons," past and present, for their rousing example of how to live a full life and passionately love a country.

A Timeless Village

Silently, the children lead the procession down the hot dusty road, each holding a small spray of white flowers in prayerfully clasped hands. In front, six barefoot girls in hand-me-down communion dresses carry a small wooden coffin painted chalk white, its lid adorned with paper flora and long ribbons that serpentine in the light breeze. The streamers are blue and white, the national colors; the flowers are pink, the universal blush of little girls.

Just behind them, a shoeless boy dressed in undersized pants and shirt proudly carries a wooden cross high above his head. His round face and protruding belly are brown, his coarse hair and squinting eyes the color of almonds.

Next to him walks a gaunt young man, his face scored by the sun. In one hand he confidently clutches a shovel, with the other, gracelessly fidgets with a straw hat.

Following close are several darkly clad women comforting one in particular, and two older men, each with colorful bandanas slung over their shoulders, the ends tied in a knot at their chests. Another man carries a maraca and wears a headpiece with small antlers and feathers. There is also an old gray-haired man with a brown and black serape draped ceremoniously over one shoulder. Other villagers, dressed in an array of colorful westernized clothing, trail loosely behind in groups of twos and threes.

Later, as the casket is laid to rest in its shallow grave, the children sing songs, then line up in single file to throw small gifts and flowers into their friend's grave. Then they gather behind the adult mourners, where the more mischievous begin teasing the others, and very shortly all join in as if on holiday. The adults eventually break up into groups, men with men, women with women and, like the children, the men put aside their sullen purpose and begin to good-humoredly socialize.

In due course, the day's revered event will merge naturally into the daily life of the village. For it is their shared belief that passage into the spirit world is indiscriminant and thus preordained by their benevolent spirit gods.

Prologue

I remember the exact moment I told him. It was Wednesday, the 6th of June 1945, and all the wars of the world were winding down. I even remember that the day was sunny and cold, as days often are in the "land of eternal spring." We were among the morass of well-wishers at the Guatemalan International airport and, as we embraced, the possibility of never seeing him again caused me to blubber like a child and frantically search for some meaningful and lasting words. After all, Ricardo was my best friend and had been all my life. We favored the same virtues and vices, traveled the same paths, shared the same secrets…in short, we had been inseparable. And now, he was leaving. So I had dramatically disclosed my enterprise as though it was an exclamation point to an argument.

I remember how inappropriate it had seemed afterwards. I had not planned to tell him; it just came out. But then, he probably did not understand what I was saying anyway. Emotions are always distracting and more moving than words during times of sorrow. But the moment stayed with me because I knew it had been out of place. After all we had been through, it was trite to mention that I was going to write about these times and the reasons for his joining the subversive underground one long year before. I know now that I was saying it more for myself, because I had felt helpless to say or do more.

I had been against the rebellion right from the start. The political situation in our country had been quite tenuous for some time and, while I agreed with the need for a change of government, my zeal on the subject was tempered. No respectable Salvadoran cared for President Martínez' tyrannical practices, but he *had* maintained social order, something that was important to my family. The Molinas have always been coffee growers; in fact, we still own several plantations. And we were survivors of the communist-led peasant uprisings in '32, and were still apprehensive that such a devastating event could repeat itself.

In this regard, my background was different than Ricardo's. He was a self-made man, full of life and bravado, and with less reason to restrain his outrage. His passion ran deep, deeper than I imagined, and for reasons about which I would only learn later.

In fact, it was right after I learned about the extent of his anti-government involvement, while desperately searching for explanations for his folly, that I also discovered how isolated and callous I had become about social issues. Then I began seeing many of my compatriots flee the country from fear or in protest of the merciless violence. So I thought writing about this period was something I could do, maybe the only thing, because I am not political by nature and would never do anything to jeopardize my family. I was not prepared to follow in Ricardo's footsteps or join those who are still engaged in the so-called "struggle for justice." As much as I cherish Ricardo's friendship, I love my Cora and our children and this land more.

Oh, I know he loved these things too, as much as I; and I do not mean to imply otherwise. His family and this country will always remain the center of his life—they make up the qualities that help define who we are. That is why I know how much he is suffering. You cannot transplant a family without stressing them to their limits any more than you can uproot and replant a mature tree. I am a psychiatrist, and about these things I know.

And I also know the questions his children will have. Without strong social roots, how will he and they successfully deal with transference and guilt and feelings of inferiority? I know how he plans to do it: he will smother them with love and attention of inordinate intensity, a variety which only someone who was orphaned as a small child and raised by perceptive and kind relatives can bestow. And that is fine. But without the extended family and the comfort of cultural traditions and significant and meaningful frames of reference, it will not be enough, and this will kill him more surely than if he had stayed and faced that firing squad.

After all, I am talking about someone who, until now, had effectively met every challenge he faced. He lived the most successful thirty years of life of anyone I know. Everyone admired and loved him. He was our hope, our *Ubermensch*, who rarely suppressed a passion. You do not abandon the expectations of such success without consequence. As it is, immigrants always travel with a backseat companion—denial. So, when the time comes, who will tell the children? My fear is that it will not be he.

All these thoughts came to me during that gut-wrenching moment at the airport. As I say, I do not know if it registered with him, but I did promise to write it, and you do not break a promise to someone you love.

I must tell you, in all modesty, that at the time Ricardo boarded that plane, I had managed to accumulate considerable data on the subject, more than I would have expected. And later, after Ricardo left for the United States, I received even more facts from many surprising sources. Frankly, I had not counted on so much information, and this begged for organization. While I am an avid reader, I am only an amateur writer. But I am fastidious about tidiness and I share Flaubert's condemnation of improvisation. So I decided to begin by spreading out my nuggets of anecdotes, memories, and historical facts on a desk in a room that I set aside at my office. After all, writing is anti-family, and the clinic afforded more privacy and discretion, commodities in short supply during these disorderly times. Having fashioned a system, I proceeded to put pen to paper.

My first decision was where to start the story—at what point? I must have stared at the pile of notes for days until I finally chose to begin with an event that directly led to the exposure of my friend, Ricardo Cruz. Some might argue that starting at this point is really starting in the middle, and they would be technically correct. But I was heavily influenced by the fact that I knew this part best. Preceding and subsequent events, during what has come to be called the "decade of iron," would have to fill in as I went along. So I chose to begin with a pivotal event that occurred on the east coast of El Salvador about a year ago.

In case you do not know much about my small country, I should tell you that it is located in Central America, northwest of the relatively larger countries of Honduras and Nicaragua. The "colossus" directly to our north is the country of Guatemala. As a point of reference, the colossus to Guatemala's north is Mexico, and the colossus north of Mexico is, of course, the United States of North America. Most of our people are descendants of the *Pipil* Indians, the agricultural cousins of the mighty Mayans, who inhabited the region some 500 years ago. The Spanish conquered us, as they did most regions of what is now called Latin America, although their only remaining trace is our national language, Spanish, and our national religion, Catholicism. Oh, and the Jesuits are still here, too. Our country is congested, but we are a hardworking and genial people, more so than in any other country in this hemisphere. The southern length of our country borders the Pacific Ocean—over 300 kilometers of beautiful beaches separated by several ports. If this description suggests to you that I am overly proud of this special land, you are right.

It was just north of the port city of La Libertad, outside a small town called Usulután, that the noteworthy event took place. Ricardo always believed that it was this episode that led directly to his downfall. I tend to disagree with his assessment. Not that it much matters, because I believe his fate was unwittingly sealed much earlier—the night he met Hugo. I will have more to say about that later, but for now, Usulután is a good place to start.

Chapter 1

El Salvador—February 2, 1944

It was a small garrison, known militarily as El Zapatillo, and located on the outskirts of Usulután, a town between the coastal villages of Puerto El Triunfo and El Cuco. Its barracks housed several companies of soldiers, although most of them were usually detailed to smaller outposts in nearby towns such as San Miguel and El Carmen. One full company, however, always remained at post. Their presence was necessary because the garrison was also home to a secret store of arms.

The munitions were strategically stockpiled for use by the larger fort at La Unión, which protected the Salvadoran coast along the contentious Golfo de Fonseca. By 1944, the perceived threat by the Salvadoran government was not so much Axis spies or marauders, as was feared by our American allies, but incursions and violations of fishing rights and legitimate trade by Honduras and Nicaragua, which also bordered and shared the Gulf. Such violations were not uncommon.

The entrance to El Zapatillo was by way of a dirt road a half-kilometer from the main coastal highway. A small wooden barricade blocked access to the road, and an armed soldier manned it 24 hours a day. Another guard post was located further down that road just outside the large wooden gates, which were the main entrance to the garrison.

The compound area took up about four hectares, and was encircled by barbed wire fencing strung on crude tree posts spaced about five meters apart. Four equidistantly placed towers guarded this perimeter. The towers, about 10 meters tall, were seldom manned; that is, except for the one on the east end near an earthen mound that camouflaged the underground arsenal. Two small cabins there were used as shelters for relief guards. In the center of the garrison, between the armory and the 12 Quonset huts used as barracks, was a large level field almost 200 meters long and almost as wide. This area was used as a parade ground for training and other exercises. Next to the barracks was a smaller building used as the officers' quarters. Two staff vehicles, a two-ton truck and a sedan, were assigned to the garrison and were parked alongside these structures.

The base commander was Captain Agustin Menin, a young officer and native of Sonsonate. This was his second posting since graduating from the military academy four years before. The sub-commander was Lieutenant Franco Eban, originally from San Vicente and on his first assignment. Both had been stationed at the garrison for six months.

The novelty of having a base so close to Usulután had, by now, worn off the townspeople. It had been constructed three years before, right after the Americans entered the war. That government had subsidized the project, which had been part of their strategic plan to increase vigilance along the entire coast of the Americas. Clearing away the heavy tropical vegetation for construction had employed many workers from the neighboring villages, even from our *finca* in Zacatecoluca. But over the years, the need for their services had decreased. Now, villagers paid little attention to the small fortification because, except for the comings and goings of relief personnel, the camp was self-contained and did not affect them one way or the other.

It was just past 3 A.M. when the dark gray oil truck left Usulután and sped down the desolate road. The driver and passenger, both wearing Army fatigues, knew that it was crucial that they be at the garrison gate at exactly 3:15 A.M. Within five minutes, they turned onto the path leading to El Zapatillo and immediately encountered the first sentinel at the small guardhouse.

The guard had been forewarned by the approaching headlights and was outside the shack in front of the barrier, his rifle at port arms. The truck stopped and the driver got out, waving a clipboard with papers.

"We have to deliver this fuel to Zapatillo, *carnal*. We got here early and need a place to park for a few hours. I have the orders here," said the driver in a friendly voice. He was approaching the soldier and pointing to some papers in his hand.

"You cannot pass without authority," recited the small young soldier by rote. Such late night deliveries were rare. The nervousness was evident in his voice.

"We do not want to pass, brother, just park. You do not want this truck on the main road where we might get robbed," said the driver, looking at his watch. "Look, here is our authority." He waved the clipboard in front of the guard's face and stepped closer to him.

The subterfuge had been enough. Blinded by the headlights aimed directly at him and distracted by the motion of the driver's hands, the soldier failed to notice the passenger, who had surreptitiously flanked him. Expertly, the man wrapped a garrote over the soldier's helmet and down around his neck. He applied just the right amount of pressure. The quick action made the soldier drop his weapon and clutch at his throat.

"Not a word," said the driver calmly. "Or my friend will cut off your head."

The noose tightened and the guard's eyes bulged. He could not speak, and found himself being dragged backwards into the guard shack. Inside, the two men quickly rolled him on this stomach and bound his hands and feet. They stuffed a rag into his mouth and secured it with a rawhide string tied around his head. The driver looked at his watch—three minutes to go.

At the main gate, the sentry had been head-nodding inside the guardhouse and had not noticed the headlights of the truck that had stopped at the first checkpoint. But then, he did not have a clear view of that location because of the thick foliage between them. A warning whistle had been their prearranged signal—there had been no whistle. On this night, however, a soldier doing punishment duty on the tower next to the gate had been more vigilant, and noticed the headlights stopped at the road's entrance. He also noticed that the lights were now slowly proceeding towards them, and he called down to alert his sleeping comrade.

When the truck arrived at the gate, the passenger quickly exited. Setting his rifle against the front fender of the truck, he approached the sentry standing at the ready in front of the gate. Speaking loudly so the guard on the tower could hear, he said, "We have an oil delivery for the garrison. We are early and will wait until the commandant wakes and can confirm where he wants to store it."

"I do not know...*no se...*" the sentry began slowly. Then, recalling his only instruction, said more authoritatively, "You cannot pass without authority."

The driver looked at his watch—any moment now.

"*Mira, manito*, look, we do not want to pass; we just want to wait here until..."

But he did not get to finish the sentence. A series of explosions at the rear of the garrison made them all jump, especially the sentry, who had been totally distracted by the unexpected prospect of having to make a decision for which he would be answerable later. Instantly, the passenger moved toward the sentry and expertly snatched the rifle away with a clean cross-body check and jerk. In the same fluid motion he spun and aimed the rifle back at the soldier.

"*No te muevas*, do not move!" he ordered.

At the same time, the driver had slipped out of his seat and pointed a Madsen submachine pistol at the tower guard while yelling, "Throw down your weapon!"

The stunned guard at the gate froze. The passenger ordered him to remove his gun belt and, pointing in the direction of the main road, said loudly, "Run, run!" The scared soldier took off without a pause.

The tower guard, however, tried to level his gun at the driver below. A burst from the Madsen caused the sentry to drop below the tower's railing.

Meanwhile, the passenger ran to the rear of the truck and opened the six-inch wide spigot, which began releasing a gush of petrol onto the ground. He smacked the side of the fender twice and the driver immediately

3

jumped back behind the wheel of the truck and accelerated. He managed to get his speed up to approximately 50 kilometers per hour before smashing into the wooden gates, which burst from their hinges and splintered into hundreds of pieces. The truck was now roaring through the center of the compound. The passenger remained by the gate firing his weapon intermittently into the barracks.

The activity inside the Quonset huts was mass confusion. The timed explosions at the rear of the garrison had taken down the two unmanned towers on the north and west sides, and these were now on fire. The rudely awakened soldiers were now crouched inside the buildings unable to assess what was happening.

Captain Menin and Lieutenant Eban had dressed quickly, but had lain low trying to contemplate countermeasures against the attacks from the main gate and from behind the burning towers. Slowly they moved to the front of the quarters. They could hear a truck roaring across the parade grounds towards the rear of the compound. Furtive glances revealed that the oil truck was discharging a great deal of fuel from its rear. Using the officers' quarters as cover from the main gate, the two men made their way into the barracks and began organizing the men.

The guard at the tower by the gate decided to make a move. He fired several rounds at the truck. The soldier then turned to search for the attackers who were firing from the gate area into the barracks. He could not see accurately, but determined that the aggressors must be hiding behind what was left of the front gates. He was raising his rifle to fire in that direction when he was struck in the upper legs by a series of shots that penetrated the tower floorboards. *The shooter was underneath him*! He screamed in pain and fright and threw down his rifle. The gunfire into the floor stopped and sporadic shots into the barracks started up again.

When the truck reached the rear of the garrison after making a direct run through the parade ground, it stopped. The driver got out and closed the spigot. He then drove the truck to the side of the arsenal, parked it, and ran back to the area where he had first stopped. He lit several flares and tossed them onto the pooled oil. The fuel ignited violently and traced across the field, leaving a flaming barrier that divided the garrison grounds in half and separated the barracks from the storage area.

The driver now joined another group of men that had already attacked the arsenal area from the east. On cue, two of these men set up firing positions behind some barriers and also fired intermittently through the blazing row of burning fuel into the barracks area.

For the men in the barracks, there was no countering the assaults. They could not see behind the sheet of flames, while the shooters could clearly see the entire barracks area through the illumination of the pyres that now

4

flanked the barracks on four sides. All the soldiers could do was hunker down and wait.

Unbeknownst to them, the assault on the front gate had been diversionary. While the truck was crashing the gate, the main group of pre-positioned raiders had cut through the wire fencing east of the compound and disarmed the lone soldier in the tower, as well as the relief guards in the two cabins outside the armory. The five soldiers had been bound and gagged and dragged into a maintenance shack, where they were deposited. After the area was secured, the raiders disbursed to predetermined locations. Two men positioned themselves behind the line of flames and joined the others firing sporadically into the barracks; two other men moved to the opening in the fence to await orders, and another two men proceeded to break down the armory doors. One of them signaled the men waiting by the fence and they rapidly disappeared into the jungle. A few moments later, they returned, leading a dozen burros tethered to each other.

Inside the arsenal, the older of the two men said, "Bring the light over here, quickly."

The other man handed him a torch and the older man rapidly assessed the cache. "*Hijos de puta!*" he exclaimed in surprise as he looked around the room.

"What is it, Hugo?" asked the other man.

"Most of these weapons are German, World War I German. Quickly, get some of the men and start loading these boxes."

He moved some boxes and took mental inventory of the others. As other men came in, he said, "Form a chain for these smaller ammo boxes."

"What are these?" asked one of the men motioning to some long oddly-shaped rifles.

"Tromblons, French gun grenades. Take them." he instructed.

"Hugo, are we taking this monster?" asked a man pointing to a large machine gun.

"No, that is a Maxim MG 08, 7.9 mm. It needs to be water-cooled. We are better off with the American Brownings, over there. They weigh less and are .30 caliber. The ammo is interchangeable with those French Lebels. We will also take all the Lee-Enfield short rifles and the Vickers; they are both .303 caliber. Take those 8 mm ammo boxes for the Madsens too."

The men worked quickly. After securing the wooden crates on the special saddling on the burros, they led the animals away into the jungle. The one called Hugo looked at his watch. Ten minutes had passed since the raid had started. He knew they had to meet the trucks outside of Usulután in eight minutes.

"Paco, we are late," he said. "Tell the men to proceed to the trucks and go with them to help load the crates onto the boats and cars."

The man ran off into the jungle with the message. Hugo looked around the arsenal and one box caught his eye. With a crowbar he opened the secured wooden top. Inside, packed in shredded cardboard, were Browning/Colt .45 caliber automatic pistols, model 1911s. He knew that a newer version, model 1911A1, was now standard issue for the U.S. military. But these were the old versions and had Norwegian markings and swastikas engraved on them. He stuck one in his belt and walked out.

One of the men jerked his head towards other boxes against the back wall. "What about those Colt revolvers?"

"No," said Hugo. "They are French-made, old, not reliable. I would have liked to take the automatics, but we cannot take any more. Get the oil truck over here."

The truck was backed up to the front of the arsenal and the spigot opened again. The fuel began pouring into the storeroom. Hugo looked at his watch—two minutes to go. He waved at the men still firing through the now dying fire and signaled a retreat. He followed them into the foliage outside the wire fence. From a safe distance, he loaded a Tromblon grenade onto the muzzle of a Lebel and aimed the vintage French rifle at the front of the armory, just behind the oil truck that was still pouring out petrol.

"*Vive la France*," he said to no one and pulled the trigger.

The missile accurately arched its way across the 50-meter distance and exploded inside the armory. The combination of munitions, combustible fuel, and explosives set off a ground-rumbling, bright, and violent series of blasts that had the raiders covering their ears and heads for thirty seconds. What was left of the truck was sent crashing into the two guard buildings, igniting them as well. After the initial blast, the men ran to where horses were waiting and rode off at a full gallop.

By the time the last of the munitions were detonated by the intense heat, the raiders were kilometers away, meeting up with others at prearranged locations on the outskirts of Usulután. In groups of twos and threes, they made their way to vehicles taking them away from the area or to the *puerto*, where they had boats waiting. By 3:45 A.M., a mere 30 minutes from the time the truck had first burst into the front gates of fort El Zapatillo, the rebels and the guns had totally disappeared.

Back at the fort, the fires were dying down. Captain Menin ordered his men to form squads and mount a counterattack. It had been several minutes since the shooting from the perimeter had stopped. Reconnaissance scouts quickly reported that the attackers were gone. Menin and Lieutenant Eban ventured out of the barracks and began a more detailed assessment.

The random shooting had wounded several soldiers, two critically. Communications with the authorities at La Unión and Usulután had been severed, so Captain Menin ordered the camp perimeter secured and the wounded taken to the civilian infirmary at the town of El Cuco. He sent Lieutenant Eban with the wounded to establish communication with the fort.

Slowly, other reconnoiters reported finding evidence that the raiders had traveled on horseback and had come and gone by different routes. There was no trace of them now. Captain Menin ordered the search expanded, but reality was starting to set in. Finally, dreading the chore, he set across the parade ground to inventory the damage at the arsenal.

What he saw, convinced him that his career, if not his life, was over. There would be no documenting the missing items or salvaging anything from the devastation that he witnessed. He would have to assume the worst. All of the hundreds of weapons including rifles, handguns, and munitions had been stolen or destroyed. That included a recent private procurement from Europe by the *Estado Mayor*, the military's headquarters, and a special gift from the Norwegian government to the President.

The attack had been executed with flawless precision and rapidity. Menin had heard of smaller rebel attacks around the capital, mainly against armed police or small outposts, but nothing of this magnitude. In each case, the attackers had only bothered with the guns and ammo and rarely killed or maimed the officials. In fact, just as in this raid, killing conscripts did not seem to be part of their tactics. If it was Hugo, and it had to be, the reason for this temperance was not clear, but the captain had heard stories.

In his report to his superiors, he would conclude that the raiders must have had inside information on the makeup, layout, and clandestine purpose of the garrison. There had been no prior warnings from their headquarters that the insurgents could be this effective or bold. Although this explanation had merit and was defensible, he knew that it would not save him. In the end, his protection of the garrison had been a total failure. And the military did not fail.

Chapter 2

During my thirty years of life, all I have ever known well and loved deeply has been confined to this small country. While I appreciate the antiquity and modernness of other worlds, nothing, not any of their wisdom or their beauty, can match the splendor of our simplicity as a people. I say these things early and in categorical terms because they explain my disposition at the start of my 31st year on earth.

My love affair with my native land started early, while a small child on the *finca*. It was there that I first learned about the wonder and beauty of our world. I was part of a full, familial, and exciting life. I did not experience sibling rivalry, insecurity, self-consciousness or any of the other childhood or adolescent ailments that I see in many of my young patients today. I worked hard during school because it was my only chore, and that left plenty of time to experiment and absorb all the joys associated with this brilliant and pleasant world.

We lived in the capital city of San Salvador near the beautiful park, Parque Cuzcatlán, but we spent considerable time at the *finca*. Visits to our coffee farm just outside the town of Zacatecolúca, about 70 kilometers east of the capital were my earliest and fondest recollections.

At least once a month my father would go there to pay the workers, and the whole family would accompany him. We also went there during the harvest seasons and holidays. Everything about those excursions was riveting to me. I recall the car rides in my father's yellow Chevrolet station wagon, the one with the wooden sides, and the drive past the ridge of forests, or *cerros,* overlooking Lake Cuatepeque and the other coffee plantations.

At the *finca*, my father and uncles would routinely take us to nearby beaches and we would swim in the warm ocean waters at the Costa del Sol beaches. We would go early in the morning before the dark sands could sizzle our feet. Afterward, we would ride a canoe along a cool feeder river with banks of more black soil, and stop at a spot where we could plainly see the origin of the earth's dark stain—that ominous charcoal mountain that spewed smoke in the day and fire at night. Even from a distance, the volcano seemed to dwarf us. At an appropriate site, we would dock and picnic under one of the *tamarindo* or *aguacate* trees that shaded the low coffee bushes, and we would admire the majesty of that natural lighthouse. We even named it "the lighthouse of the Pacific."

I remember my father would spread out blankets and have the servants, who had come by horse and cart to meet us, lay out baskets containing *pupusas* of cheese and *chicharón* and meat *pasteles* wrapped in cotton cloths to keep them warm. They also brought large brown clay jugs filled with *refrescos de ensalada* made from the *marañon* fruit, and more *canastas* filled with other tropical fruits and *aguacates*, and my favorite, green mangos coated with lime juice and salt. I remember that the *anona* fruits were as large as *fútbols* and without blemishes, not like the small ones you find in the markets today. I can still taste the milky insides with their large perfectly smooth seeds that my brothers and I used to play marbles with on top of the blankets. And there were *nances* and *mangos* and *platanos* and *sandias*, and...I could go on for some time. We would feast until we could not eat more.

Then my father would tell us stories about the Mayan gods and the Pipil Indians and the *siguanava*, the evil witch that preyed on vagrant children. But we were protected from her, he said, because we were respectful and worked hard at our studies and did not go out alone after dark. Wide-eyed, although sleepy from the feast, we would furtively nod, still unsure of the meaning of his uneasy smile.

My father enjoyed these holidays with his family and friends as much as we did. It was during these times that the festive and mischievous side of him came out, not unlike the personality traits of all my countrymen, which I cherish so much. I miss him today and every day.

I remember that after our picnic at the side of the river, he would place us into a waiting oxcart for a ride back to the *finca*. The methodical sway of the ox's lumbering gait and the heavy meal were potent narcotics, and we slept until we reached the ranch house. There we would wake up still full of excitement and find our mother and aunts relaxing in hammocks, which the servants had strung up along the wide veranda for the afternoon *siesta*. It was now our turn to tell of the day's adventures while they intently took in every word. This then was the routine of my youth.

Later, as an adolescent, I would add more adventures, mainly due to the influence of my best friend and fellow pirate, Ricardo Cruz. After my father died, when I was ten years old, my personal world was not as beautiful or exciting. But, as if sent by my father from heaven, Ricardo came swashbuckling into my life. The transference of affection was timely, natural and definitely therapeutic. Ricardo was also searching, and we fit together comfortably as a hand does inside a well-fitting glove. I did not have to hide my sentiments about losing my father, because Ricardo had lost both his parents much earlier, and so was the one person I knew who understood my pain. Despite our different family backgrounds, how could I not love him?

Ricardo Cruz Carranza was three years old when both his parents died from unrelated illnesses a year apart. Urban aunts, Concepcíon and Catalina

Cruz, adopted him and his two brothers. The sisters had never married, and ran the strict home of spinsters. They were very knowledgeable about politics and maintained close business ties with influential people. They were known to be very conservative, savvy, and opinionated.

It was in this environment that Ricardo developed his insight and direction. He had a romantic and soft side that, according to knowledgeable relatives, reminded them of his mother, Maria Luisa Carranza. She had been the kindly and loyal wife of León Cruz Orantes, a successful businessman. When he succumbed to a sudden illness, she had died shortly afterward, of a broken heart, some said.

While his brothers inherited the business tenacity of their father, Ricardo's personality reflected the lithely and convivial traits of his mother. The individualism of the Cruz brothers was not lost on the aunts. Early on, they had decided on the course their three nephew-wards would take. First of all, the three would avoid what the sisters considered the "socialistic poison" being doled out by the Jesuit priests. They decided that the boys would study under the more moderate Marist Brothers at Liceo Preparatory. Then, when it came time to select a profession, the sisters steered the young men into careers that insured the best use of their inherent skills. Raphael, the meticulous one, would become a teacher, León, the analytical one, an engineer, and Ricardo, the adventurer, a dentist.

Ricardo and I went through *primaria* and *secundaria*, the primary and secondary schools, at Liceo together and have stayed best friends ever since. Although Ricardo was citified, our excursions to my *finca* and the farms of his uncles near the Guatemalan border also made him passionate about the country life. Neither one of us enjoyed hunting, but he did have a passion for target shooting and was a marksman with both pistol and rifle.

During our school years, we were notorious for our outlandish and mischievous pranks. And we continued challenging the patience of our professors all through the university years. Only the fact that we were at the top of our classes scholastically saved us from being in more serious trouble with school administrators. As it was, we took many a beating early on from the good Marist brothers for our misbehavior.

But we survived and, before we knew it, in August of 1936, the 23-year-old Ricardo received his doctorate from the University of El Salvador in surgical dentistry and I received *my* doctorate in clinical psychology. At the same time, another dramatic change in our lives took place. Our legendary romantic escapades took on a different and more responsible quality—we both discovered the more serious and compelling side of romantic love.

I had already fallen deeply in love with Cora when Ricardo met Teresa, or "Teco," as we called her. The story of their meeting and courtship is very *simpatico* and I will digress a moment to tell parts of it.

It started out as another one of Ricardo's conquests. Cora, who worked part time with Teco at the Librería Caminos, a bookstore located in the business section of the city, had told me that Ricardo and Teco had been eyeing each other through the bookstore's window for weeks. It had been humorous for us to observe them, because we had just been through the courting dance ourselves and my antics must have appeared as ludicrous to others as Ricardo's did now.

In games of the heart, men are definitely clumsier, with their farcical and overly solicitous overtures. Ricardo was no different. Occasionally, he and Teco would exchange shy smiles as he passed by the bookstore. Then he began appearing regularly each day at noon, tipping his white Panama hat to her. She managed to be fidgeting with a window display at about the same time and would nod back. Cora had already told her about Ricardo's background, so both women marveled at his formal dress on these occasions. He always wore a three-piece suit, white shirt and tie. It was much too proper for a laboring dentist out on a routine walk downtown. But as I say, there is no controlling the male's preening ritual during these times.

Their meeting could not have been avoided, but a formal introduction was required. That is where Cora and I came in, and we scheduled it for an afternoon tea at a café near the bookstore. Despite the summer heat, I remember both were purposely overdressed. Ricardo wore his off-white suit, white shirt, a royal blue tie, Panama hat, and white and brown shoes. Teco was wearing a mid-calf one-piece black and yellow print dress, heavily padded at the shoulders, high-heeled shoes, and a black wide-brimmed hat.

When Cora ceremonially introduced them, they acted at first as if they did not hear; their eyes were so locked on each other. Then, slowly, he took her hand, smiled while bowing his head and said, "*Con mucho gusto*, pleased to meet you." He also raised a Rudolf Valentino eyebrow high over one eye, a gesture which, I must admit, I had never seen him make before. I was impressed, but had to suppress a guffaw as I looked over at Cora, who was fighting off over-romantic tears.

"*El gusto es mío, caballero*," Teco quickly replied, displaying her own coquettish smile.

And that had been that. They had uttered the words by rote while communicating the real message with their eyes. They were instantly and totally in love and we all knew it—no thought, just sensation. Other formalities would follow as was expected, but the outcome was inevitable. They would see each other every weekend and talk almost every day until, in December of 1939, less than a year later, they were wed.

It was greatly as a result of their prodding that my Cora and I were wed just a month later. At this point in our lives, Ricardo and I felt good fortune and prosperity were blessing us even beyond our expectations. Our careers were set, we had married the two most beautiful women in this, the most beautiful of countries, and there was no reason to expect that we would not continue to reap the most beautiful of futures.

So what when wrong? The lines I now write about Ricardo only add to the confusion. You see, my friend was not self-destructive, but rather self-consumed and self-delusional—not uncommon traits among the self-made.

He was the type of man other men wanted to look and be like. He was tall for a Salvadoran, over six feet, and strong and big-boned. He loved fast cars and horses and was expert in both. He had also been a champion long-distance swimmer at the university and competed in the Pan American Olympics. His swimming style was even compared to that of the American Olympic swimmer/actor of the day, Johnny Weissmueller. Ricardo's overall demeanor was confident but not aggressive. Even his gait reflected this trait—slow and deliberate.

But it was his inner size that set him apart. His greetings were festive, his smile and laugh contagious. You were cheered by his presence and drawn into it. And you missed him when he left the room. Some said he looked like the popular Mexican *charro* singing actor, Jorge Negrete. He was unsure of the comparison, but admitted he did love to sing, especially with friends.

I remember that when he was courting Teco, he would often serenade her with a *trio*, one of the many three-guitar minstrel groups that hired out by the hour for such occasions. Over the melodic harmonies of the guitars and the baritone and soprano voices, the now-quartet, would weave a romantic mood the envy of any Latin. One of the songs he sang was "Negra," a soft Latin love ballad that cast a spell over her. *"Negra, Negra consentida, Negra de mi vida, no me hagas llorar..."* These soft words of love and sentimentality along with the swaying melody were so enchanting to them both that he endearingly began calling her *"Negra"* and she would call him *"Negro"* in return.

Although he stayed physically fit, after marrying, Ricardo put on weight. And since Salvadorans are not shy about *apodos*, nicknames, I naturally started calling him Gordo, and that tag stayed.

I remember also that the first four years of our respective marriages passed quickly, what with the arrival of the children and the exercise of setting up our respective clienteles. This is not to say that there was no time for festivities; Salvadorans do conduct festivities often and very well. There were baptism parties, birthday parties, engagement parties, bachelor parties, and even parties in honor of our patron saints. And that is not counting holiday outings at the lake, the *finca*, or Ricardo's favorite, *la playa*, the beach. As far as Ricardo and I were concerned, we had discovered the meaning of life, and so tended to reject all negativism. I am sure that, at least for three of those years, Ricardo felt the same.

It was therefore inexplicable to me when I first learned of his involvement with the underground, why this man risked it all for such an unfettered cause. I know that he did not tell me about it at the time because he wanted to protect my family and me. He understood better than I the difference in our backgrounds, and how that difference made it unrealistic for me to join him in this venture.

His later involvement with the guns made him a seditious and dangerous man. He also knew that although he did not take part in the raid on El Zapatillo, it did not matter. Just as being present at the scene of a crime is no conclusive evidence of guilt, *not* being there is no clear indication of innocence. He believed that the attack on the armory precipitated his downfall, because that embarrassment caused the military to step up its persecution of suspected subversives. About that he was right. Two weeks after the burglary, on a quiet Monday morning, the ripple effect reached our neighborhood and our lives.

Chapter 3

San Salvador, February 15, 1944

"*Gracias, Lucha*," Ricardo said as the maid placed a dish with his favorite breakfast pastry, *semita*, and a cup of coffee in front of him.

"*Por nada, Doctór*," said the respectful servant.

He folded the *El Diario de Hoy* newspaper in half and set it to one side as he reached for the cup.

"*Mas café, señora?*" Lucha asked turning to Teco, who was seated next to him at the breakfast table in the patio.

"*Ay, si, Lucha, gracias*," said Teco holding out her cup. The maid poured, wiping off the excess at the spout with a napkin. "And, Lucha, bring the plate of *frijoles y plátanos* with some more warm tortillas for the *Doctór.*"

"And the cream, too, *señora?*"

"*Si, Lucha, gracias.*"

The maid nodded and quickly made her way into the adjacent kitchen. Ricardo resumed reading an article in the daily with fixed attention. Teco sat quietly but let a faint smile crease her lips.

She was secretly enjoying the sound of the reference, *Doctór*, and the social standing it gave them. It was still a relatively new feeling.

Ricardo had finished his internship at the Hospital Rosales over a year before and opened up a clinic near the center of the city on Primera Calle Oriente with a colleague, Rodrigo "*El Choco*" Mendez. As a licensed dentist with a paying clientele, Ricardo could now afford a small residence near the new subdivision, Colonia La Esperanza, where he and Teco had settled earlier in the year with their two children. He could also afford to indulge himself with electronic gadgets that he enjoyed so much, like the latest phonograph player or convincing me that we simply had to have personal telephones in our homes and offices, despite their limited and dubious service.

Teco, on the other hand, was not materialistic. She was satisfied to embrace her wifely and motherly duties. She was not disillusioned with the often-unexciting routine that accompanied these responsibilities, probably because they were in sharp contrast to her more humble and turbulent beginnings, where she had to protect her portion of life's attention.

Lucha returned quickly and began serving the second helping of the morning meal. Teco glanced furtively at her husband, who had not relaxed his focus on the news article. Although his profile was mostly silhouetted against the sunlit foliage of the back yard, she thought he looked especially striking in his surgeons' attire, all white down to the shoes. She shifted her attention beyond him to her garden, lush with flowers and ripening fruit. She noticed that some of the limbs of her favorite *aguacate* tree were overburdened and ready for harvest. She would have Felipe cut some down before the ripe ones started falling. Such a peaceful morning, she thought. There was but the slightest of breezes and the sun had not yet started to scorch the day. She smoothed the pleats of her white linen blouse and reached past Ricardo for a piece of pastry, mindful not to interrupt his reading.

Suddenly, Ricardo slapped the front page of the newspaper with the back of his hand. Teco jumped back, startled.

"*Es el colmo!*" he blurted out. "They are threatening to close the university again. It is as though the university and the students are the cause of all this unrest." He read more, then added sarcastically, "It says they fear disorderly protests. *Por Díos!* Protestation is a symptom, not a cause. Why should students have to meet secretly to debate questions of public interest? Where else do they expect examination of issues to take place? On the streets? You had better be armed with more than words if you are going to discuss politics on the streets these days."

Teco reserved comment, as was expected, but sensed the serenity of the morning dissipating.

Ricardo continued, "I tell you, *Negra*, they are a pack of imbeciles!" He finished reading the article, put the paper down and, still irritated, said, "That is enough! I am going with Chepe to see the regent today."

While this appeared to be just another of his spontaneous outbursts, this time she ventured a remark. "I would rather you did not, *Negro*," she said purposely. She stood, took the coffee urn from Lucha, and dismissed her. When the maid was out of the room, she began pouring him more coffee, and without noting his reaction, continued softly. "And please do not drag Chepe into this; you know he does not want to be involved in these things. Cora has even mentioned it to me. Besides, how do you know the regent will not betray you? I worry about you. The other day Juanita told me that she overheard your name in a conversation at a party. Some people she did not know were saying that you are involved in some kind of plot…"

She was planning to continue, but noticed that he was staring at her, almost wincing. She put down the coffeepot. Intuitively, she decided to change tact. "*Negro*, it is just that…"

But he broke in angrily, "Just a minute! Let us be clear about something. I know Chepe better than you do. *Somos compadres.* He and I feel the same way about these things. And by the way, I do not care *dos pitos* what your sister says or what she heard from those vagabonds she and her friends party with. Let them talk. That is the problem, all they do is talk. They did not see what I saw in the military reserve—the ignorance, the arrogance!"

He paused. She remained silent.

Then, less emotionally, he said, "Even you said that I had changed when I came back from the *Guardia*. You remember the talk about Choco. And I did not tell you everything. Things have not changed since those days. Martínez has become a tyrant. He sees communists everywhere—in the press, the University, the unions. Someone has to speak out against their abusive practices. It is for you *and* your sisters that I get involved."

He was looking at her sternly, but was starting to cool and slowly looked away, embarrassed by his outburst. He reached into his shirt pocket, removed a cigarette from a pack, and lit it. Normally, he would have lit two and handed her one. Instead, he turned his chair and sat staring blankly into the yard.

She stood silently beside him looking down at her interlocked hands. She was hurt, but could not bring herself to be combative. She had been up most of the night with Ana Maria. But it was not just the baby's illness that troubled her; she had not been sleeping well for months.

She said quietly, "*Es que te quiero mucho, Negro*, I love you. You know I defend you. But I worry. I do not complain much and I try to keep my opinions to myself. I only ask that you be more prudent. I am afraid for you. I am afraid for all of us. *Disculpame*, I am sorry."

Her obsequious words took their effect. He slowly stood and looked down at her. The dark smudges around her eyes made her look even frailer than she was. His large arms encircled her. After a moment, he kissed her, long and passionately. When he persisted, she let herself be led back into their bedroom.

She had won the moment, she thought; she had managed to reach him emotionally and physically. Maybe, with patience, another kind of passion and reason would force him to see what he was risking with his recklessness. But she would need time...did she have the time?

By midday, the harassing heat had replaced the morning's pleasantness and the children's fretting started uncannily every twenty minutes before and after the hour. Teco had adjusted to Ricardo León's antics, which had more to do with a three-year-old's mischief. He was currently recovering from a scratch inflicted by *Lalo* the cat, who had defended its tail from being used as a pulley.

Ana Maria, however, was another matter. Her vexing was of a darker, more troubling, variety. Her doctor's relaxed attitude about possible causes did little to calm the mistrusting Teco. Although she was married to a dentist and constantly socialized with his professional peers, her opinion of doctors was jaded from years of listening to their bravado and their inability to admit that there was actually some medical factoid they knew nothing about.

Her "university" had been the *barrio* of a small town where she had grown up an orphan. She was prone to superstitions despite being a devout Catholic and having been raised by an uncle who was a priest. She constantly prayed to Our Lady of Perpetual Help for her daughter, but she also kept the ashes of burnt Palm Sunday leaves in a small bag nailed to the foot of the baby's crib.

During this time, the lives of the four of us and our children were quite intertwined. For example, it was customary for Ricardo to lunch with me at least a few times a week. And Teco would look for excuses to visit our home with the children during the day. Likewise, Cora would often arrive unannounced at their home to gossip with Teco. And this day had been no different.

"Teco, how are you feeling?" Cora asked after settling into the living room couch. She was bouncing Ricardo León on her lap.

"*Bien*, Gringa," answered Teco without much zest. She always called my Cora, Gringa, because of her fair skin.

"What?" probed Cora, who knew too well Teco's transparent moods.

"No, it is nothing, the usual. Ana Maria is not sleeping well. Victor just says we must be patient, that she will grow stronger in time."

"What does he think is the problem?"

"He is not sure. He is still running tests."

Cora looked at her for a moment, started to say something, but decided to change the subject, "Are we going to the Lake this weekend? I told Chepe that we would."

"No, we cannot, Gringa. We are having dinner with Ricardo's aunts. It is Connie's birthday." Teco pursed her lips.

Cora smiled. "What? They still have not accepted the beautiful *Señora de Cruz*?" she kidded.

"Did I tell you, Gringa, about how I first met them?"

Cora's eyes lit up. "No, tell me." She put the boy down and he ran off to get a toy from his room.

"*Mira*," Teco said intensely with an air of theater, "it was horrible. Ricardo arranged the obligatory tea one afternoon soon after we started dating. You remember how I doted on everything he said?"

"It was pitiable to watch," Cora said dryly, urging her on.

"Well," Teco said switching to a dramatic voice, "nothing he had said prepared me for that meeting. Even though it was Ricardo's home, we had to be announced and escorted into the formal living room. And there they sat—motionless. Only the overhead fan was moving. The two aunts looked like stout twins in matching white cotton dresses dripping with lace. The only difference I could tell was that one was heavier than the other. Their salt and pepper hair was meticulously coiffured in large buns that made their heads seem even larger than they were. I knew then where Ricardo had inherited his bulk."

"*Ay*, Teco, you are so exaggerated," laughed Cora.

"No, I am serious, Gringa. And not a smile between them! Ricardo walked over and kissed them on the cheeks and said jovially, '*Tías*, let me introduce you to Teresa Marroquín.'"

"And what did they say?" Cora asked absorbedly.

"There was only a slight painted cordial smile on their faces and one of them said, 'Concepcíon Cruz, at your service.' She offered a hand." Teco mimicked the gesture. "And, I took it and said very formally, 'Maria Teresa Marroquín.' 'Catalina Cruz, very pleased to meet you,' said the other." Teco stuck her nose up when she copied the aunt's voices.

Cora was laughing and Ricardo León joined in the laughter as he showed Cora how the toy train crashed into the wall.

Teco continued her play, "'It is my pleasure to meet you, *señora*,' I said quickly, but Catty corrected me, '*Señorita*, if you please,' she said this with an inflection that noted more satisfaction than irritation."

"*Ay*," Cora winced while snapping her index and middle finger.

"I was embarrassed of course, and tried to recover. I said, 'Ricardo has told me all about you. I am so pleased to finally meet you.' Then Connie says, 'Ricardo says you work downtown.' 'Yes,' I said, 'at the Libreria Caminos. Do you know it?' 'Of course,' answered Catty, 'Gustavo Caminos has been a friend of our family for some time.'"

"How condescending!" said Cora seriously.

"Oh, wait," said Teco putting out her hand in a halting gesture. "So I said, '*Señor* Caminos has been very kind to me. I have only been there for a year since moving from Santa Ana. My sister Juanita helped me get the job.

"And then I could not stop talking. 'Juanita de Imeri?' I said. 'Her husband, Ricardo Imeri is a very well-known photographer. Have you heard of him?' I asked. And Connie says in a puffed-up voice, 'No, we have not had the pleasure. We use Miller Photography for the boys. Paco Miller is considered one of the best and, of course, we know his family.' Then, she turns to Ricardo, who is oblivious to all of this and says, 'you know Paco, *Tata*. We have been to his home for dinner. They always ask about you and your patients. I believe he would like to send you some business. Give him a call.' Like I was not even in the room, Gringa! And he just says, 'Of course, *Tía*,' like some puppy dog. I could have killed him."

"And how long did this last?" asked Cora gleefully.

"Oh, I cannot believe I had not told you this before. It went on all afternoon. One aunt rang for tea and the light conversation continued, mainly among them. It seems I did not have much of anything interesting to say. The afternoon ended like a formal letter, with closing amenities. It was all I could do, Gringa. They are the only parents Ricardo and his brothers have known."

"I know, Teco. You were very patient, more than I could have been. But I am sure none of this crossed your mind when you were eyeing Ricardo through the bookstore window for all those weeks."

"No, you are right, they would not have made any difference," said Teco.

They talked for a while and Cora stayed for lunch. When she left afterwards for home, Teco was in better spirits.

Later that day, Fernando Sager, Teco's nephew, came by with another cadet from the military school, Paco Iraheta, and took Ricardo León for a walk at the Campo Marte, the military parade grounds. The respite gave Teco a chance to take care of some chores in the children's bedroom while the maid played with Ana Maria in the backyard under the protective eye of their female German shepherd, Balalika.

This relief also gave Teco a chance to examine Ricardo's motives for risking their idyllic life over political affairs that were unlikely to change no matter who was running the country. She suspected that he relished the intrigue. More and more, he was going off secretly in the evenings. She had thought at first that it was another woman, and now she almost wished it had been. She could have competed with that type of threat. But the idea was quickly erased when, the week before, he had brought home rifles and pistols and hid them in the backyard outhouse. There had been nowhere else, he had explained; informants were everywhere. It was right after that time that the sleeplessness started and her baby's milk stopped flowing.

She was reflecting on these things when several loud explosions in the street startled her. The gunfire had been loud and close.

"*El niño!*" she screamed instinctively. "Where is my son?" she pressed Lucha, who had come running into the house from the back yard with a crying Ana Maria in her arms.

"I do not know, *señora*; Don Fernando and Don Paco took him out for a walk a while ago," answered the scared maid between short breaths. Defensively, she added, "You gave them permission to take him."

The women's reaction to the shooting outside the house had also frightened Balalaika, and she barked in confused alarm, looking at one woman then the other.

"*Ay, Díos mío!*" Teco wailed ignoring the maid. "*Callate* Bal," she admonished the dog as she paced aimlessly.

She knew instinctively that running out into the streets in search of her son was not a viable option. Meanwhile, the maid and the dog watched her, poised to recoil if necessary. It would not be the first time that without cause they had become objects of her wrath.

"You should have gone with them; you're the nanny!" Teco fired off illogically. Then she said, "Go take care of *la niña.*"

The obedient maid walked quickly down the corridor, the dog following. Both protected their retreat with occasional backward glances. Teco moved to the front-room window and carefully parted one end of the sheer curtain and peered past the window. Nothing was moving. Silence. Only the increasing humidity in the air seemed to stir and add to the discomfort.

She stared at the false calm and repeated quietly, "*Ay, Díos mío!*"

Chapter 4

Fernando and Paco had taken the three-year-old to a nearby playground for a late afternoon walk. They had been gone for about an hour. Fernando liked the boy and the feeling was mutual. Even the boy's unusual Latinized name, Ricardo León, which coincided with the legendary English lion-hearted king, appealed to the chivalrous and romantic Fernando, although he affectionately called the boy, "*El Chinito*" because of his small slanted eyes.

Fernando was comfortable interacting with the boy's family. Although Teco was his aunt, he did not think of her in that way, since they were close enough in age to be siblings. He also got on well with Ricardo, whom he regarded with approbation, as he would have the father he never really knew. His parents were divorced and being an older cousin to Ricardo León allowed him to borrow their family ideals.

The mischievous side of Fernando had also learned a side-benefit to being seen with the young boy in public. Walking an affable toddler around the neighborhood attracted many young ladies. As was the custom, single males and females would often queue in opposite directions and parade along the park walkways of the Plaza Dueñas or the Plaza Barrios, inspecting each other as they passed.

"*Ay, que lindo el niño,*" the interested maidens would coo the compliment. "*Como se llama?* What is his name?"

"*El Chinito,*" the boy would jovially blurt out on cue.

"*Ricardo Corazon de León,*" his gallant wards would add with flirting glances, waiting for their turn in the attention game.

Without the boy, it would have been unseemly for unchaperoned young ladies to engage in public conversation with military cadets. The tactic did not fool anyone, but neither did it matter. The approach was *simpatico* and always worked. Meanwhile, *El Chinito* played his unwitting role very well; he also enjoyed the attention of the young ladies.

The afternoon had started out like all others. The park was full of eligible young women and the cadets had already met several of them. Two even agreed to meet them later behind the soccer stadium at the *barrio* Flor Blanca.

Paco was impressed. He came from a small town and, though a third-year cadet, knew very few people in the city. Although his dark complexion and shy attitude afforded clues to his rural background, being with the fair-skinned and citified Fernando gave Paco social heart. At the same time, Fernando liked Paco's quiet but determined attitude. Fernando was more outgoing and personable, but he suspected that Paco came from strong stock and would one day make as strong a leader as he was determined to be. Their personalities and styles were different, but they shared common values and complemented each other.

They made their rounds in the park and had started back to the house. Each was holding one of the boy's hands and swinging him up and down rhythmically, keeping time with the boy's pleading song for more, *"Otra, otra, otra."*

Suddenly, the sound of sharp gunshots reverberating off the cobblestone streets ahead of them shattered that wholesome and tranquil portrait. All three jumped in alarm at the same time. Pedestrians, who routinely reserved the early evening for social walks alongside neighbors from the less affluent Colonia Mejicanos, were sent scurrying in all directions. Fernando saw several men about a half block ahead running with abandon towards them. As these men crossed the street in front of them, Fernando saw another group of running figures turning the corner at the next cross-street. At this distance, the figures were only silhouettes against the twilit sky but he could see that they wore helmets and carried rifles. He, Paco, and the boy were in the line of fire!

Fernando's training and instincts took over. *Get down. Anywhere. Lay low. Assess. That thick hedge near the sidewalk two meters away.* Fernando picked up the boy and dove for the thick foliage, burrowing low inside the enclosure. Paco followed them into the nook without comment. Fernando was alarmed, but his demeanor remained calm and his thoughts were clear.

What luck! he thought. He had heard about skirmishes with dissidents around the city, but this was the first time he had been this close to one. At the *Escuela Militar,* cadets were drilled on the current political situation. It had been explained that the government's position was very clear:

"There can be no peace without respect for law and order. Subversives are criminals who have to be weeded out by force. They can not be allowed to contaminate the populace with their destructive propaganda. Law-abiding citizens must be protected. The military's mission is not only to defend the country from external threats, but also to support the authorities involved in the internal security of the nation."

Fernando was comfortable with these precepts. He had learned early the mantra of "duty, honor, and obedience," and displayed these ideals proudly in daily interactions. This credo could be the deciding factor in how one dealt with a battle or the trials of everyday life. He knew or cared little about power politics. What he did know at this moment, however, was that whatever was occurring in front of them had nothing to do with the three of them. *Stay down*, he told himself. *Do not panic. It will pass.*

Meanwhile, Teco continued her vigil by the window, occasionally wiping her brow and cheeks with a handkerchief. Tears and sweat mixed on her face. Anger, fear, and frustration randomly exchanged places in her scrambled thoughts. She hated feeling helpless.

Like Fernando, she did not know or personally care about politics. *One crusader in the family is enough,* she thought. Her mind was recalling the now long-ago morning when she and Ricardo had clashed. She knew Ricardo would not avoid risks, such as bringing home guns to hide. The guns, she suddenly remembered. She had forgotten about them. The thought of them hidden in the back yard snapped her back to the present. *Dios mío! What if they search the house?* She felt anger, then a cold chill on the back of her neck.

Again she heard gunfire in the neighborhood. Very close. Three short popping sounds. A handgun. She had heard that sound on the *finca* where Ricardo and his friends would go shooting. Then three cracking reverberations. A louder, sharper set of shots followed by another set. Rifles, she thought. *Jesus, Maria, y José…*she began praying.

Her husband was out there, too. Were they shooting at him? Another flash of anger swept through her. *If they were, he had brought it about!* Then fear again. *Ricardo León was barely three years old. What did this have to do with him?* She heard a single crack. *This miserable country,* she thought! She wanted to scream. But she would not allow herself to panic. She continued her vigilance by the window.

Although many considered her emotional, Cora and I knew Teco was mentally tough. We knew about her childhood and her more recent recovery after losing her second-born. Jose Maximiliano was six weeks old when he succumbed to complications from a hernia and pneumonia. Then, there was the time when Ricardo León fell in the *pila* while being bathed and the blood had been unstoppable from a two-inch gash to the side of his head. With horrified maids watching, Teco had removed a block of ice from the icebox and broke the foot square block into pieces over her leg. Applying a piece to the head wound, she had managed to stop the bleeding. After the drama, she had emotionally recounted the frightening event over and over to us. But those who were there told a different version, and knowingly stressed that Teco had another subliminal side.

In our tiny country, people's pedigrees might as well be published in the newspaper. Newcomers are socially classed the moment they leave the room. So the background of the Marroquin sisters was well known to us even before my Cora met Teco at the bookstore.

She was the youngest of nine children. Her mother had died when she was eight years old and she had never known her father, who had drowned in a flood when she was less than a year old. Because of her age, she was sent to live with her priest uncle in Santa Ana. As a result, Maria Teresa Marroquin-Contreras had to fight for the meager attention doled out in the ever-serious and pious environment of her clerical foster home. She had been a rebellious girl who would sneak out at night to socialize with the youngsters of the street. Then, in her late teens, she blossomed into a stunning young woman and was dispatched to live in San Salvador with her married sisters. Compliments were sincere and slowly bolstered her scarred confidence. Many of her avid movie-going friends said she looked like the new American movie star, Ava Gardner. It was this combination of boldness and good looks that had attracted the young dental student.

Now, in her mid-twenties, married with children, she was drawing on past cunning and prayer to handle the frustration and fear of having her son in harm's way.

Ricardo León had been frightened when Fernando and Paco pushed him under the bushes. His eyes were no longer small and slanted but large and frightened. He was still lying under the shrubs, held down by Fernando's hand on his chest. Fernando and Pablo were also lying on the ground. Fernando smiled at the boy and told him not to say anything, because they were playing a game with some friends who were shooting off *cuetes*. That had calmed the boy, because he loved firecrackers. His father and his friends were always shooting them off at the farm. His father called some of the fireworks, *pistolas,* and once his father let him shoot one.

"Nando, those *hijos de puta* are close," Paco said. "Can you see anything?"

"No, nothing. Wait a minute. Hush, be quiet."

A series of pistol shots exploded close by, and three dark figures came running down the street. Then three shots erupted from semi-automatic rifles behind them. One of the men fell on the street about 20 meters from where they were hiding. The other two kept running. More rifle fire. There must be at least three of them with Mauser rifles, Fernando thought. Mausers were now standard issue for the infamous *Brigada Jaguares* of the *Guardia Nacional*.

The figure on the ground was moaning. Four soldiers in distinctive pith helmets slowly approached the downed figure. They stopped, looked around, and started talking among themselves.

Fernando knew what was coming. So did Paco. Fernando slid his hand up to Ricardo León's mouth. He brought up his other hand slowly and put a rigid index finger up to his lips, all the time smiling at his young cousin. Ricardo León smiled back just as the report from the rifle reverberated along the ground and hurt the child's ears. Fernando put pressure on the young boy's mouth and kept the forced smile. The boy grimaced, but his trust and affection for Fernando eased his apprehension, although it did nothing for the pain in his eardrums. After a moment, the soldiers trotted away.

Fernando exhaled and told his young cousin, "We are going to stay here a while, then we are going home."

When he released the pressure on the boy's mouth, the child started crying, "I want to go home, Nando."

"*Si, mi hijo,* we will go now."

"Nando, we have to get out of here. If we run into soldiers, we will just identify ourselves." Paco said.

"I do not want to take a chance with the boy." Fernando said looking behind them. "Besides, they are *Guardia*, and who knows what those illiterate bastards will do if we surprise them?"

Paco understood. The *Jaguares* were renowned for their ruthlessness. Most conscripts in the military were young men, recruited or just taken from mainly rural families and forced into military service. Very few had any education. Some were singled out for their tenacity and ability to follow orders blindly. These were assigned to the *Guardia Nacional,* whose main mission was to police the rural areas. But recently, the *Jaguares* had been active in the capital against dissidents. The timing was not right for explanations.

Against a nearby hillside, Fernando saw a few of the cardboard shacks that were becoming prevalent around the *barrios*. Plummeting coffee prices and the subsequent peasant's revolt in '32 had unsettled the traditional peaceful country life of the *campesino*. Now, it seemed, many of them were blindly migrating to the city in larger numbers and squatting on the outskirts or wherever they found space.

One of the shacks, about 50 meters away, was constructed of wood and mortar and had electricity, because Fernando could see a light inside. There was an open area between where they stood and the house. It was partly fenced for use as a corral, although Fernando could not see any animals. He made a decision.

"We will go to that house," he said, pointing. "Walk calm but quickly alongside the fence line. I will take the boy."

They heard more shooting, and then some construction trucks with soldiers piled in the back drove by. The trio kept moving. It was getting darker and clouds from pending summer rain helped mask their way. The trucks did not stop.

When they reached the shack, Fernando began pounding on some boards that served as an entrance. He used the authoritative voice that he practiced daily as an upperclassman. "Open the door!"

"*Quien*?" a tremulous voice said from inside.

"*El cadete* Fernando Sager! Open the door."

The door opened slightly and Fernando, Paco and the boy moved in without waiting to be invited. The cadets quickly assessed the inside. The shack's flooring was dirt, with pieces of cardboard strewn around like mats. Several dirty mattresses, a table, and a few chairs were the only furnishings. The rest could best be described as groupings of litter, what the Salvadorans colloquially called *chunches,* just things.

"We were just going to bed," said a short, toothless, pregnant woman hurriedly.

She looked old, but Fernando knew better. There were a half- dozen children huddled in corners of the room and a brittle old man, wearing white, or once white, pajama pants. He was barefoot, unshaven, and his chest reflected the shadows cast on the even rows of bowed ribs. Too old to cause trouble, Fernando thought, and his demeanor softened.

"*Mamacita,*" he addressed the woman in a diminutive and affectionate tone. "We have to stay here for a while. The boy is my cousin and I do not want to take him on the streets right now because of the shooting. I want you to put him in bed with you as your son. If the soldiers come, I will tell them who we are and go with them. Later, I will come back for the boy and give you a little gift. But do not worry, the soldiers will probably not come. We will wait a while, then leave. *Me comprende?*"

His voice was soft, but direct. He held eye contact with the woman, looking for a reaction. There was none. Fernando and Paco did not wear uniforms; they did not look like cadets except for their short-cropped hair, but it was enough.

The woman did not answer, only glanced slyly at the old man. He said nothing, moving back into the shadows and sitting down on a mattress next to some of the children.

Neither did she object as Fernando led her to another mattress and coaxed her to lie next to the boy. He smiled at Ricardo León, who said nothing and did not return the smile. Fernando turned off the light bulb that was dangling low over the table by a thin wire. He and Pablo sat on chairs and waited. No one spoke.

Outside, sporadic shots could be heard, but more distant now, like a retreating thunderstorm.

"*Tía*," Fernando called loudly as he and Pablo entered the house with the youngster. "The party boys are back."

Teco came running from the back bedrocm carrying Ana Maria. "*Gracias a Díos!*" she exclaimed handing the yea:-old child to Lucha. She ran to Ricardo León, lifting him off his feet and squeezing him so hard he started to complain. "*Baboso!*" she screamed at Fernando. "I have been waiting for hours not knowing anything."

She began to weep. This part of the crisis over, she vented stored up frustration.

"I did not know what was happening. Were you killed? Hurt? Lying in some gutter? Nothing!"

Ricardo León and Ana Maria, both confused with the loud complaints of their mother, started crying, too.

"You are scaring the children, *Tía*," Fernando said, smiling. "Nothing happened. We stopped off to see one of *El Chinito's* new girlfriends. She was trying to seduce him," he added with an impish grin. "She even took him to her bed."

"You can joke if you want, but you cannot take him out anymore," Teco said emotionally.

"*Tía*, that will break too many hearts. Right, Paco?"

Paco wisely chose to reserve comment.

"*Baboso!*" Teco repeated and threw a half-hearted punch at the cheery Fernando. Gratitude was starting to replace anger and fear. "*Gracías,* Nando," she said earnestly, wiping away tears.

She composed herself quickly while the loquacious Fernando recounted the conquests they had made at the park and how *El Chinito* had distinguished himself as a conspirator in their courting. Then he told her about a new girl he had met, Amalia was her name, and how they were going to start dating soon. But Teco was only half listening. During a break in Fernando's stories, she politely offered him and Paco something to drink, and they eagerly walked back to the kitchen icebox for *refrescos.*

Teco loved Fernando as a brother. She had lived with her sister, Fernando's mother, and the young boy when she had first moved to the capital, barely a young woman herself. Fernando was a mischievous child, sneaking off after bedtime to meet with his pals and taking the candies her suitors brought her—*travieso*, mischievous. They bickered and fought and were often punished together. But when it mattered, she would defend him. After she was married, they stayed close, and she spoke to Ricardo about exercising his influence or *cuello*, as we Central Americans call it, to get the floundering teenager into the military school. Acceptance into the Gerardo Barrios military school was difficult. Success there insured a student and his family security and social standing.

"So, where is my uncle, still at the clinic?" asked Fernando when he and Paco returned from the kitchen.

"I do not know," replied Teco. Then she added, "He probably is. They say the telephones are out all over the city."

"That is not unusual. I keep telling my uncle he should have invested in a driver instead of that toy. Those telephones never work right. But he will be all right," Fernando offered. "All that shooting outside was just the *Guardia* chasing some communists. But it is all over."

Teco looked past Fernando's words into his eyes. Seeing nothing, she reflected on what he had said and became visibly calmed. "*Si, todo está bien*, Nando; you know that I worry easily. I am sure you took good care of Ricardo León. Look, I know you and Paco need to get back to the *cuartel*. Go, I need to settle the children anyway. Do not worry, we will be fine."

"You are sure? We can stay a little longer if you want."

Teco forced a smile and said it was not necessary. Fernando nodded back, then went over to the children's room and tried unsuccessfully to console them. It was 6:00 P.M., Teco told them, and for some unknown reason, children always fret during this time.

"Give them a kiss from us later," Fernando called from the door as he and Paco left.

"*Que les vaya bien*, have a safe trip back" she said to them.

And they were gone. Teco just stared blankly at the back of the closed door.

Chapter 5

Before I go any further, I must tell you about Teco and this special relationship she and I had. Conceivably, it started because I was Ricardo's best friend and a trained listener. But I can see now that she had a special need to better comprehend why her husband was so fixated with politics and, at the same time, give vent to her own feelings and opinions. In this regard, she was walking a fine line and had to be circumspect, because I was not supposed to know anything about Ricardo's involvement with the underground. Teco would make light of her reasons, claiming that Ricardo dismissed her views. So I listened. Now, this personal requirement makes more sense.

She did not understand, for example, why a revolt was always necessary to change a government, only that it had always been that way. It was how Martínez had ascended into power and probably the only way he would relinquish it. She knew the last elections were fraudulent and, even though women could now vote, she was convinced that the next elections would be just as marred. Women would not be a factor; they never were.

She told me about the effect Prudencia Ayala, the *Santaneca* who had tried to run for president in 1930, had had on her. I had heard of Ayala, but like most of my colleagues, I had ridiculed the notion of a woman president. But Teco, like other modern women, admired Ayala, who had stood up for women's rights and the plight of the growing number of illegitimate children. Mistresses were as numerous as the hungry, and it was common for men to have a *casa chica,* as a second home was called. Occasionally, fathers and sons would pass and greet each other on their way to their "other" families.

During her campaign of over 20 years, Ayala was mocked, beaten, jailed, and exiled for her "crime" of challenging the social injustices of the day. Before she died in 1936, some visionaries were starting to proclaim her cause just. The fact that Martínez retained power for all these years and someone like Ayala remained in virtual obscurity spoke volumes to Teco. She, and other women, would concede the folly of men's politics because they had no choice. All they could do was abhor the situation in mordant silence. What did it really matter to them, this dictator, or that one? They were all the same. Besides, during a raging World War, a strong leader was probably beneficial.

As Teco would confide these personal thoughts, I could see that they were expressed passionately and it was doubtful that she had ever articulated them to anyone else, least of all Ricardo. And frankly, on the latter points, I could not agree with her more. Capitulation, like ignorance, occasionally has its rewards.

During these sessions, I came to the conclusion that Ricardo intimidated her, not only with his superior education, but with his zest for living. She was no euphemist, but when it came to political banter, she was *his* listener. Early in their courtship, before he met Hugo, Ricardo was always boasting to her, and to me for that matter, about his political views. I was used to this tone from our university days and tended to agree with him on some points. It was common, especially over libations, that he would become even more animated and quite selective in his political and historical commentary.

"Let me tell you about *cuello*," he would say jokingly to us when we were just sitting around in each other's homes. "Great influence lies in the hands of the very few wealthy landowners—present company included."

He would toast me and I would snicker and shake my head in protestation.

"Do not deny it, *compa*," he would say. "You know that it is the skillful handling of investments on behalf of the government by you oligarchs that ensures they even have a budget. In turn, the military protects your interests and ensures that the 'right' government is always in power—the pun *is* intended. So why should we criticize? It seems to work very well."

He would toast us again and we would all laugh.

In those days, we did not see any hidden meaning in his words. My family was economically comfortable, that was true enough, but our holdings were small compared to the Meléndez' and the dozen or so other families, who formed a very elite group that owned most of the land and the country's wealth. Coffee accounts for 90 percent of the country's exports, and it was through the combined strength of the *cafetaleros* that we survived the devastating effect of Brazil's flood of coffee into the market in the late '20s.

Meanwhile, Ricardo and Teco were part of an emerging middle-class, and still needed patrons for certain privileges and favors. It had been through such an influential contact, for example, that Ricardo and his guardian aunts had supported Fernando in getting his appointment to the military school. Ricardo had a point about *cuello*; it is an accepted practice in my country. But parenthetically, getting Fernando into the academy had more to do with proving Ricardo's deep love for Teco.

And while we are on the subject, let me point something out here about their relationship and I will present it comparatively: The love my Cora and I share is like no other; I feel this in my very soul. We complement each other in so many ways. We share similar values and traditions; our respective families are themselves friends, and our ancestors have always been successful business and professional people. We are interlocked into the shared fabric of a comfortable life in this wonderful land.

Having said that, I also do not know of any other relationship that is as unique and exciting as that of Ricardo and Teco. It is as intense as what my Cora and I feel for each other, but much, much more extraordinary. For one thing, they bask every day in a glow of affection that neither had ever come close to experiencing before. Having both been raised orphans, they adopted the maverick ways of those who, without having experienced parental love or the succor of the extended family, gravitate to self-taught traits and habits. Their love replaced loneliness with purpose. In many ways they are more genuine with each other and unaffected by the trite social draping that seemed to wrap and consume the rest of us.

I remember that when they were courting, they would commiserate about those early orphaned days. It was a world of solitude that only they understood, a state of mind where nostalgia was fondly welcomed, much as the godless embrace alienation and purposelessness. From early on, they confidently stood apart and scoffed at those needing the patronage of doting parents. They often visited the pain and desperation of their childhood, their "secret place," they would call it, and felt they were stronger because of these trials. It was an intimate bond, stronger than compassion; it was soulful and made other relationships seem superficial by comparison.

Cora and I also viewed them as a study in contrasts. Teco had an earthy side that made her popular with those who appreciated naturalness. While apathetic about physical sports, she had a passion for games of chance, especially poker. She enjoyed smoking and coarse talk, which were carry-overs from those early evenings behind the rectory with the neighborhood vagabonds of Santa Ana.

She had not been a vagrant, but understood their wonton idleness and promiscuity. While tolerant about most vices, she was antipathetic about social drinking and refused to participate even when urged by Ricardo. She had witnessed first-hand what liquor did to men's brains and other parts of their bodies. She had learned well in the school of the *barrio*. Yet, despite this unique insight, she was not judgmental, and as a result, she was neither a joiner nor a leader.

In comparison, Ricardo loved life and was an avid fan. Life returned the affection by adorning him with charisma, respect, and popularity. He studied social and physical sciences and vicariously participated in the major social events of the day. He enjoyed having friends and being around them, and could not fathom partying without the stimulus of alcohol. He was athletic and loved competition. He did not consider gambling, however, a sport or very exciting.

31

As astute as he was intellectually, he lacked first-hand experience and understanding of the customs and mores of the less privileged. He trusted and loved many, and was an easy mark for the less sincere. Thus it was that over time we began commenting that the colorful couple confirmed the truism that opposites did attract.

And oh, how we loved to party with them, frequently at social events and dances at the newly remodeled Casino Salvadoreño. They would literally stop conversations when they walked into the room. The tall handsome figure in an evening tuxedo and his beautiful companion, dressed in the latest style, looked like celebrities. I remember when American movie stars, Clark Gable and Tyrone Power, and later the famous orchestra director Leopold Stokowski visited El Salvador, the couple was automatically added to the organizer's' guest list, and they would drag us in with them, so popular and pleasing was their presence. During these times, we openly displayed our love for music and festiveness and the four of us would dance the waltz, tangos, foxtrots, and sambas all night.

I do not want to suggest that we did not have serious conversations about politics and other affairs, because we did, especially when President Martínez would discredit himself publicly, which he did often. I recall one time in particular. It was when the Spanish poet and writer Rafael Alberti, who had been exiled from Spain by Franco for his socialist views, called on El Salvador.

The event was part of the new chic ritual of international luminaries visiting new emerging nations. The world was more available after the Depression, especially with the emergence of air travel. Alberti was just another of several celebrities to visit El Salvador, but this time from Mother Spain. Ricardo and I were *aficionados* of Spanish literature and of Alberti in particular, so when the event was announced, we had enthusiastically offered to help escort him during his stay. To our delight, the organizers had agreed.

On the assigned day of his arrival, I was called with the shocking news that Alberti was being detained at the Ilopango airport. I drove directly to the Hospitál Rosales, where Ricardo was still seeing patients, to confront him with the information.

"Alberti has been arrested!" I proclaimed agitatedly. *"Ese imbecíl* Martínez will not let him into the country because of his anti-fascist writings. He has called him a communist."

"He cannot do that!" said an incredulous Ricardo. "Alberti is a famous writer, not an infamous politician. Besides, he has not broken any laws here."

"Since when does that matter?"

"But this is different, Chepe. This is not just anybody. They need lawful grounds."

"Martínez *is* the law. Besides, you know his admiration for those European fascists. My God, Ricardo," I said dolefully, "he still sees communist ghosts everywhere. I am surprised we do not have a swastika added to the national flag."

"Is there anything we can do?" asked a dejected Ricardo.

"No, I talked to the *Camara*, but Alberti is furious and will no doubt take the next plane out of here. And I do not blame him."

Ricardo was silent for a moment, then, grimacing, he asked rhetorically, "Chepe, what the devil is going on here? As a country, we are humiliated by his ignorance. Martínez is not an internationalist. Look at the fiasco he caused over Manchuria. First, he appoints one of our most noted authors, León Sigüenza, for a second term as Consul General in Tokyo. Then, when the Japanese invade Manchuria and establish a puppet government, he recognizes them without even consulting Leo!"

We were both shaking our heads at the embarrassing episode. Leo had lectured at the university in our early days there.

"The Americans are furious," Ricardo continued. "And they have a right to be. What was he thinking? If war comes, whose side do you think we will be on?"

"I do not know, Gordo," I said equally disheartened. "Martínez is brutally unconventional. Look at this preoccupation with the occult. What the devil does he call his bizarre cult? Theosophy?"

"Yes, he supposedly read about this combination of Buddhist and Brahman philosophy in a New York magazine."

"But a son, Ricardo! He let his own son die of pneumonia rather than be treated with real medicines. He actually thought his ludicrous blue waters would cure peritonitis!"

"What did you expect? You heard what he said right afterwards: 'It is a greater crime to kill an ant than a man, for when a man dies he becomes reincarnated, while an ant dies forever.' Where does he get these thoughts, Chepe?"

"I do not know. He has no background other than the *cuartel*. He is anti-poor and anti-intellectual; he is pathetic."

It is true that we were both being emotional and dramatic, but my outburst was a result of being totally disappointed at not meeting Alberti. Ricardo's grievance, I now know, went deeper. Teco told me later that the Alberti incident seemed to be the beginning of Ricardo's preoccupation with getting rid of the *martinistas*.

I had also noticed the change, but did not think it was any worse than some of the complaints of our more vocal friends. But he did begin blaming

33

Martínez for all the political and social ills the country was experiencing, especially after the World War began in earnest.

"He is profiting from the war," Ricardo proclaimed to me one day. "I know it. Remember when the Americans wanted the property of German, Italian, and Japanese citizens living here seized? Martínez did not object to that, even after all of his anti-*gringo*, pro-Hitler sermons. Blacklists were started. And why? Because it fattens his personal coffers."

This observation did have a ring of truth. I recall that whole families had been deported because of the "blacklists." Rich families fleeing Europe before the war, such as the Baums, the Liebes, and the Lewinskys had become Salvadoran nationals to avoid the possibility of deportation and interment in Nazi concentration camps. Some had been sent to prisoner-of-war camps in the U.S. while others had been able to buy Salvadoran citizenship from the *martinistas*. So these latest "accommodations" by Martínez did have a perception of profiteering.

Then, another time he said, *"Mira compa,* this government has the power to force change, however gradual. I am not saying like Araujo; he was a communist sympathizer and was influenced by Stalin's gloating after the collapse of '29. I mean more like his predecessor, Pío Romero Bosque, *Don* Pío, who knew how to balance the political Left and Right."

It was true. I recall that *Don* Pío, as we all called him, ruled with a tight fist, especially against foreign propaganda, and did support the poor as long as they did not unionize. My family supported him.

"And we had a free press then, *compa*, not like the censored papers of today. *Don* Pío also tried to reform the role of the *Guardia* and the police. But the power brokers never understood him. It was not his fault that the world price of coffee dropped from 24 cents to seven cents a pound. He was a realist. He allowed the hungry to vent their frustrations. Now he is blamed for permitting the *Ligas Rojas* and the communists Marti and Mármol to become influential and start the revolt of '32."

I must say that even through whisky-induced bravado, I was impressed with his analysis of national history. But then, I am, at most, apathetic about geo-political affairs. What I do know is that in this small country governance is all about who holds the reins of power. About concomitant world events such as the Mexican and Russian revolutions and their influence on our region, I am less attentive.

The truth was that we had lived through the prosperity of the Twenties and had witnessed the transformation that accompanied the migration of wealthy *cafetalero* families from their plantations in the *campo* to the capital. Their money funded a cultural renaissance in El Salvador. Fine arts, higher education, and modern facilities had been instituted. The wealth of the rich had built this country and we were the beneficiaries.

We now attended social events at the modern Club Internacíonal and the Casino Salvadoreño. Our children had been born in the new Hospital Rosales. The wealth of these rich families had also built the new Estadio Olimpico, where Ricardo had competed in the Pan-American Olympics. Salvador was no longer a backward country of peasants. All this was new and exciting and formed part of the world we cherished. We did not take this bequest for granted and, if it had been anyone else but Ricardo, I would have resented any criticism of it.

But given his persona, I could understand Ricardo's reactions at the time. After all, he was generous, gregarious and kind, while the government was impersonal, pitiless, and apathetic. But I would never have understood any action on his part that would place his family and career in jeopardy. Like me, he is passionately patriotic.

But by then Teco knew he was involved in more than just rhetoric, and so sensed the danger of this paradox better than I. At this pivotal moment, Ricardo's internal conflict could change their lives and the lives of their children and their children to come. To this day, neither she nor I is sure whether this enthusiasm was misguided pride, profound courage, or both.

It was about an hour after Nando and his cadet friend Paco left her home that Teco first heard noises coming from the back patio. Suspiciously, she rose from the sofa to look out the back window, through the dwindling light of dusk and the few streetlights, but could not make out anything out of the ordinary. When she asked Lucha, the maid replied that she had heard nothing. It must be nerves, Teco thought, and went into the baby's room to check on her. Ana Maria was sleeping fitfully. She picked her up and sat on the rocker that we had given her when the baby was born.

Suddenly, she heard the noises again, this time from the front of the house. There was clearly movement just outside the door. Her heart began to race. *Ricardo?* She walked from the baby's room into the corridor where Balalaika began barking uncontrollably. *It was not Ricardo.*

Then, a loud pounding on the door, "Open up, military police!"

Lucha was half running to the door, but Teco ordered her to stop. "Here take the baby and stay with the children. And take Balalaika with you." She handed the crying Ana Maria to Lucha, then looked at the dog and said, "*Vaya, vaya con Lucha.*" The dog continued growling, but reluctantly obeyed.

Another loud bang at the door and Teco heard movement in the rear of the house. She was terrified, but remained outwardly calm. With her posture erect, she walked slowly to the door, her high heels making an unhurried steady clicking on the marble floors.

"*Voy*," she called out in a calm voice.

She opened the door with the same controlled pace and faced four battle-dressed soldiers with rifles at the ready.

"What has happened, is there something wrong?" she asked with an appropriate quizzical facial expression. Her tone was concerned, but steady and deliberate. She might be shot dead in the next few minutes, but there was an inner, unexplained energy soothing the burning urge to break down emotionally. She surprised herself at this, and if it were not for the circumstances, she would have felt a sense of pride in her self-control, as if she were outside herself witnessing this calm performance.

"We have orders to search all the houses in this neighborhood. We are looking for subversives," the older soldier in front said quickly, his eyes darting past her to take in all that was in view. Then, he focused on the strikingly beautiful young woman before him and paused.

She had also distracted the other soldiers behind him, who had been poised for action. Her tailored blue housedress accentuated her small waist and well-proportioned and well-endowed figure. Her back was straight and her shoulders proudly balanced. Her dark curling hair was pulled back around her ears, showing off a matching set of diamond earrings.

Keeping the same expression, Teco said, "*Jesús*, in this neighborhood? This house? This is the home of *Doctór Ricardo Cruz*. My husband is not at home, but I am his wife. There are no subversives hiding here, I assure you; there is no one here but the children and the *muchacha*."

Teco had put a strong emphasis on *Doctór*, knowing that soldiers were influenced by status. The soldier started to speak, but Teco cut him off.

"I do not think that the *Doctór* will like knowing that soldiers are searching his home. He works at the Gerardo Barrios military school, where he volunteers his time. But..." she softened her voice, knowing that to argue would be pointless, "We do not have anything to hide either, and you have your orders. I understand. But please, the children are in bed and I do not want them scared."

Her attitude and response surprised the soldiers, who had been ready to force their way through.

"You are right, *señora*, I have my orders," the soldier in front stated evenly. This time, he made eye contact with her. "There are soldiers in the back yard, but they will not come in," he added.

He turned to the other three soldiers and told them to look around the house, but not to touch anything. The soldiers communicated something with eye and head gestures, and three of them went to the rear of the house, leaving Teco and the older soldier in the foyer. In one of the rooms, she heard Ricardo León say something about *cuetes* and her heart leaped.

The search was cursory. They did not go into closets or the maid's room where Lucha had put the dog. It was more of an assessment, thought Teco. Further glances were exchanged among the soldiers. Words outside her hearing were spoken in the back patio.

When they had finished, the older soldier returned to Teco and said, "We will be leaving two soldiers in the back patio and two in the front until your husband returns. For your safety, should someone try to hide on your property."

Teco looked into his dark eyes but could read nothing. They would not be doing this to every house, she reasoned. Displaying maturity far beyond her years, she quickly said, "That is very kind of you, *gracias. Buenas noches.*" To herself, she thought, *Ricardo, where are you? I do not know what all this means!*

The soldiers left the house, but she could hear voices and occasional laughter coming from the back and front. She went back to Ana Maria's room. Nervously, she sat on the rocker and blankly stared at a painting above the baby's crib. Some children about Ricardo León's age were running peacefully along a beach. She was terrified and numb at the same time. *Until your husband returns...Now what?* she asked herself. *I cannot warn him. Will I be arrested, too?*

Not since her mother's death had she experienced such anxiety. What of the promises and optimism she and Ricardo had pledged each other? *Stop thinking about that!* After a while, her mind returned to that sanctuary of thought, their walks on the *playa*, like the children in the print, where the wind moved her hair and the black sand possessively gripped her naked feet.

Suddenly the ringing telephone brought her back from her reveries. She was jolted and almost dropped the baby. It took her a moment to clear her thoughts. *The telephones are working again*, she thought. Ana Maria was starting to stir, and she quickly put her down in her crib.

"*Lucha, ve a la nina*, see to the child," she yelled as she raced from the nursery to the foyer where the telephone was. Her heart was pounding as she lifted the instrument, uncradled the receiver, and put it to her ear. Behind her, the baby started to cry.

"*Alo?*" she said into the speaker in as calm a voice as she could manage.

"*Negra*, I must speak quickly." His tone was urgent.

Her heart began to sink and she whimpered faintly, "*Ay, Negro*, what is happening? Soldiers are here. They are waiting for you to get back before they will leave. I think they are looking for you. And there was shooting outside. I did not know if it was you. I am so scared..."

"*Escuchame!*" he interrupted firmly. "We have been betrayed."

He was speaking in a voice she had never heard before. *Was it fear?* She did not like what she was hearing.

37

"You will be all right. But I have to leave the country tonight. I will send for you and the children. Talk to Chepe about preparing yourself to join me. He is not involved in any of this, and he can help. I cannot talk now, but do not worry."

Despite her pain, she could sense the heavy tone in his voice. *"Ay, Negro,"* she repeated weakly and started to cry.

"Yo sé, mi amor. Discúlpame. I am sorry. In a few days we will be together in Guatemala. Everything will be all right. Be strong. I love you."

*"Yo tambien te quiero...*I also love you..."

But the phone was dead.

He has to flee, she thought, remembering his words. *He is sorry. He will send for me. In a few days we will be in Guatemala. Guatemala?*

The magnitude and the implication of his words overcame her capacity to absorb them. Whatever strength had kept her together these past months, this night, this moment, suddenly abandoned her.

Before collapsing to the floor, she said aloud, *"La niña!* She is so frail. *Díos mío!"*

Chapter 6

As much as it pains me to remember, I will now detail how I learned about his crimes. And I use the word "crimes" purposefully, because that is what they were—high crimes. It is only now, when these extreme actions have been vindicated, that the word seems inappropriate. But at the time I heard it from his very lips, they were very serious and frightening charges.

What I recall of that day is that Ricardo had sent a messenger in the late morning to cancel our scheduled lunch. I thought nothing at the time, since our hectic schedules often forced last minute changes. But I was somewhat surprised, later in the afternoon, when my receptionist told me that he was on the telephone and insisted on speaking to me.

"*Ola*, Gordo," I said jovially. "I missed you at lunch."

"Sorry, *compa*, I could not avoid an emergency with a new patient. *Mira*, can you meet me right away at that place where we had *pupusas* last week, in about a half-hour?"

The request was unusual and I sensed something in his voice. I paused, then regaining my composure, I said lightly, "*Por supuesto*, Gordo, and I will bring some *Pico de Gallo* and the dancing girls." I forced a giggle and added quickly, "See you there." I hung up and tried not to think about the call as an emergency, after all, we both loved our *pupusas*, but the premonition was distracting.

I should mention that *pupusas*, which are freshly cooked tortillas filled with beans and rice, cheese, or ground pork meat called *chicharón*, is without question the Salvadoran national food. We all love our *pupusas*, and *pupuserias*, as the makeshift cooking stands that serve them are called, are ubiquitously scattered around neighborhoods and roadsides where laborers can easily access them for a late *almuerzo* or early dinner.

We all have our favorite *pupuseria* and Ricardo and I had found ours months ago off the main road to Santa Tecla. We had been going there at least once a week with our families, but never this early.

When I arrived at the small crude diner, my eyes quickly found Ricardo sitting in the back, smoking a cigarette and staring at a half-full bottle of beer. The tables were mostly empty and the customary swarms of flies had gathered to inspect the invisible morsels left on the tops of the oilcloth-covered tables. A very young couple sat towards the front of the *pupuseria*, against the wall. They were holding hands across an empty table, silently gazing at each other and furtively touching knees.

An older woman sat on a chair behind a counter that separated the restaurant tables from the *comales* used to cook the *pupusas*. Salvadoran *ranchero* music blared scratchily from a radio as the woman sorted pieces of wood that would be used fairly soon to heat up the clay skillets. She did not look up as I made my way to the rear of the room.

The expression on Ricardo's haggard face immediately confirmed my suspicions and my heart sank. I managed a cheerful, "*Ola, compadre.*"

"*Ola, compa,*" said Ricardo with a wistful smile, getting up from his chair.

We exchanged the usual embrace, but this time Ricardo's clasp was a tad stronger and more in earnest. As we sat down, I called out to the woman to bring me a beer. For a moment, neither of us knew how to start. Ricardo managed a faint smile, but avoided eye contact.

Looking down at the top of the table, he finally said, "I have really made a mess of things, *compa.*"

"Tell me what happened," I said seriously.

Ricardo spoke slowly, "You were right not to get involved, Chepe. I would not listen and now I am paying the price."

He paused while the woman behind the counter walked over to our table carrying a bottle of *Pilsner*, the local brand of beer, and a napkin with sliced lime and salt. She set them down in front of me and walked away.

"We were betrayed," Ricardo said directly. "What I am going to tell you is just for you. You know some of it already." He paused, then said, "I have been part of a group that collected and hid weapons for the underground."

I felt an emptiness in my stomach, but said nothing.

He looked intently at me and began explaining, "A few weeks ago I took some rifles and handguns to my house to hide."

"Ricardo!" I could no longer hold back the shock.

"I know, I know. It was stupid. Teresa was furious. But at the time I had no choice."

No choice! I thought to myself angrily. Then I looked into his reddened eyes and saw his need to release some of the pressure that had been building inside. I said patiently, "Gordo, tell me what happened today. Is this why you cancelled lunch?"

"Yes," he said. "I was warned and fled. Then I called Tere."

I wanted to know the extent of his troubles from the beginning, but he insisted on talking about Teco and his family. He was speaking urgently and so I merely let him tell it in his own way.

He began by describing his brief conversation with Teco earlier that day. He said that after he broke off the connection with her, he had stared blankly at the telephone for a while, as if in a trance. He *had* needed to talk to her; he owed her that much and more. But the words had failed him. She had been right all along; their world was falling apart and he was to blame.

What had he been thinking? Then he thought of what she had said and felt chilled. Soldiers were at their home waiting for him. He felt he had to do something about that. So he had risked a cryptic call to his aunts.

"*Residencía Cruz*," the maid had answered after the third ring.

"Let me talk to *mí tía Concha*," said Ricardo.

"*Si, Don Ricardo*," she said, then speaking away from the phone, he heard her say, "*Es Don Ricardo, Doña Concha. Quiere hablar con Usted*; he wants to talk to you." Back to him she said, "*Ya víene, Doctór*; she is coming."

Between the two, he preferred to have serious conversations with his aunt Concepcíon. Socially, he favored his other aunt, Catalina, because she was more personable and affectionate, but she was not as astute as her sister. Concepcíon sought out responsibility and demanded compliance. This situation, thought Ricardo, demanded her perspicacious and shrewd attention.

"*Ola, tía*," Ricardo said when she got on the phone.

"*Y esté milagro, tata*," she said.

"No miracle, *tía*, I am always thinking of both of you." Usually, the amenities were expected to go on for some time, but he got right to the point. "Listen closely, I have to tell you something and also ask you for a favor." This tone and approach were not typical. He had used it deliberately, hoping she would appreciate his intent.

She did. "Go on," she said stoically.

"I have to travel to Honduras for a conference. A colleague is driving me tonight and I will be gone a few days. I just spoke to Tere. She says that there are soldiers at the house. Apparently there was some trouble in the neighborhood and they are waiting until I get there. Unfortunately, I have to leave, but I want you to call Colonel Gutierrez or whomever else you think appropriate to complain about these soldiers. Tere does not deserve this inconvenience or worry. Do you understand my concern?"

She paused, then stated, "I will call Memo immediately and complain about this abuse. Will Teco be needing anything while you are gone?"

Gratefully he realized that she did understand. "I do not think so, *tía*. These last-minute trips come up so often, she is used to them. I will be talking to Chepe Molina, and he will stop by to see her. I will tell him to come by and see you as well."

"Yes, please do that. We love Chepe very much." There was another pause, then she spoke first, "*Y tata*, we also love you very much. Be very careful and have a safe trip."

She wisely rang off before either was tempted to say what they no doubt were experiencing inside. Again, he had been unable to say what he wanted to say: *I am sorry if I disappointed you. I love you and will miss you.* The people he loved and who loved him most were all being hurt. He reflected on the telephone conversations. No one was surprised, he had noted. No doubt they were sorry for him, but not surprised. It was almost as though they were expecting trouble. Was he that obvious? That reckless? Had he only been fooling himself that it would not come to this? His family had been more prepared for this eventuality than he was.

Telling me this now, he was getting overly emotional and I said, "Calm yourself, Gordo, things will work out. Tell me about this morning."

He nodded and finished off his beer. More composed, he proceeded to tell me in great detail how he had learned about their betrayal.

He had been busy with a patient when his receptionist came into the examination room to announce that a young man named Enrique Veliz needed to see him right away. He was in the waiting room, she had said, and he had an important message he wanted to deliver personally.

Ricardo felt a numbing sensation. He told his patient *Señora* Ramirez to excuse him; he was almost done and would be right back. He did not often pray, but at that moment he closed his eyes and made a brief petition. He walked to the door of the reception room and faced the young man, who was distracting himself by reading the inscriptions on the professional certificates that hung on the wall. He caught sight of Ricardo out of a corner of his eye and turned.

"*Doctór* Ricardo Cruz?" the young man asked as he approached.

Ricardo nodded.

"I was sent to tell you that you need to go to the home of your *padrino* right away." The youth looked at Ricardo intently, as if to insure that the message had registered.

"*Gracias*," Ricardo said slowly, maintaining the eye contact.

The young man did not hesitate. He nodded back, turned, and walked out of the clinic doors.

Ricardo stared blankly after him. *It was the worst.* No, he thought, the police could have delivered the message, that would have been the worst. He continued to stare at the vacant doorway. He had not been sure how he would react if the moment came. The thought of police crashing into his office at any moment flashed through his mind and he did a mental double-take.

Quickly he dismissed that tactic as illogical. Why send the messenger in the first place? To lure him outside? He had not seen it in the boy's eyes. No, it had to be the prearranged signal. He analyzed the circumstances and calmed slightly. He turned away from the door and walked to the receptionist's desk.

"Sarita," he said evenly, "I need to make an emergency visit to a relative and I do not know how long I will be gone. See that *Señora* Ramirez is attended. Tell her that I will see her next week. Also, reschedule this afternoon's appointments. Oh, and inform Dr. Mendez of my absence, but do it after the midday meal, in case I can get back."

Sarita was making notes as he spoke. When he stopped, she looked up at him. "Is there anything else, *Doctór*?" she asked.

"Yes, tell Narciso I want to see him."

"*Muy bien, Doctór,*" she said stepping back into the reception room.

Ricardo went to his office and removed his smock. His mind was still racing. He had known this day might come, but he was still not prepared. He knew he had to tell Tere, but how? When? The telephones were not working, he recalled.

He had thought that if he had to leave, it would be to a neighboring country like Guatemala, where he could practice his profession and wait for a change in government. But he did not have a plan in place. *Why had he not prepared?* He knew the answer. He had not thought it was a possibility; he was too consumed with this cause.

He was putting on a *guayabera* over his undershirt when the gardener knocked on the frame of the open door.

"Narciso," Ricardo said, "I need you to run an errand for me right away."

"*A la orden, Doctór,*" said the short, thin gardener.

"I want you to go to Dr. Molina's office. You know where that is, on Primera Calle?" He waited for Narciso to nod, then continued, "Give him a message. Tell him yourself, only him, that I will not be having *almuerzo* with him today; something has come up. You understand?" Narciso nodded again. "Good. Go on now. Oh, and Narciso, has anyone outside been asking for me?"

Narciso thought for some seconds, then said slowly and very seriously, "No, *Doctór*. I have been cutting the grass outside all morning and no one has been asking me anything. Just the street vendors selling fruit and cheeses. I did send the woman who sells the *queso de leche* that you like in to see *Señorita Sarita*. That was all."

"Very well, Narciso, *gracias*. Go now. After you have delivered the message, come back and Sarita will pay you for the day."

"*Gracias, Doctór,*" the servant said, putting his straw sun-hat back on as he left.

Ricardo gathered up his personal effects and left the clinic through the back door. As he walked down the side street to where he garaged his car, he was glad he had thought to keep the .38-super automatic pistol under the seat of his car. Even though he had a permit to carry it, he did not want anyone detaining him on the street to be prejudiced by the fact he was armed. He did not plan to resist, at least not at this moment. He would take his chances on his reputation and all the influence and outrage his aunts could marshal.

When he arrived at his car, he motioned to the *guardían* to open the gate. Once behind the steering wheel, he set the choke and throttle and hit the starter and gas pedals simultaneously with his right foot. The Chevrolet coupe started right up. He reached under the front seat and removed the gun, still in the soft leather holster, and placed it inside his pants at the small of his back. He pulled the *guayabera* over his waist and pulled out of the garage.

During the drive, police "ghosts" haunted him. He purposely stared at those he suspected of being *cuilios*, as Salvadorans call police. Hugo had said that, when on surveillance, *cuilios* avoided eye contact. But no one was reacting suspiciously. He circled several blocks, looking in his mirror for cars that might be following him. He drove through narrow alleys, using a technique Hugo called "funneling," and pulled over periodically and suspiciously inspected the occupants of the cars that passed him. He stopped at the Mercado Cuartel open-air market and walked around on the pretext of pricing some hammocks. He detected no furtive or sudden movements from traffic behind him.

When he got back to his car, he asked the street boy, who had volunteered to watch his car, if anyone had been around the auto. The small barefoot boy shook his head. The boy reminded him of Ricardo León, and Ricardo swallowed a slight lump in his throat. He patted the boy's matted hair and gave him a five-cent piece. The boy ran gloating to a group of street kids across the road. It seemed to Ricardo that there were more of them these days.

He arrived at the prearranged safehouse about 2 P.M. No one was there except the maid and her gardener husband, who lived in a small cabin on the grounds. They recognized Ricardo when he arrived and let him through the iron gates.

The chalet was on the outskirts of the capital, near the town of Santa Tecla, and belonged to Tomas' parents. Tomas was a member of their five-man group. This was the place each knew to use when the signal was given. Ricardo went into the house and waited.

One by one, members of the group began arriving, each without any information, until the last, Carlitos, came in around 5 P.M. and delivered the ominous news: Someone had betrayed them.

"Teco will be all right, Ricardo," Carlitos assured him. "All the military has is part of a name, no evidence. The *Guardia* is vicious, but they would not harm her or take any action without more information. But they will be watching."

Jose Carlos Escudes, whom they called Carlitos, was a lawyer in his thirties who taught *Derecho* at the university. I did not know him well, so I was not that surprised when Ricardo mentioned his name. Carlitos had been with the group for a short time, but had been actively campaigning against Martínez since '32, Ricardo said. The group trusted him and he acted as their leader.

"Nothing will stop them if they think there are guns hidden there" Ricardo told Carlitos.

"They could not know about the guns," Carlitos said. "Their informant is from another group. Hugo was smart to break us up. On the other hand, as soon as the authorities learn that you are hiding, they will have every reason to search the house."

"Tell me again," Ricardo asked. "How much do you think the police knows?"

"As I said," Carlitos answered, "they know about me, and that there is a dentist named Ricardo in this group. The informer, Dominguez, was with me in another group before I joined this one. That group was responsible for distributing information leaflets around the city, but mainly at the university. We have to assume Dominguez has told them all about that operation."

"How did you find out?"

"This morning, one of the people I knew from that group called to warn me at home. He said that he had barely escaped being picked up himself, and that I was probably next. He suspected that it was Ernesto Dominguez who had betrayed us. I have been able to confirm this through another friend."

"How sure are you?" Ricardo pressed.

"Well, it seems that Dominguez was picked up by the police a week ago and released the same day. No one had thought anything about it because the police are always harassing the students. From the day he was released, however, he has been asking questions about others in the movement. Then this morning the police started picking up people from his group. One got away. He is the one who called me. My friend thinks that, to save his skin, Dominguez agreed to spy for them."

"Why did they decide to take the action now?" asked Tomas.

"Apparently Dominguez was too obvious about it and did not get anywhere. The police probably became concerned that Dominguez, who is not too bright anyway, was tipping off the groups with his provocative questions. So the *cuilios* started picking up our people today. Dominguez had been asking to see me all this week. He said he wanted to help get weapons, that he knew where they could steal some."

"When did my name come up?" Ricardo asked.

"Yesterday, Dominguez asked my friend about a dentist named Ricardo. My friend told Dominguez that he did not know anything about our group or any dentist, but said he would try to contact me and pass the message along. The truth is, my friend does not know anyone in this group except me. I was going to report all of this to Hugo when everything started happening. That is why I decided to call us in."

The others just nodded.

"What about the man you sent to my office to warn me?" Ricardo asked.

"He is a *coreo*, runs messages for us. I know him and his family personally. I also left a sign for Hugo to contact us. By now I am sure he knows, but he cannot help us at this moment. We have to decide what to do next ourselves."

Ricardo was still unsure about the extent of the information the police had on him and the expression showed. He frustratingly shook his head.

"Look, Ricardo," Carlitos offered, "you know how these bastards work. They have a list. To them it does not matter how a name gets on it or what you are suspected of having done, everyone is guilty. It is as though the sons of bitches, those *hijos de putas*, have their own religion. They are the gods and we are the sinners. They advocate confession and penance, but not reconciliation."

"Yes," another man, named Leo, said, "Once you are on their list, there is no way to get off. If you are lucky, you are forewarned and leave the country. If you are able to evade them and have enough *cuello*, you might be asked to leave. But if they get their hands on you, they will force a confession whether you have done anything or not, and then the best you can hope for is a quick bullet to the back of the head."

Carlitos said somberly, "My name is now on that list, Ricardo. I have no choice. And, perhaps every dentist in El Salvador named 'Ricardo' is on that list, too. You may not have a choice either."

Ricardo slammed his fist on the table. "You knew this piece of shit Dominguez from before, but I am the only dentist named Ricardo in this group. How did he get my name?"

"*Por Díos*, Ricardo, we do not know," said Carlitos calmly. "Hugo and those of us here are the only ones who know your involvement, and you can be sure it was not one of us. But it is a small town. You could have mentioned…"

"Do you think I would be so stupid?" Ricardo interrupted angrily. "This is the most dangerous assignment, and *we* are the only ones who know each other."

He had put too much emphasis on "we," and three of the men looked away.

But Carlitos patiently said, "Ricardo, it could be a guess on Dominguez' part. You are well known. People outside this group know your strong feelings. They also know your background. You were a national shooting champion. People know that you have a permit to carry that *escuadra* around with you. Think about it. Would someone like you be satisfied pasting leaflets on walls around town in the middle of the night? It was probably a guess on someone's part—a good guess, but a guess. That is why you need to assess what you will do next. If they knew for sure, they would already have you. They could be going to every dentist named Ricardo in El Salvador with some pretext just to see who runs."

Ricardo was thinking. After a moment, he said in a cooler and more contemplative manner, "Now you are being naïve, Carlitos. If it was a calculated guess, then they already know my last name."

Carlitos raised an eyebrow and half nodded. "A good point, *mi amigo.*"

"Where is Dominguez now?" Ricardo asked intensely.

"Most of his group have been picked up and he is hiding. By now, Hugo will have people out looking for him. They will find him."

"That *hijo de puta* will get his," said one of the men.

"He is a man without a country," said Leo. "He failed us and he failed the police. And you know the military hates failure more than treason. He is a dead man without a soul."

"Ricardo, you cannot take the chance of going home," said the young Tomas. "If they suspect you…"

"Let us analyze this for a moment," Carlitos weighed in. "For now, it is only I who cannot return home. Dominguez has given them my name, and others who are now being questioned will be forced to give it, too. They could have taken me earlier, but they waited. No doubt I have been watched, but luckily we have not been active. They were also probably waiting to see if Dominguez could deliver more information."

"You were very lucky," agreed Tomas.

"Yes, if my friend had not gotten to me early this morning, I would surely have been picked up in their raids. If they are able to arrest me now, you will have to assume that they will make me talk. Forgive me, I am brave and I will resist, but I am also a realist, *compañeros.*"

He bowed with a half smile. The others nodded knowingly.

"On the other hand, if they cannot find me, they will have no proof except the statements of people who knew that I had been part of a group that distributed leaflets around town. A forgivable offense after this government leaves power. The only proof is what some poor miserable *infeliz* has told them. And, as Leo says, if we do not kill him, the police will. So it is clear what I have to do. In fact, I am leaving the country tonight by private plane from the *finca* of a friend. I have already made the arrangements."

He looked at the others. A few winced at the thought, but knew that the statement was rational.

He continued, "There is no reason to believe that anyone has given them your names. After a few days, Hugo will know if you are on any lists. My guess is not."

Then, he turned to Ricardo. "There is no debating what we have to do, but you, Ricardo...Well, if they have your name and it involves the weapons, they will be relentless. If you are caught, they will try to get everything they can from you and then..."

He left the sentence unfinished. Then he reached over and put a hand on Ricardo's shoulder.

"Look, there is room for one more on that plane. Of course, once you cross that line, there is no turning back. You will have confirmed what they now only suspect, but they will have no proof. As for hiding here..." He smiled. "No offence, my friend, but you do not blend in easily."

Ricardo accepted the comment, and said, "So what are you saying?"

"My opinion, Ricardo, is that either way it is too great a risk for you. Come with me."

Ricardo had come to the same conclusion the moment he received the coded words from the young student who had come to his office that morning. He could not explain it, but a piece of him had been excited. Exiled, he could write editorials, continue the fight with his family safe, even open up a practice.

But the thought of Teco and the children chilled him. This campaign had taken its toll on them as well. If it were just he, there would be no question. He would stay, hide, and fight them as Hugo was doing. But that was not the case. He would have to leave and send for Teco and the children from Guatemala. They would all return later, during better times.

Ricardo nodded his head slowly and said, "I will have to make some arrangements first. I need to talk to my aunts and Chepe to see that Tere and the children are safe."

"Of course, Ricardo," Carlitos said understandingly. "I will wait as long as I can."

"And that brings us to now," Ricardo said to me, pausing.

I could not help myself, and just uttered, "But *why*, Gordo?" It was the wrong question, I knew immediately, but by now the implications of his actions were hitting me fast and hard and I needed to vent. "I am sorry," I corrected myself. "I do not mean to judge, it is just…I do so much want to understand…" I let my words trail off because I was starting to choke on them.

He looked at me understandingly and said, "It is all right, *compa.* You have every right. Let me ask you something instead. Have you ever heard of Hugo?"

"Yes, the name, but Ricardo…"

"No, listen, please. Hugo is the one who organizes things for us. He is our contact with the other groups." Then, in a pleading voice, he said, "Chepe, you have to understand that there are hundreds of us dedicated to bringing down Martínez."

He waited for a sympathetic reaction. Getting none, he continued with eyes lowered.

"Several weeks ago, after the armory in Usulután was broken into, Hugo's spies got word about a plan to step up arrests. You remember that some guards died in the raid. The military was incensed, even more so because they were embarrassed. And you know what happens when the military gets embarrassed, they get violent. Many innocent people were tortured and killed in Usulután. Anyway, the guns I had were part of that cache. Our group was afraid to take them to the usual hiding places, so we decided to split them among us and…well…I just could not think of any other place where I could get to them fast." Ricardo frowned. "They are still there," he added slowly.

"*Dios mío*, Ricardo, if they are found, Teco could be arrested!"

"I know, Chepe. That is why I need a favor. And it has to be tonight," Ricardo said studying my reaction.

I was apprehensive and it must have showed, but I did not say anything.

Ricardo continued, "I must know she is out of danger before…well…before I leave."

"Then you are going?" I asked carefully, although I already knew.

"I have to, *compa.* They have my name, no evidence, just my name, but that is enough. Chepe, please, the favor?"

"Tell me," I said without hesitation.

"There are soldiers at the house. My aunt is calling Colonel Gutierrez and others to have them removed. I am asking you, my friend, to go to my house and make sure the soldiers are gone. Nothing more. When you are sure, call this number." He handed me a piece of paper. "Just say, 'the prescription for the *señor* is ready to be picked up at the pharmacy.' That is all. After you make that call, and only afterwards, I will leave." Then parenthetically, he added seriously, "Chepe, remember what happened to Choco Mendez."

He emphasized the words with penetrating eyes. I nodded.

After a moment, he said, "Chepe, when you see Tere, tell her everything. Tell her that I will get word to her from Guatemala. And tell her…tell her that I love her."

"*Por supuesto*, of course, Ricardo."

"Chepe, please help her prepare for this."

"*Hecho*, Gordo," I said, still serious but more relieved.

I would do anything for him and Teco; we were that close, *compadres*, godparents to each other's children. We even half-joked that someday we might even be in-laws, my Jose Carlos or Enrique with his Ana Maria, or my Rosa Maria with Ricardo León.

As close as we were, though, he knew that I vehemently stopped short of anything that implicated me, and by extension my family. But he also knew that what he was asking me to do did not place me in great risk. Having me check on Teco and make a call to Tomas was close to the line but did not cross it.

"Chepe," Ricardo said working on a smile, "I will come home when this is over. These bastards will not continue for long. Already more and more people are insisting on change. I do not regret getting involved, only the pain I have caused others because I took on responsibilities that have put them in jeopardy. I did not think that it would come to this. I should have, but I honestly did not. You know I love my family. I wanted it both ways. I want to believe that I am true to myself when I say that I did it for them, for you, for all of us."

He looked pleadingly into my eyes.

I returned the gaze and said warmly, "The fact that after all of this you sincerely want to believe it, Gordo, means that you probably do." Then added, "About that I know, clinically and otherwise." I was now feeling the full weight of what Ricardo was carrying and my eyes started to water as I added, "I will miss you, Gordo. You are a good person and we will always be *compadres*."

"Gracias, *compa*." Ricardo said, his eyes also moist.

Chapter 7

I was in a daze as I drove to Teco's. My mind was congested with sentimentality and I had to force myself to concentrate on Ricardo's request. If it had been anyone else, I would have run in the other direction as fast as I could. Still, I owed our friendship this much. But something he said bothered me. It was Choco. *Remember Choco*, he had said to me. And of course, I did remember.

The incident, as it came to be called, happened soon after Ricardo was inducted into the reserve-training program of the *Guardia Civil*. We were still working on our doctorates and he had just started dating Teco.

As I mentioned before, Ricardo's aunts had only managed a partial deferment for him from the mandatory induction into the military; he would only train as a reservist for a year in the *Guardia Civil*. And in truth, he did not put up much of an objection. I, on the other hand, did object and, because of my eyesight, my family was able to arrange a full exemption. I remember Ricardo needling me about this because many others with bad eyesight, like our friend Rodrigo Mendez, whose vision was so bad we had nicknamed him *El Choco*, the blind one, had not been excused. But then, admittedly, they had less *cuello*.

I did not care; I would have done almost anything to get out of the rigors of basic training; I abhor all types of regimentation. But Ricardo had been enthusiastic about the physical training and the idea of soldiering, unlike many of the other recruits, who complained bitterly about the interruption in their studies and their fledgling careers. After all, having to spend two training days a week for a year interned in a *cuartel* caused quite a disturbance. But in the end, most acquiesced, as he had.

However, their assent quickly turned.

At first, there had been military drills, physical fitness exercises, classes in defense, weaponry, and military strategy, all of which they tolerated, and as I say, a few like Ricardo, even enjoyed. But after weeks of physically exhausting the recruits, there had been a concerted effort to indoctrinate them in *martinista* policy. This part none of them abide.

The new recruits were a mixed bag of young men from all walks of life, but most were university educated, some even had doctorates. But the lectures on political philosophy were banal, opinionated and clichéd, and the more scholarly of the conscripts considered them pure autocratic propaganda.

It was not that they were elitists; many felt that the military's decision not to tailor the lessons to their backgrounds lacked foresight. The organizers could easily have used the skills of these educated reservists to remedy, for example, the perception of a stoic military image. Instead, instructors preached about the responsibility of social institutions, such as universities, to blindly accept policies aimed at insuring stability and order. Harnessing the ability of the conscripts to challenge the *status quo* was the antithesis of what these young successful men stood for, namely, academe and intellectual debate.

Still, the insulting regimen could have been forgiven and forgotten were it not for the overreaction of certain anti-intellectual military instructors who took great pleasure in making the seemingly haughty young men uncomfortable. Undeterred, many recruits continued to face up to their instructors on logical and moral grounds. There was no war or emergency to even justify this draft, they argued. It was illegal, a misuse of military powers. And stamping out internal rebelliousness was a job for the police. To use the military against its own people was tyrannical. The military instructors considered these confrontations insubordinate and made a determined effort to break the recruits' defiance. In turn, the young professionals believed that the disciplinary measures were purposeful acts on the part of the military to humiliate them. This the recruits could not pardon or ignore.

The incident occurred during the second month of their training, in the evening following a heated classroom session. For the reluctant trainees, most lecture sessions had become opportunities to discredit the officers, who continued to read their lessons from manuals, and did not invite discussion. When the student recruits insisted on challenging a point, the classes became unruly and void of military bearing. One-sided discourses and shouting often broke out. This would often provoke frustrated officers to leave before completing their lessons, to the delight of the "victorious" students. The day of the incident had been no different. The rage on the face of the young lieutenant as he bolted out of the classroom had been the brunt of jokes throughout the rest of the day and until they retired that night.

It was about two in the morning when a persistent call began outside the window of one of the barracks.

"Ricardo! Ricardo Cruz!"

It took a while for the subsequent tapping on the window and the call of his name to finally wake him and several of the other men. Ricardo jumped out of his bunk quickly and peered outside. He saw a man in tan uniform trousers and an undershirt, a reservist from another barrack. He did not know the man's name but knew him to be an engineering student. The man was excited.

"What is it?" asked Ricardo when he managed to get the window open.

"It is Choco *Mendez*," said the engineer. "He has been hurt, beaten, and wants to see you."

"Wait for me!" said Ricardo, shuffling to find clothes, the anger beginning to build.

He knew that Choco always sought him out, ever since they were in primary school. They had recently completed dental school together, and planned to partner in a clinic after finishing their internship. Choco was a small man and, by appearance, seemed feeble. But he was quite athletic and had starred in track and boxing at the university. Only his eyesight kept him from being a better pugilist. What set him apart, however, was his strong will and brilliant mind.

Ricardo put on his tan uniform pants, boots, and undershirt. Before climbing out the window, he pulled out a couple of handkerchiefs from his duffel bag. He wrapped one around each set of knuckles and held them in place with tight fists, a technique Choco had taught him.

Then he proceeded to follow the engineer to another cabin. As he approached the barracks, he saw several men watching from an open window. No lights were on. He recognized the somber faces of most of the men and nodded to them as he drew near.

"What happened?" he asked as he climbed through the window.

One of the men said grimacing, "It is bad, Ricardo."

The men walked with him to a far cot where a man lay in the darkness with a blanket covering him.

"They just dumped him at the front door about a half hour ago and ran away," said another. "He was unconscious, and we would not even have heard them had we not been up waiting."

"Yes," said another, "a couple of uniformed men came for him earlier, just before lights out. They said the *comandante* wanted to see him. It did not sound right, but Choco went without objection."

As Ricardo approached the cot, he could see that the man, who was lying on his side in a fetal position, had dried blood around a swollen nose and forehead. Choco was conscious and tried to smile when he saw Ricardo, but that seemed to hurt, and all he managed was a contortion. Ricardo could not remember ever seeing Choco without his thick glasses. His squinting swollen eyes made him look alien in the shadows cast about the room by the moonlight.

"*Que pasó,* Choco?" Ricardo asked softly as he knelt alongside the bed.

Choco tried again to smile. He started to talk but his voice was slurred, as though his tongue was twice its normal size.

After a moment, Choco managed to say, "I got two of them pretty good before the others took me down, Ricardo." His eyes tried to do what the corners of his mouth could not.

"Do not worry, Choco, we will get them," said Ricardo feeling the fury mount inside him.

"No, Ricardo!" Choco blurted out, and Ricardo could see that it hurt him. "That is what they want. Besides, I do not know who these men are. I do…but I do not. You understand?"

Ricardo nodded, although still confused. He could see that it hurt Choco to talk, so he said, "We can talk later, Choco. I will get you to a hospital." He looked around questioning at some of the men as if to say, *Why have you not taken him yet?*

One of the men answered his look. "He did not want us to. He wanted to talk to you first."

"Ricardo," Choco called. "I need to talk to you…now. It is important that I do that." He was emotional but in control. "They said they were taking me to see the sergeant. But instead, we went to a shed by the woods where four other men were waiting. Two tried to grab my arms, but I went into their bodies close in with fists and they were not expecting that. They were soft and went down easy. But the other four came at me at the same time. They hit me but without much strength. Then they tied my hands and held me down on the floor…"

He broke off and looked away either from physical pain or anguish; Ricardo could not be sure which. But he could see that there were tears welling up in Choco's eyes.

"Ricardo, there is something else," said one of the other men in the room quietly. "It was not just a beating."

Ricardo stared at the man and began to comprehend what he was saying. The rage gagged his throat and heated his face. Knowingly, Choco put a hand on Ricardo's arm just at the right moment, not to hold him back because he knew he could not, but as if to say, *Stay in control, I need you.* Ricardo had never felt such anger, but he also had never seen Choco emotional before, and this tempered him.

When they would party and drink together, it was Ricardo who was the soppy and over-romantic one, especially during the maudlin songs of the Argentine, Carlos Gardel. He was now recalling the poignant lyrics of one of the melodies: *Adios muchachos, compañeros de mi vida…*farewell my life's companions…

Compared to him, Choco was a quiet drinker, an intellectual who loved to listen and study the habits of other people. It was Choco, the logician and philosopher, who had lectured Ricardo on how to drink correctly or, as he put it, how to be correctly drunk.

"*Mira*, Ricardo," he would say, "the only difference between being a social drinker and a social drunk is simply knowing when to stop.

Comprende? That is the only bit of wisdom I bestow on you. Anything else would be a waste; you enjoy it too much."

Ricardo just looked at his friend lying there on the cot. They had not gone after the vocal rabble-rousers like him, he acerbically thought. No, the cowards had gone after the bespectacled, soft-spoken, diminutive one. Almost on cue, the calculating Choco began patting Ricardo's arm.

One of the men in the barracks, a last year medical student, said to Ricardo, "I examined him. There are no symptoms of internal bleeding as far as I can tell. There are tears of course but they are superficial. There are minor cuts and bruises on his body, the most severe are on his wrists. His right wrist is dislocated. He probably did that himself trying to fight the bindings. His nose is broken but he is breathing well. He has two broken teeth. I do not think the jaw is." He paused then said less clinically, "I am a medical doctor, Ricardo, not a psychiatrist. When something like this happens..."

Ricardo broke in, "Choco, I will kill those *hijos de puta!* I promise you!"

"No, Ricardo," Choco said in a calm and deliberate voice. "I want to tell you what happened, in detail; then we will try to put it behind us. My body will heal, Ricardo. You will make me new teeth and Roberto will fit me with new glasses. I will heal. Do you understand?"

He looked intently at Ricardo. He was not squinting now.

"As for the other...well, I first must tell someone, my friend. I must not deny what has happened. And then, I must forget about it. You can help me by doing the same. Tell me you understand."

It did not take long for Ricardo to comprehend the words uttered by this small giant. This was not a plea based on the emotion of the moment. It was something that had been well thought out by someone who actually thought he could force himself to forget. He needed someone to confide in, as a penitent needs absolution. But what he was asking for was enormous. *As large*, Ricardo thought, *as the affection he has for me. But at that moment, all he saw was hate.*

What Choco was asking was for him to put that aside, to have as much strength as he did when he pushed against the bindings to suppress the pain. *He wants me*, Ricardo thought, *to join him spiritually.* The lyrics of the song came back to him,...*compañeros de mi vida*, my life-long friends.

Ricardo nodded. Then Choco told him everything and they wept together. When it was done, it was a very old Ricardo who turned to the other men who had been huddled out of hearing range.

He said to them, "I will take Choco to the military hospital later this morning. Your story is that unknown men took him and assaulted him. They were dressed like soldiers, but you did not know them. There will be an investigation, and your statements will be taken. Say what you know except for one thing. I was not here until later this morning, and he did not say anything to you about what happened. What you suspect is not relevant, and it will die alongside their cursory and meaningless investigation."

He looked at each one. They nodded. Then, he went back to Choco and sat next to him. He had visions of self-righteous officers gathered in some corner of the Officers Club toasting the strong message they had delivered to the dissidents who had infiltrated and berated their institution. He imagined the satisfied winks and nods that accompanied the "completed mission," the boisterous mockery and vulgar jokes about the soft recruits. He craved revenge, but instead stayed with his friend until reveille sounded.

Ricardo kept his promise about not telling anyone what Choco had confided to him, but it was clear to me that the incident had affected him deeply. He did not talk to me in depth about it until later, after his aunts, who were concerned about his brooding, insisted that he seek the advice of a close military friend of the family, who also happened to be the director of the *Escuela Militar*.

"*Ricardo,* please come in, *por favor, pasa adelante,*" said Colonel Guillermo Gutierrez Ruiz as he walked around his desk to greet Ricardo with a broad smile.

He was a short, square-shaped middle-aged man, balding on top, with his few remaining hairs graying at the temples. He had a thin mustache above large purplish lips that seemed to divide his round face. His freshly pressed uniform was spotless and his movements precise.

He stretched out his arms, and after a warm embrace, asked, "To what do I owe this miracle? How long has it been? Let me guess. It was six months ago at your aunt's' New Year's party, am I right?"

"That is correct, Colonel," Ricardo said, smiling back. "They send their best regards, and this *quesadia* from San Lucas that they know you like so much."

"How kind of them to remember. I will save it for this afternoon's *almuerzo.* Let me get you some coffee." Without waiting, he called his aide and ordered two coffees. "Let us sit over here by the window where it is cooler." When they were seated, he asked, "So, what brings you to the *Escuela*? Do not tell me you want to accept a commission? It is not too late you know," he said jokingly.

"No," Ricardo said putting up his hands in resignation. Then, more seriously, "No, it is a personal matter. I was hoping you could give me some advice."

"Of course, Ricardo; you know that I have always felt that you were like a son to me. I have followed your career since you were getting into trouble at Liceo with that other *chavacan*; what was his name? Molina, I think. What happened to him?"

The sergeant came in with two coffees and set them down on the table in front of them. Ricardo only took a sip, because it was quite sweet. The colonel drank his in one gulp.

"Chepe and I are still best friends," said Ricardo. "We graduated together, and he has started his internship as a psychiatrist. In fact, I have managed to stay in touch with all of our classmates. It is a matter related to that fellowship that has brought me here."

"Oh, and what might that be?"

"Colonel, you have a high regard for education and have always encouraged us to study—as you put it, to not lose our curiosity. But I am not sure others in the military share your views."

"Ah, yes. I heard what happened to your dentist friend Mendez at the *cuartel* a couple of weeks ago," said the Colonel seriously. "In fact, I was going to call you about it, but thought best to let the investigation continue uninterrupted. Had you been directly involved, I would have certainly called. How is Mendez doing?"

"He is much better. He is very strong and will recover. His spirit is not broken, but the rest of us are not as understanding. You see, we do not believe that this attack was directed against just one of us. We think there is a vendetta against us and, as a result, our relations with the instructors at the *cuartel* are polarized.

"All discussions in the lecture sessions, for example, have stopped. They think this is an improvement, but it is only a sign that things are worse, not better. We are silent because we are angry, not afraid. They do not recognize that their attitude is breeding contempt. Is not the purpose of instruction to enlighten? There is a growing antipathy among the recruits that is not healthy. And, none of the instructors or officers considers the matter important. I just think that this situation is wrong, and should be brought to the attention of the high command."

Ricardo knew from his aunts that Colonel Gutierrez had a reputation for fairness and believed in the integrity of the military. He had a soft-spoken and professorial demeanor, which some of his peers had interpreted as timidity. Ricardo's aunts thought that this perception had caused the colonel to be passed up for several cabinet posts. He was the Director of the Military School, which was a prestigious post, but it did ostensibly keep him out of the more influential and thus more lucrative positions. But those who knew him well acknowledged that he was more levelheaded and cerebral than his peers. Ricardo felt he could expect a direct answer from him.

The colonel put a hand on Ricardo's arm. *"Mira, Ricardito,"* he said slowly, after pausing for a moment to prepare his reply, "if you will permit me, I am going to talk to you about this as a father would to a son."

"Gracias, coronel."

The colonel nodded and said, "I have been in the military all of my life. I came up through the ranks because President Meléndez closed the Polytechnic Institute, which was the military academy of my day. Later, other officers and I established the new Gerardo Barrios Military School that you see here, and it has survived all this time. I have come to know and trust my peers from those days; it is they who are currently in power. If I have any influence it is because I can call on any one of my fellow officers, including the President, I might remind you, and speak to them with the esoteric bond of a Masonic brother. Do you know what that means?"

Ricardo shook his head.

"No, of course not, how could you? But take my word for it, there is a strong union and loyalty among us. Idealism is not just for the young, my son. Frankly, such romantic optimism is wasted on them, because the young lack depth and organization. Present company excluded, of course," he said smiling and with a slight bow.

"True idealism," he continued, "is profound and tenacious; it matures with age. In the military the fire of those years of youth and camaraderie stays with you forever. Loyalty, duty, honor; these are values that do not dissipate with time. That is one reason why I love the military so much and defend it, right or wrong."

Ricardo interrupted, "Even when that includes raping the innocent citizens they are supposed to protect?" He had not been able to hold back the impertinent comment, and regretted it the moment he said the words.

Gutierrez was stung and glared at him.

After a moment, he said solemnly, "Ricardo, please do not abuse our relationship. You are young and you are angry about what happened to your friend, so I will overlook it." He stared at him, driving home his admonition. Then, he broke off eye contact and looked pensively out the window.

"I am sorry," said Ricardo penitently. "That was insolent and discourteous."

Gutierrez waved off the apology and instead said, "Although your question does not deserve a reply, I will answer it anyway. No, our duty does not include committing heinous acts against honest citizens, and those who systematically practice such things are not patriots. They are criminals and traitors. Is that straightforward enough for you? You might be shocked to know that most of us in the military do not condone these acts or agree that they are necessary."

Ricardo started, "I did not mean to imply that you…"

"No, let me continue. Do such things happen? Yes, but they are done by the overzealous, the ones who are too ignorant to conceive a more effective plan. In this regard, the military is no different than other institutions. Your brother dentist pulls out the wrong tooth. Do his fellow dentists attack him? No, privately they might criticize, but they will make excuses for him to those outside their 'brotherhood.'

"I do not agree with some of the practices being carried out today by my brethren. I wish more thought and counsel preceded their decisions. But they do not act this way for treasonous reasons anymore than your brother dentist pulls the wrong tooth on purpose. These people may not be as skillful as other statesmen, but I assure you they are patriots.

"Look at the situation with theft in this country. The people are sick of thieves. One of my brothers is very forceful and focuses on this cancer and is trying to eliminate it. Who is more immoral, the thief or the overzealous policeman? Even the Koran permits mortals to use extreme measures when the security of the populace is threatened. My brother's practices are moral by a standard that is accepted by the majority. Maybe not by you and, confidentially, not by me either, but he is in a position to do something to help his countrymen and he does it. Some say to excess. Well, that could be. But you do not hear anyone complaining, do you?

"When it is your daughter who is raped by a burglar, or your hard-earned possessions that are plundered, believe me, you will say his 'excess' is not enough. So, he interprets their silence to be acquiescence and acquiescence to be his mandate. Is he wrong?"

"I do not think we are talking about someone accidentally pulling out the wrong tooth or how to deal with burglars and rapists," Ricardo said heatedly. "This is a case of people in the military being offended by our demeanor and taking violent actions to chastise us for something as petty as debating with instructors. What they did to Mendez was unconscionable. You have to agree with that."

"If a member of the military is responsible, I agree. But the last I heard, it was still being investigated."

Ricardo bit his tongue. He had already shown his impertinence once and did not want to alienate the colonel further, but he could not help making a skeptical face.

The colonel ignored the expression and thought for a moment. He then said, "Ricardo, let me think about this. I have not wanted to get involved, but you have raised a valid concern and I am grateful that you came to me with it. There was a time when I would have done everything in my power to get you to join us in a military career. We are in desperate need of good leaders. You are a good and respected young man with the future ahead of you. If what is occurring at the reserve training camp is turning people like you against us, then that must be assessed. Let me think some on it and I will get back to you in some way with a better response."

"*Gracias, Coronel,*" said a relieved Ricardo.

"Now tell me about you," Colonel Gutierrez asked, changing his voice to a lighter tone. "Catalina tells me that you are engaged. When do I meet the lucky girl?"

"Very soon I hope. Her name is Teresa Marroquin-Contreras; she is from Santa Ana."

"Are they the Contreras related to the Hinez?"

"Yes, I think so."

"I know Luz and Polo from Santa Ana. Luz is Hinez de Vides I believe."

"Yes, Luz is Teresa's aunt."

"You know, when I mentioned the Masonic brotherhood, I was thinking of Polo. He is a Mason and travels to conventions all over the world with them. He wants me to join but I have to 'knock on their door' first, he says, because they do not recruit. A couple of us are thinking about it, but you know the Church. They have condemned the Masons.

"I imagine there is some interesting history there, because there was a time when every Pope was a Mason. Did you know that? You cannot get any more universal, holy or true than that. Interesting, no?" He laughed at his musing, then added, "Please give my best to the beautiful *Señorita* Marroquin. I know she is beautiful because I know your eye. Now, tell me, are you still drinking good whiskey? Remember my two rules: you cannot trust a man who does not enjoy a good drink, nor can you trust one that does not look you straight in the eye when he is talking to you."

"I remember and I am," said Ricardo smiling, "If it was later in the day, I would prove it."

"Well, I have something right here." The colonel made a furtive move towards a desk drawer.

"*No, gracias,*" Ricardo held up his hands, laughing. "I have to get back to the clinic. But you can count on me regardless."

"I know I can, Ricardo. I know I can." The colonel stood and gave the much taller Ricardo an embrace. He then held him out at arm length, and said, looking up at him, "Seriously, Ricardo, wait for my response before you do anything you may later regret. These are difficult times and judgments are often confused. Stay with us. I can protect you only so far." Then, shifting gears as if for a different audience, he said in a loud voice, "As for what we have discussed, I cannot tell you how pleased I am that you came to see me about your concerns. They say volumes about you, your patriotism, and what is in your heart. And that is how I am going to report this visit. *Que Dios te guarde mi hijo.* May God watch over you."

"Thank you, colonel; I hope to see you soon."

As Ricardo drove away from the military school that morning, he felt better. He would wait, and counsel the others to wait. He understood that the military would probably not do anything about the incident except hypocritically condemn it; after all, they were the ones who had ordered it in the first place. But Colonel Gutierrez' concern seemed genuine. He would wait to see what the colonel reported back.

Meanwhile, despite Choco's wishes, it had been impossible to keep the subject from being sensationalized and turned into a *caúse celebré* at hushed gossip sessions. The news of the outrage was rampant. It was at this point that Ricardo sought me out professionally. At first, he used the pretext that it was Choco who needed the help. But from my social observations of Choco, that ruse could be easily countered. Choco was adjusting just fine— Ricardo, however, was not.

We spent several "sessions" at my house with our usual medicinal inducements and, as he was apt to do after about four whiskeys, he would espouse his most troubling concerns. Heretofore, I have described him as a man's man, proud and passionate. But during these times, I detected an inordinate preoccupation with "the incident," and I began drawing out deeper feelings. After a while, I began to believe that there were aspects of his *own* sexuality that troubled him.

"It was not just an assault," he would often say, "they abused him sexually." It made him queasy to even think about it, he would add, similar to seeing a child being abused or any underprivileged living creature being maltreated. He confessed that he did not understand his overreaction and that this lack of comprehension gave him pause. Ricardo was quite analytical, and these doubts did not sit well with him.

I told him that, as a therapist, I saw nothing wrong with his self-analysis; it was honest. But now I know that there was more to Ricardo, more than my advantaged upbringing allowed me to perceive at the time. And part of my guilt today as I write this is that I failed to diagnose that inner struggle, his "illness," if you will, that drove him right into Hugo's hands.

But the incident did not end there.

As awkward as it was for them, Ricardo and the recruits returned to the *cuartel* for the rest of their training. Then, four weeks after the attack on Choco, their level of unease was raised even higher.

Early on a Saturday morning, as Ricardo and the men in his company were drilling in a field near the barracks, they noticed a commotion at one end of the parade ground. A group of men were gathered near a thicket adjacent to one corner of the field and several of them could be seen running back and forth to a nearby administration building. The company continued to march until they were close to the area and the drill sergeant called them to halt.

The lines held in place while the sergeant broke ranks and walked over to where the group of men, including a lieutenant, were bent over some thick grass about five feet from the edge of the field. About ten enlisted men, some carrying machetes to trim the grass around the field, were standing or squatting around something on the ground. Ricardo could hear some of the comments made to the sergeant as he approached them.

"*Es El Chato Olivedo*," said one. "We found him lying there about ten minutes ago with that sign on him."

"We found him when we were cutting this end of the field," said another man.

Several of the men were now staring at the reservists still standing in formation, still at attention. Other men from the offices were now joining the huddled group. The lieutenant stood up and told the men to back away and then said something to the sergeant. The sergeant acknowledged him and slowly walked back to the formation. Ricardo could see the anger in the stocky veteran's eyes.

"The lieutenant orders you to return to your barracks immediately," he said brusquely. "Stay there until you are told otherwise. Dismissed."

The men slowly began to disperse. Some of the recruits just looked at each other uncertainly. Others shrugged and started walking away, and still others just stared back, expecting more information. Ricardo was in the latter group. When he saw that no more was going to be said, he unshouldered his rifle and began walking past the sergeant towards the huddled group on the edge of the field.

The sergeant said to him sternly, "You have been ordered to your barracks."

Ricardo slowed some as he turned to the sergeant and met his gaze with his own insolent stare. "And that is what I am doing," he said defiantly as he continued to close the distance to where the men were staring at the object on the ground.

The men who stood in the tall grass stared at Ricardo as he approached. He noted they had the same angry stare as the sergeant. Some looked away as he neared; others deliberately turned their backs. The lieutenant, intent on looking at the body on the ground, did not notice Ricardo until he was about five feet away. When he did, he stammered angrily, "You men are ordered to return to your barracks!"

"*Si, señor*," Ricardo saluted him and began to arc away, but not before glancing at the body lying on the ground near the lieutenant's feet.

As he turned away, he heard clearly the smothered comments from the men who had been standing with the lieutenant. From under their breaths, they were uttering profanities at the recruits, calling them cowards, "*Hijos de puta! Hijos de once mil putas. Cobardes!*"

Ricardo continued to walk, but was poised for anything. He slung the rifle onto his right shoulder and cocked his cap to one side. As he logged some distance from the group, colleagues who were making their way back to the barracks approached him.

"What was that about, Ricardo?"

"I am not sure," he said. "There is the body of a soldier lying in the brush. I saw corporal's stripes on his shirt and heard one of the men refer to him as 'Chato.' He had dried blood on his throat and quite a bit on his shirt, but none on the ground. He must have been brought out here. And there was a sign with letters in red paint. They spelled the words, '*PUTO*' and '*MARICÓN.*'"

"Really?" said one of them. "The man was a homosexual? I do not understand, and what has that to do with us? Those men and the sergeant acted as though we had something to do with it, like we were responsible."

Ricardo shrugged. Then said cryptically, "Maybe because we were."

The voice of Colonel Gutierrez kept coming back to him: *I will get back to you in some way with a better response.*

Chapter 8

As I approached Ricardo and Teco's home, I was extremely anxious, and searched for any sign of the authorities. I saw none, but that did not make me feel any less nervous. I did take some comfort in knowing that, since we visited each other almost daily, my presence there would not seem out of the ordinary. Still, the hairs on the back of my neck were prickly as I walked up the path to their door.

The maid let me in and led me to the living room where, Teco was trying to calm an upset Ana Maria. We gave each other a feigned, yet knowing, smile that revealed to each other that we both knew about Ricardo's situation. Teco gave the child to the maid as soon as she could and came to me. She fell into my arms and began to weep. We embraced for a moment and then she insisted on emotionally recounting in detail what had happened after Ricardo's call. Despite the anxiety I felt just being there, I listened patiently.

"And after I collapsed, *compadre*, Lucha aided me to bed, but I was too nervous to rest. Ana Maria kept crying, and Lucha was back and forth trying to attend us both. I could not focus; only pulses of thoughts came to me, like heartbeats reverberating in my brain."

She was half crying, half talking and I held her hand and let her get it out.

"I kept saying to myself: I must be strong, we will come out of this, Ricardo is alive. I prayed to Our Lady of Perpetual Help, 'Holy Mother of God, you have always answered my prayers and I need your help now. I beg you as a mother to give me the strength to see to the welfare of my children and my husband.' I began reciting the rosary. But before I started the final creed, Lucha came back into my room with more frightening news."

I did not know about this and sat up straighter. It was a remarkable tale, and I am writing it the way it surely happened.

"The soldier who spoke to you before is back and wants to see you," the maid said.

My God! Teco thought; she had not even heard the knocking. She looked at her watch. It was 8:30. More than two hours had passed! She thought she must have fallen asleep before and lost track of time. "Tell him I will be right there."

She tried to arrange her hair and put on a fresh coat of lipstick. She managed to straighten out her dress and, as composed as she could be, hurried to the front door and opened it.

"*Sí?*" she asked the same older soldier who had spoken to her before.

"*Señora*," he said, "I have been ordered to leave the area, and I wanted to personally apologize if we caused you any inconvenience."

Teco was relieved, and quickly composed herself. "You have nothing to apologize for. You were only doing your duty and you and your men have been respectful. I will so report to my husband when he returns. He called a while back and said he was delayed, but he will be here soon."

"You are very kind, *señora*." The soldier was looking right at her and made no movement to leave.

What? I do not recognize that look, she thought, *he wants to say something else.* She noticed the soldier had stripes on his sleeves, a sergeant perhaps. She could tell he was rural, from the *campo,* but his face was not weather-beaten like the other regular soldiers. He was about her height, but stocky, and there was something about his demeanor that was familiar to her. Without the threatening uniform, the man could have been a merchant at the *mercado.*

Given her background, Teco had always been comfortable making small talk with *campesinos* and people of lesser means. It came naturally to her.

In a more casual tone, she asked, "Where is your family from?"

"Atiquizaya, close to the border," he answered without hesitation.

"Yes, I know it," she said confidently. "I grew up in Santa Ana, not far from there. My husband has an uncle with a farm in Atiquizaya. Raul Siliesar, do you know him?"

"Of course, *señora.* Everyone in Atiquizaya knows *Don Raul.* My family still works for his neighbor *Don* Enrique Prado. I grew up on his farm." He said, and his eyes met hers again.

Teco looked at him more intently. Prado was the name of the Guatemalan *cafetalero* who had sired the famous Ernesto Interiano in Santa Ana. She also knew that the beloved Ernesto was killed the year before in a police ambush at the age of twenty-five.

Although he had not lived long, Interiano's romantic adventures and defense of the poor and the less fortunate were legendary. He was eight years old when he witnessed the violent death of his pet dog, Satanás, poisoned by an overzealous public official. It was said that on that day his anti-authoritative spirit was set.

His exploits since were likened to the English story of Robin Hood. He generously gave money to the poor and violently sanctioned police and military officials who abused street vendors and other deprived people in the rural areas around Santa Ana. In turn, these people protected him. Martínez had sought Interiano for years; even proclaiming him public enemy number one after an altercation over a woman at Lake Coatepeque resulted in the violent death of a police official.

Interiano was then rumored to have tried to kill Martínez near La Libertad, although the townspeople placed Ernesto on his ranch, La Montañita, in the foothills of the volcano Santa Ana at the time.

Teco had met him when she was younger, and recalled how he had flirted with her even while in the arms of another woman. She also knew that many common conscripts in the military were secret admirers of the brave Ernesto. They had not liked the way the *Guardia* had arrested and abused his sick mother to lure him into a trap. Despite warnings, the brash Ernesto, who had been in the process of fleeing the country with his paramour at the time, had tried to see her and was gunned down.

But even in death, Ernesto had left his celebrated mark. As he was falling, he killed the Olympic sharp-shooting champion, Rodrigo Salazar, who had been employed by the police for the ambush. Salazar had been Ricardo's teammate at the Pan American Olympics, where they had both medaled. Ricardo told Teco later that it had been a single shot from the falling Ernesto that had felled the champion.

Was this sergeant an Ernesto sympathizer? Teco wondered now. "What a small world," she said to him earnestly, and thought, *What does he want to say?*

"*Señora*," he paused and was no longer making eye contact. "My soldiers and I are leaving, but we will be around the area." Again, the pause. Then slowly in the flaccid argot of the *campo*, he said, "I know that your husband is *Don* Raul's nephew and, well...*Don* Raul is...I mean...you and your husband and *Don* Raul are good people. *Señora*...tell your husband to be careful. I cannot say more. I have to leave, *con su permiso*." The last part had been uttered quickly as he was turning to leave.

But Teco stopped him with her words. "Wait. I...I do not understand," she said guardedly.

"*Señora*," he said half turning and in a whisper. "I was assigned to this platoon because I know what your husband looks like. Please, I am telling you this because I also know of your family, the Marroquín. *El Padre* Marroquín was my confessor and it would not be right for harm to come to you. I am an office clerk at the *cuartel*, not the *Guardia*. In saying this to you, I am putting my life in your hands. I was ordered to bring your husband in by whatever means, but I have heard what they have done to others, and it would not be right."

She could see that he was as scared as she was. It was not an emotion familiar to him; she could tell from his expression of almost pain. She looked into his eyes and started to protest, but stopped instinctively. She lowered her eyes as well. It was her turn to take a chance. She said evenly, "What do they call you?"

"My name is Rodolfo Maria de Jesus Mendez, *a sus pies, señora."*

Teco said solemnly, "I am grateful for your confidence, Rodolfo, and your words are safe with me. My husband has no reason to be fearful of the military, but I understand that mistakes are often made and sometimes they have grave consequences. You are obviously a good and brave man, and I will remember you in my prayers. *Vaya con Díos."*

"God watch over you too, *señora."*

Teco watched the *campesino* in his dirty tan soldier's uniform, sagging gun belt, and slung rifle, walk down the stone path. He opened the wrought iron gate and took a last furtive glance back before stepping onto the street where six other soldiers waited for him. Straightening his posture and gait, he gave some instructions, and they all started walking down the street. It was then that she noticed that her heart was pounding almost audibly beneath her sweat-soaked dress. *Madre de Díos, you have always been there to rescue me in my hour of need*, she prayed. *And now when I most need it, you have delivered me an honest man to intercede as your messenger. I will be eternally grateful.*

I do not much believe in divine intervention, but the story of the compassionate soldier gave me pause. What are the odds? I was speechless.

"Chepe," she said, "after he left, I returned to my room and finished the rosary. It was a short while later that you knocked on the door."

"Do not worry, Teco. Cora and I will be close should you need anything."

I consoled her, but she continued crying. I did not dare mention my own apprehension. I had noticed troops on the streets, but none around the house. My Cora and I lived just three blocks away, and I was familiar with the neighborhood. As was our routine, I had instructed the chauffeur to wait outside for me, and I was anxious to get home and bring Cora up to date. It was no telling what she was wondering, since I had been gone all this time.

When Teco's sniffling subsided, she said, "*Ay, compadre,* you do not know how happy I am that you are here." She managed a smile.

"*Comadre*, you look tired. You must get some rest tonight."

"Of course, I will try," she lied. Tears welled up and she began to sob again. "You know about Ricardo? He is leaving. Chepe, what are we going to do?"

"Everything will be fine. I was with him a few hours ago. But first things first. Right now we have to think of you and the children."

I walked her over to a sofa and we sat. Lucha came into the room and asked if we needed anything. I asked for some water and she left.

"Chepe, how is he?"

"Distraught. He did not see it coming and is guilt-ridden. He is concerned about you and the children and has asked me to help get you to Guatemala. We need to make arrangements, but not now. That can wait until tomorrow. Cora and I will be back in the morning and we will plan. Tonight you must rest. Now, tell me about Lucha. Can you trust her to watch the children while you get a night's rest?"

"Chepe, I will not rest. We have much to think about. But do not worry about me."

"Nonsense. You cannot concentrate without relaxing. You will rest; I promise you. Tell me about Lucha."

"She is good with the children. But…"

"No 'buts.' I am the doctor and I know what I am talking about. You will need all of your strength when the time comes. Now, I need to use your telephone for a minute. You said it was working again."

"Yes," she said. "You know where it is."

I went to the hall and asked the operator for the number Ricardo had given me. When a man answered I merely said, "Tell the *señor* that his prescription is ready to be picked up. Do you understand?" The man said he did. "Good." I paused for a second, then added, "And assure the *señor*, if you would be so kind, that everything *is* going to be all right." I hung up without waiting for a response and returned to Teco.

"Ricardo will be leaving for Guatemala now. He will be safe there. Now, for you." I reached into a shirt pocket and took two pills out from a small brown envelope. Lucha was just walking into the room with a glass of water and some tea. I handed the pills to Teco. Lucha turned to leave, but I stopped her.

"Lucha," I said, "the *señora* is very tired and needs to sleep. I am giving her some pills now to help her do that. You have to mind the children tonight. Do you understand?" Lucha nodded. "My wife and I will be here in the morning. I am leaving our telephone number right here by the phone. Any concerns, call me. Do you understand?" Lucha nodded again.

In another room, Ana Maria started crying and Lucha looked at both of us for permission to leave.

"Lucha, the soldiers are gone and will not come back," I continued. "If you have no questions, please go see to the *niña*. Here, take these; they are for you." I handed her some coins.

Lucha thanked me and left the room. Teco's eyes followed her down the hall then turned back and stared at the pills. In the back room, the baby was still crying. She gave me a pleading look.

"No, Teco," I said sternly. "Take the pills, kiss the babies goodnight, and go to bed. I will not leave until you are asleep."

"Chepe, there is so much to talk about…"

"I know and we will, tomorrow. Now take the pills."

She did. Within a half-hour the drug took its effect and she succumbed.

While I was comforting Teco, Ricardo had returned to the safehouse to wait for my call. While there, he gave Tomas instructions on how to deal with the guns.

"Simply cut the rope that suspends the wrapped guns under the stool in the outhouse," he said. "Do not try to salvage them. Let them fall into the cesspool."

"Ricardo," Tomas said, "the guns were difficult to get; people have died. I should try to retrieve them if I can."

"Cut the rope!" Ricardo repeated said adamantly.

Tomas just nodded.

"It is too dangerous, Tomas. The house is being watched. Besides, it is only fitting," Ricardo remarked bitterly, "Like this phase of my life, the guns should also turn to *mierda*."

"Ricardo," Carlitos said, "I have to leave. I know I told you that I would wait, but I cannot."

"Just a while longer," Ricardo appealed.

"No," Carlitos was firm. "You will not leave until you know that the soldiers have left, and I do not blame you. But I cannot risk missing this departure. I will wait as long as I can for you at the *finca*."

Ricardo just nodded.

After Carlitos left, Ricardo sat alone in a hallway chair and waited. No one, except me, knew how much the soldiers scared him. Waiting, without information is its own form of terror.

Ricardo was still sitting quietly in the hallway when the telephone rang a half-hour later. Tomas, who was passing by when it rang, picked up the receiver. Ricardo was immediately at his side.

"*Alo*," Tomas said. He listened for a few seconds, then said, "*Gracias*, the patient will be much relieved. *Adios.*"

"Was it Chepe? What did he say?" Ricardo blurted even before Tomas had hung up.

"He said, 'The prescription for the *señor* is ready to be picked up at the pharmacy!'"

All the men started congratulating Ricardo.

Tomas smiled and added, "Then Chepe said, 'Tell the *señor* not to worry; that everything is going to be all right.'"

Ricardo closed his eyes and gave an audible sigh.

"And now, Ricardo," said Tomas. "Go!"

"Yes, for God's sake, go," said another. "We will pick up your car from the *finca* and take it to your home. And we will take care of the guns the first thing in the morning."

"Good-bye my friends," said Ricardo, and embraced each one. "Keep up the fight. We will be back together soon."

"To better times," they each said.

Ricardo left immediately, following closely the instructions Carlitos had given him.

"If Chepe calls," Carlitos had said, "it means that your aunts had enough *cuello* to have the soldiers removed from your home. But they will be watching, so do not go there. Come directly to the *finca*. Now remember, be careful and do not overreact if you are stopped. Police outposts do not have telephones and you will have a safe window to travel to the coast. If you are stopped, show your certificate from the military school; it awards you status. And have your story ready. Tell them you are going to meet your family at your *ranchito* on the beach; you were delayed with an emergency at the military hospital. And above all, stay calm."

The directions to the ranch were not complicated, and Ricardo did not encounter any roadblocks. But despite Carlitos' admonition, he was prepared to use his automatic pistol if it came to that. The rain had muddied the dirt back roads and his Chevrolet coupe almost got stuck several times. It was 3 A.M. by the time Ricardo saw the lights of the farmhouse and maneuvered towards them.

As he approached, he saw that there were several cars parked in front. He recognized Carlitos' car, a Hudson, but not the other three. Although tired, he was alert. The adrenaline from the night's ride had not dissipated. The lights inside the house were on and he could see shadows in the front room moving about. He had made no effort to hide his approach, and kept the car's headlights shining on the front of the house. He also kept the engine running and the car in gear. The automatic was at his side, the hammer cocked.

After a long minute, the front door opened and Carlitos stepped out. Shading his eyes from the car's lights, he called out, "Ricardo?"

From inside the car, Ricardo asked, "Is everything all right?"

"Yes, come on in. Hugo is here."

Hugo, Ricardo thought. *Why am I not surprised?* He took a deep breath and uncocked the automatic.

Chapter 9

"And finally, the famous Doctor Cruz," Hugo said rising from a sofa chair as Ricardo entered. They shook hands, then Hugo turned to face another group of men just rising from a couch. "Ricardo, let me introduce you to a colleague, Armando Solis. And I think you know Paco Poveda."

Ricardo shook their hands as well. He knew everyone except Solis, a short, thin man with an expressionless face, the type who usually went unnoticed. Ricardo had met Poveda through Teco's sisters. He was a former military officer who had turned pilot five years earlier, and now flew mail and commercial cargo for a fledgling air service that he had helped to start. He was a big man for a pilot, almost as tall as Ricardo, and heavier. Carlitos was very high on him, although Ricardo knew he had a reputation as a philanderer, something the pilot took great pride in propagating.

Hugo's presence was unplanned, but by now Ricardo knew that Hugo often succeeded at being where he was not expected. He was not a large man, about the average height of Salvadorans, slender, and light-skinned for someone purported to be the son of peasant farm workers. He had dark curly hair and fast eyes, which seemed to be constantly taking in everything. Ricardo had not seen him often since the first time they met. It was Hugo who had convinced Ricardo to join the underground. And, after all these months, Ricardo was still unsure how he felt about him. He did not feel this awkward with anyone else in the room. But then, he recalled, their relationship had been uncomfortable from the time they met.

It was in August, almost a year before. I recall the episode, although I took little notice of it at that time. It had been an innocent night of festivities. A women's club patronized by Ricardo's aunts had staged a large and colorful costume ball at the new Casino Salvadoreño for the benefit of an orphanage. We had planned extensively for the event, renting professional costumes and practicing for a talent contest.

Ricardo looked dashing in a white Cossack outfit complete with sword and high top boots. I was roguish in a crimson pirate outfit, and Teco and my Cora looked wild and sensuous as gypsy dancers. There was a carnival atmosphere, with everyone in high spirits. We danced to a large twenty-piece band and later, during the talent contest, Ricardo and I had sung our duet, while Teco and my Cora jokingly chided us for our clowning antics on stage. No one had any intention of being serious that night.

The evening was winding down and, during a music break, Ricardo had walked across the dance floor to get us another round of fresh drinks. From my vantage point at our table, I managed to see a man in his thirties, dressed as an Argentine *gaucho*, complete with spurs, approach him at the crowded bar. Ricardo must have heard the spurs, because he turned and was sizing him up when the man unexpectedly addressed him. They spoke for a while, and then Ricardo returned to us with the drinks.

When I asked, Ricardo told me the man was someone he had met casually at the university, no one important. I thought nothing of it as I did not know the man nor did I get a good look at him. As it was, I never saw him again. It was only after Ricardo's exile, when we had an occasion to meet in Guatemala, that he confided what had really taken place, and, how the encounter had changed his whole life.

"So you are the famous *Doctór* Ricardo Cruz Carranza?" the brash stranger had said to him loudly over the noise of the conversations around them.

A surprised Ricardo had said, "Well, I do not know about the famous part, but I am Ricardo Cruz. I do not think we have met."

"No we have not. My name is Jorge Villareal; I am a student at the university. But you are being modest, *Doctór*. An Olympic swimmer, a decorated sharpshooter, a prominent dentist with friends in high places, please. I was wondering if we could have a word; I have been trying to meet you all night."

He had stuck out his hand, but Ricardo ignored it. He was starting to feel his drinks and was annoyed by the stranger's patronizing tone. "No offense, but you seem a little old for a student. And why do you want to meet me, anyway?"

"Well..." the man said, forcing a strained laugh, "I think we have some things in common. As for the student part...I started late. You see, I was exiled in Europe until recently."

He slowly pulled back his hand, reached for a pack of cigarettes in his pocket instead, and offered Ricardo one.

"*No, gracias*," said Ricardo, whose hands were already busy trying to balance four drinks. With an annoyed expression, Ricardo turned to leave.

"Then later perhaps," called the man. "I would like to buy you a whiskey, with just a splash of soda, I believe."

Ricardo turned and looked at the man again. This time he did not hide his irritation. "Look, I do not know you and I do not want to. And I do not like games or people spying on my habits. Incidentally, you should know that the spurs ruin the outfit." He turned to walk away again.

"I am sorry if you are offended," the other man called after him. "But perhaps it is because you have already had one too many. Choco always says that knowing when to stop is the key to drinking."

Ricardo stopped and looked at the man curiously.

"Yes, I know Choco and what they did to him years ago," the man said moving closer. "Not a secret, I grant you. But it is partly because of him that I wish to speak to you. You see, I also know how they set you and the others up to be blamed for the corporal's murder. I also know how they got back at Memo Gutierrez for trying to help. But more important, I know what they are up to these days, and how they plan to continue raping others who disagree with them."

Ricardo was stunned. Jorge Villareal's sharp words were sobering. The man was no longer just the arrogant pest in a comical cowboy outfit. He was clearly in his element, confident and self-assured. Ricardo turned his head slightly, but maintained eye contact with the man. The man's eyes were darting but totally serious. He had said these words passionately and with an ardor Ricardo recognized as genuine.

"You and I need to talk," said Villareal.

"I do not want to talk about this now…here," said a disarmed Ricardo slowly.

"*Esta bien,* Ricardo," the man said. "Tomorrow is Sunday. Go to the Cathedral for the eleven o'clock Mass. I will find you."

"I do not go to Mass," Ricardo said lamely. It sounded trite the moment he said it and he was embarrassed.

"What a man does spiritually is his business. Just because you are at Mass does not mean you are in attendance, despite what the priests say. Go. I will find you there. We have much to talk about."

The man was confident, no longer condescending. There was understanding and steadfastness in his voice.

And so Ricardo had gone to the Cathedral and Villareal had found him. They had walked to a downtown café, where Ricardo had ordered a beer and Villareal milk; for an ulcer, he had explained. When he pushed the chair back from the table to cross his legs, Ricardo noticed the same fancy gray cowboy boots, this time without the spurs.

"Choco Mendez told me you would be attending the costume ball, and he gave me some words you might recognize to get your attention," Villareal began. "He has been telling me quite a bit about you. He respects you very much and recommended that we speak. You see, Choco is with us and thinks you should be, too."

"He never mentioned it to me," Ricardo said casually. He held back that he had already talked to Choco that morning before going to the Cathedral.

"Listen to what he has to say, Ricardo. Then make up your own mind," was all Choco had advised. Ricardo had not pressed him. He trusted his friend's judgment and was also somewhat intrigued.

"He was not supposed to," said Villareal. "At first, he did not think you should be involved, but now he is convinced otherwise. He believes that you would be of great assistance to us during this last phase of our plan to get these bastards out of office."

"Who is 'us'?"

"I will get to that, Ricardo," Villareal said, taking a sip of milk. "As you know, there are many people who are dissatisfied with the *martinistas*. I am helping to organize the opposition. The government has their inaccurate and indiscriminate list of dissidents, and well...I have mine, two lists actually, and very accurate. The names of patriots against Martínez are on one, and those who are with him are on another. Until now, they have attacked the names on their 'list.' Now, those on my list, the ones who are truly against the tyrant, are organizing to fight back. Preferably through the political route, but by force if necessary. We are smarter than they are and we will win. You have no idea how stupid they really are."

"Go on," said Ricardo, expressionless.

"Let me take you back five years. You remember when your friend, Colonel Memo Gutierrez resigned after the Choco incident?"

Ricardo narrowed his eyes and nodded.

"But do you know why?"

"I guess not," said Ricardo.

"He was forced out," Villareal said, sipping more milk. "In fact, many of Martínez' supporters wanted Memo exiled or worse for taking sides with the recruits. But Gutierrez and Martínez are colleagues; they came up through the ranks together. So there had to be a compromise. When Memo presented your argument about the recruits being harassed, he approached the issue at a much higher plane. He made an impassioned plea for Martínez and the *Estado Mayor* to recognize the value of having young professionals like you support the institution.

"He argued that co-opting the minds of these very influential young men was in the best interest of the country and the military. He recommended that a new training policy be adopted to tailor the instruction of new recruits to fit their aptitude. He even offered to take on the drafting of a new policy and implementation plan for Martínez' approval. He also recommended that, concomitantly, those responsible for the attack on Choco be punished for exceeding their authority. It could be handled internally, he suggested, so as to avoid publicity, while at the same time sending a clear message that such acts are unworthy of the institution. It was quite a speech. As you know, Memo is a man of vision and principle, and quite articulate. It was a brilliant argument, but it had one basic flaw." He paused to drink more milk. "He was addressing imbeciles."

"How do you know all this?" asked Ricardo skeptically.

"I was told by someone who was present at that meeting. Now Ricardo, I am confiding in you because I am sure that when you hear me out you will see how you were duped, as was Memo, and hopefully…as a result, you will join us."

"What happened to Memo's recommendation?" asked Ricardo.

"Well, Martínez could not argue with Memo's logic, and congratulated his classmate for his patriotic support and wisdom. He told Memo that he would look into the matter, since all this was news to him. But after Memo left, there was another meeting attended only by Martínez' closest advisors. General Marcos Chulio Lopez, the head of the *Guardia*, dominated that meeting. Chulio accused Gutierrez of being soft and said that his recommendations were treacherous. Chulio said he had an alternative resolution with a more favorable outcome."

Villareal paused as some patrons walked by and sat a nearby table. Ricardo took the occasion to order another beer. The conversation turned to small talk until they felt that they could speak in privacy.

"Martínez let Chulio speak," Villareal said in a quieter tone. But insisted that any counterproposal should not demean the integrity of the *Guardia Civil* program. Chulio said that, in fact, his plan would make the curriculum stronger. Then he began reciting pure *martinismo*. What was needed, he said, was order. Catering to the students was out of the question. They were subversives, bent on overthrowing the government, and had infiltrated the universities. He knew of only one answer to such treachery, their total elimination and the exile of any sympathizers."

The waiter brought Ricardo's beer. Her could tell that Villareal was not used to interruptions and was anxious to continue. When the waiter left, his eyes found Ricardo's and continued.

"Then, Chulio outlined his diabolical plan. You should know that Chulio is Martínez' *protégé*. He and the 'witch of the blue waters' are two of a kind. They even look alike, no?" he asked rhetorically. "Well, it seems that the man who staged the assault on Choco, was a troublemaker himself within the brigade. His name was Jesus Olivedo, but everyone knew him as *Chato*, because of his pug nose.

"Olivedo was an enlisted man who had been accused by several women of rape, some of them wives of workers at the *cuartel*. The man was a habitual drunk and difficult to control. He had been demoted to corporal the previous year for insubordination, but remained quite popular with the enlisted men."

"I did not know his name," said Ricardo. But I do remember someone calling him Chato. I never understood the signs that referred to him as a homosexual, though."

"It was supposed to be a message that only you and Choco would understand. You see, Chulio's plan was simple. Olivedo's unexplained murder would appear as retaliation for the assault on Choco. You and the others would think Olivedo was executed under 'military code.' It would be suggested to the abused women at the *cuartel* that it was justice for what he had done to them. Gutierrez would be silenced, because he would suspect that it was an internal action as he himself had suggested. The young officer corps and the enlisted men would find it easy to blame the incorrigible recruits for the murder of a popular soldier and that, in turn, would strengthen the *esprit de corps* of the program."

Villareal paused to let the implication of such a depraved plan by a government leader sink in. Ricardo was dumbfounded and just shook his head.

"And here is the most despicable part," he continued. "The *brujo* thought the plan was brilliant. Martínez ordered Memo informed that his recommendations would be taken under advisement since Martínez himself had at one time been head of the *Escuela Militar*, and was more than qualified to administer this program. Since everyone knows that Martínez has no use for advisors, Memo would recognize those words as a vote of no confidence and resign. Which is exactly what he did."

"You told all this to Choco?" Ricardo asked thoughtfully, taking it all in.

"Yes, I sought him out as soon as I learned of it. That is why, and incidentally, when, he joined us."

"Choco has been in the underground all of this time?" asked Ricardo incredulously.

"Yes. He is free to tell you himself."

Ricardo was crestfallen. Slowly, he said, "And for all these years, I believed Colonel Gutierrez had caused the retaliation against Olivedo. I remember that when he came to my wedding, he was gracious, but solemn, and we never spoke about this. Now that I think back, I was misreading his seriousness. I remember thinking that the killing was a somewhat inelegant tactic for him, but I also thought that somehow he had honestly raised the issue and that others had acted on it."

"In a way," Villareal said, "that is true, and you should not blame yourself for bringing it up. Both you and he acted nobly and in good faith. Not even he suspected how deeply the *martinistas* had buried the honor of the military."

Ricardo was shaking his head. "Now Memo is a ruined man. Everything he stood for, his mentoring of the young *tandas*, his faith in the military, all these ideals destroyed. For a man of principle, this is worse than exile or imprisonment."

"Yes," agreed Villareal. "Now, all he does is some consulting when the military needs him for some meaningless task. He does not know it, Ricardo, but he is still respected by many people, including those of us in the movement." He paused and looked intently at him. "Ricardo, listen. There is a way to get people like Memo back in power, but first this fascist government must fall. You are respected, and with your participation we can make this happen."

As astute as Ricardo was, all this information was too much for him to consume in one sitting. "You will have to give me some time to think about this," he said.

"Of course, Ricardo. I will contact you in a couple of days."

Their discussion was over and both rose from the table. This time, Ricardo took the stranger's extended hand and shook it.

"And, incidentally, as you no doubt have guessed, my name is not Villareal. I go by the name of Hugo."

"Of course," said Ricardo knowingly.

He had not needed a couple of days. That night, a dubious but invigorated Ricardo made up his mind. He mentioned some of this to Teco, but held back the details. He also warned her about telling anyone, especially me. When he later described the extent of his relationship with the underground, I recall being astounded by the level of detail and stratagem involved. Ricardo started attending meetings with Hugo right away. After each meeting, Hugo would set a date, time, and place for the next meeting, and even signals and a fallback place should the first be compromised.

Ricardo was not one to immerse himself in anything halfway. He began absorbing the insight Hugo divulged about current political events. After several months, Hugo called for more aggressive action and that suited Ricardo, who also felt that the time for dialogue was over—Martínez had to go. Hugo had known about this trait of Ricardo's from his conversations with Choco. And he knew one other thing: Ricardo was the right man for the perilous task of arming the movement.

"Paco will fly us out just before dawn," Carlitos said. "He knows of an airfield that the German government built for the Guatemalan military before the war broke out. It is in Alta Verapaz, a province just north of Guatemala City inhabited by Quiché Indians."

"Yes," Paco said, "the Germans vacated the station, but several Nazi sympathizers who own plantations there still maintain it. The Germans had ambitious plans for this remote outpost and built barracks, storage sheds, and a tower near the dirt field. Since that time, local ranchers and a Guatemalan Army detachment near the town of Flores occasionally use it. I have flown into the field several times with equipment for an oil company. If we should be questioned by anyone, we will merely say we are businessmen making our way to British Honduras, but there should not be any problems. We will need good light, however, to navigate the mountains north of Guatemala City. If the weather does not cooperate, we will return here to wait it out."

Carlitos added, "I have made arrangements to have some friends wait for us with horses and provisions at the airfield. It will take us a couple of days to get to Alta Mirano, which is the nearest town with good roads. From there a car will drive us to Guatemala City."

"I think your decision to leave is wise," interjected Hugo. "There is no question that the *martinistas* have stepped up their campaign. They do not know much for sure, but they will go after those they suspect. They have lists of names, but no proof."

Ricardo and Carlitos just nodded pensively.

"Ricardo," Hugo said, "I would like a word with you in private if you do not mind. We can go outside."

"Of course," Ricardo said and followed him out.

When they were on the porch, Hugo lit a cigarette and offered Ricardo one. He took it and spoke first, "Hugo, what about Paco?"

Hugo smiled while shaking his head. "Paco is a curious person, but he will not betray us. He has been tested many times and that is not his game. No, he is an adventurer, much like you, only not as passionate. The military loves him. He befriends them and whores around with the young military pilots. Flying is nothing more than a big Ferris wheel ride to them. Paco is a good pilot and this gives him a certain standing with the colonels, but they do not take him seriously. Meanwhile, he absolutely adores Carlitos. It goes back to some boyhood oath or something. One owes his life to the other; I do not know the details. It will be interesting to see what happens now that Carlitos is leaving."

He took a deep pull on his cigarette and let the smoke out slowly. Then he continued, "Paco has been acting as interlocutor for me, Ricardo, but I want to make a change. This is what I wanted to talk to you about. You see, Paco has been a messenger between us and the Americans in Guatemala."

"The Americans?" Ricardo asked furrowing his brow.

"Yes. Look, there are some things you need to know. But first, I need to ask you if you are willing to replace Paco as our liaison with them in Guatemala. It will be a different kind of work from what you have been doing. I will give you some background if you would like."

"Yes, of course," said Ricardo.

"There is an American with their legation who wants to stay informed about the politics over here. Because of the war, Washington's interest in this part of the world is limited, but they still need reporting, watching the 'back door' and all that. And, there is some sympathy in their camp for our cause. The Americans have not forgotten how the *Chapines* allowed the Germans to set up a base camp in the northern jungle province called the Petén.

"The intention of the Nazis was obvious: Co-opt the other military governments in Central America. The Americans also know that Martínez is a secret admirer of the European fascists. True, he has been obediently following some of the decrees of the allies, but only superficially, such as sending over two hundred of our young men to fight with them in Europe and the Pacific. But this is because our tobacco and coffee growers have been profiting from the war.

"Did you know, for example, that this country exported over a million sacks of coffee and over twenty-six million packs of cigarettes last year? Most of it for the allied armies. That is a record. The *gringos* know all this. Now that the Germans are losing the war, some Americans will want to settle scores. Ricardo, we are at a pivotal moment in our battle against Martínez. *Carpe diem*, my friend. I want you to speak for us with the Americans; we need them."

"Why me?" Ricardo asked, although he was clearly intrigued. "Surely there are more qualified people. I do not have the international background. Besides, I am totally preoccupied with my family's situation."

"I do not mean right away. Get your family settled in Guatemala. I will help in any way I can. In a few weeks, things will improve for you. And incidentally, you are wrong about not being qualified. You are a patriot and a quick learner. You must know that permanent change will not come without strong internal and external pressures. We live in an international world, and need to convince the Americans that peace in this region will only come about with drastic internal changes.

"Frankly, Paco is not an enthusiastic enough spokesperson. He likes the scheming, but sees nothing wrong with flying mail for Martínez on the side. I believe the man is totally apolitical. No, Ricardo, you are respected and articulate. You have the enterprise and judgment we need at this moment. Say you will do it."

79

After thinking about it for a moment, Ricardo said, "I will not say no." He was clearly flattered by the request and fascinated by the possibilities. "Let me get established there and I will get word to you when I think I am ready."

"*Hecho*," said a confident Hugo, and offered his hand. He had not read Ricardo wrong and knew the importance of timing. A temporarily deflated person, like the proud Ricardo, would unhesitatingly grasp at a mission of importance. Hugo thought he was perfect for the job of wheedling American sympathy and aid. And with the war winding down, there would be many opportunities for those who sided with the Americans.

"*Buena suerte, mi compañero*, good luck," Hugo said to Ricardo as they walked back to join the others.

Inside, Carlitos and Armando were listening to the garrulous Paco recount an erotic encounter with a female guest of a prominent Salvadoran general.

"It was a favor," Paco was saying. "I was ferrying her to Mexico City for him. Well, she had never flown before and was scared. So when we leveled out, I told the copilot to take over and I went to the back, you know, to comfort her." He smiled roguishly. "Besides, she had been giving me the eye...and well, one thing let to another and..." He made some pumping motions with one fist. "And every time the plane hit an air pocket, she would tense and tighten up those legs around me...*Ay Chihuahua!*" He laughed heartily and the other men winced gleefully.

Ricardo and Hugo entered in time to catch the punch-line and also laughed. Hugo's cackle, however, was a bit exaggerated. On previous occasions, Ricardo had noticed that Hugo was not quite comfortable with expressions of levity, like the overstated *gaucho* costume when they had first met.

As the laughter subsided, Hugo walked around and patted each man on the back. Then, he announced, "*Caballeros*, let me introduce you all again to Armando." He had his arms around the Solis' shoulders.

The men shook off the lightness of Paco's story and focus their attention on Hugo.

"You should know that Armando Solis is a very special person in our cause. Some, and I am among them, think he holds the most important key in this struggle."

He paused to let the meek-looking man smile and begin to humbly protest.

"No Armando, I mean it." To the others he said, "Armando is a newspaperman. Like Napoleon Viera Altamirano, he is one of the most respected men in his profession. Why have you not heard of him before, you ask? Well, simply because of the fascist practices of the *martinistas*, who have tagged him a communist!"

The others saw that Hugo was taking center stage, and picked a comfortable position from which to listen to him. Hugo started walking around the room as he spoke.

"Let us look at the facts," he continued. "When Martínez took power, our economy had been in crisis, as was true of most of the world after the crash of '29. Then, when the Brazilians glutted the market with coffee, prices dropped to nothing and our people started to grow hungry. There was no end in sight to the misery.

"Historically, that has been fodder for revolution. The Soviets, still reveling over the plight of capitalism, started establishing roots in these small dependent countries, and that was a threat to the *status quo*. Arujo, before Martínez, had tried to keep the peace by giving the communists a voice. The *Partido Communista Salvadoreño* and the *Federación Regional de Trabajadores Salvadoreños* both grew strong during his time. But, when the effects of 'Black Thursday' reached our borders, Arujo packed his bags and fled. And up steps *Generál Maximilliano Hernández Martínez*, an eccentric, opportunistic nobody, to fill the void and save the country. You remember those days and how scared we all were about what the next day would bring."

The men in the room nodded their heads, a few raised eyebrows. This was not new history to them; the psychological scars of self-doubts had not healed. These were uncertain times and Hugo was their beacon of hope. And if he now sounded preachy, they did not seem to mind.

"But to remain in power," Hugo continued, "a dictator is required to take care of certain rich stakeholders. Martínez promised them order, and to the rest of us he promised nationalism, no doubt plagiarizing what the German people were hearing from their 'savior.'

"Then came the fraudulent elections. You cannot elect a 'nobody' with an honest process. For the most part, he has delivered to the oligarchs the law and order they needed to bring back prosperity. But at what cost? Limiting the migration of certain nationalities, including leading artists and professionals, was foolhardy. But the biggest mistake of all, the biggest threat to our liberty was his suppression of a free press. And that is his Achilles' heel."

Hugo paused to light a cigarette. Carlitos drew the cart with coffee, *pan dulce* and cigarettes closer to the group and let them help themselves. It had been a long night and it was not yet over.

"Until now," Hugo continued after the hiatus, "we have clandestinely embarrassed the *martinistas* by exposing the hypocrisy of their government. We had no choice, because Martínez denied gifted men of integrity and renowned internationalists from freely publishing public views. He is protecting his power base by limiting freedom of expression. He thinks that his Tuesday radio announcements are convincing. But he is wrong. My old *maestro,* Francisco Gavidia could not have put it better when he wrote, 'Intellectual indifference is a treason to democracy, a theft perpetrated on the country, a swindle on liberty, while art, armed with a sword, is the most beautiful of God's Archangels.'"

Hugo paused again. His own words had moved him as well as the others. When he continued, he was speaking slowly and fervently.

"When Martínez began censoring the press, he sealed his own demise. You remember his suspension of the newspaper *Patria*, and his efforts to try Guerra Trigueros for treason, followed by the expulsion of Quino Caso, the founder of *El Nacionalista*, and the suspension of the *Diario de Santa Ana* and *Diario de Occidente.* In the past eight years, *El Diario de Hoy* has been suspended six times, not to mention the various student newspapers. Many of us still remember those ludicrous newspaper editions with whole sections left blank after the police and *gobernacíon* got through with them. Imagine—police editors. What idiocy!"

Hugo walked over to where Solis was sitting and stood by him.

"This is where Armando comes in," Hugo said. "He worked with Trigueros and Caso. He is a student of Alirio Garcia Flamenco and has been editorializing for *La Voz* for the past four years. He has the respect of many of the editors of *El Diario.* And when this dictator falls, it will be Armando who will write the headlines and the history.

"It should not come down to a choice between fascism and communism, because in neither case are the people free. Armando has the ability to articulate this position. The new government's constitution must ensure representation and a free press. We will not be a liberated country without those guarantees. That is why I consider Armando the most important piece on our chessboard. He is recording what we stand for and how we are comporting ourselves in defense of this cause. That is why I wanted him to meet some of the key players first-hand."

There was not much left to say after he finished. Satisfied with his dissertation, Hugo walked around and tearfully embraced each of them.

An hour before dawn, the single engine Cessna took off from the dirt airstrip adjacent to the farmhouse. The occupants were crowded in the small craft as it circled the coast to gain the necessary altitude to clear the mountains to the north.

The flight from the coast would last about three hours, according to the unflappable pilot, who predicted good weather all the way. This news did not change the mood of the two dejected passengers, who merely stared in silence at the ground passing under them.

Although flying was new to them, fear was not a preoccupation. Each was consumed with what awaited them in Guatemala and beyond; each knew they were starting a new chapter in their lives, and each feigned certainty that he would return to his native home one day, maybe even to a hero's welcome. *When* that would be, they did not know, and that was cause for further trepidation. Much depended on how successful Hugo and the others were. At least for now, these two were out of the fight—exiled.

Their minds raced with indiscernible thoughts. A myriad of arrangements and tasks lay before them, but during the flight, they maintained an empty focus. Not even the ominous creaking and jostling of the small plane distracted their stares at the nothingness outside, that invisible air that surrounded and magically suspended them.

They were subdued by tired and unfocused thoughts of the events that had brought them to this moment, events now becoming as imperceptible and distant as the microscopic items on the ground below. Accepting responsibility for one's life often requires this humbling introspection into past choices. And so, they reflected on their fate as the land continued to pass slowly beneath them.

Chapter 10

When Ricardo began telling me about Hugo that day at the *pupuseria* and describing him in such glowing and heroic terms, I was barely able to control my feelings. I did not know, nor want to know, anything about the man. He and his cause threatened everything I cherished. It was only in an effort to understand my friend's situation that I later began taking note of this man and the myth that surrounded the mere mention of his name.

He was reported to be everywhere, secretly recruiting anyone who would listen. Yet in the weeks and months to come, he never approached me directly. I found this strange, but surmised that Ricardo must have discouraged him from doing so.

Although I was not drawn into their schemes directly, I am sure that he manipulated me in some tortuous fashion. I study human behavior; that is my discipline, what I am most curious about. Somehow, from a distance, Hugo understood this trait and used it to indirectly involve me.

I remember that after Ricardo left for Guatemala, I began receiving unsolicited information from casual friends about Hugo and his work. I realize now that it must have been purposefully done. His ability to use people wittingly or unwittingly was uncanny and boundless. I know Ricardo did not know about this and I never brought it up to him, mainly because by this time it had become clear to me that Ricardo idolized Hugo. In those days, I must admit I was jealous.

It was while researching Hugo's background that my long-held sentiments about the peasant revolt of '32 began to change. I had only heard the version espoused by *cafetaleros* and other landowners who had lived through that terrifying period, including my parents. I had been programmed to be leery of stories vilifying the military's role, as well as other socialist ruminations about social causes and reforms.

I had witnessed first hand how we cared for our *campesinos*, how we treated them with respect and love and they reacted in kind. I have never seen any with an ambitious bone in their bodies except that planted by some false foreign prophet. We do God's bidding in caring for these people and I will believe this until the day I die.

But in the case of the peasant's revolt, there was another side, which, at least in my family, had gone untold until I began to document it with Hugo's help. There is no question that Martinez' slaughter of thousands of defenseless men, women and children, who had been misled by conniving socialists, is an abomination in itself. That this government had somehow managed to conceal or avoid debating these facts is also wrong. And frankly, that is why I have never had an interest in politics or politicians. It and they are corrupt and inhuman and there is no moral victory in their labor.

Having said that, it was by way of this fragmented information, attested to by those who were there, that the brief history of this extraordinary man Hugo began to unfold before me.

It was about at the time Ricardo was being discharged from the *Guardia Civil* training program that this elder economics student began organizing dissidents at the *Universidad de El Salvador*. Under his leadership, students launched a formidable seditious campaign against the *martinistas*. Their enthusiasm was aided by the Administration's policy of gagging any form of academic political debate. *Opinion Estudianti!* and *La Verdad,* the periodicals that were the traditional voice of the students, had been declared subversive and simply disappeared. Unauthorized gatherings of students, even within the university campus, were routinely raided and dispersed.

Hugo began filling these empty spaces with his clandestine periodical *La Voz.* As a result, he was immediately targeted and declared an enemy of the state. This in turn gave him celebrity status among the students, and together they began exploiting what he considered the seeds of *martinista* self-destruction—their arrogance and their ignorance.

Over time, as his notoriety grew, stories spread about the man and the true motives behind his strong anti-Martínez feelings. If it were not so terrorizing, it would have made for great theater. Which of the two, Martinez or Hugo, was more mythical? The saga could have been billed as the "battle of the mystics." But no matter which story about the genesis of their notoriety I was told, they all seemed to originate at the same time and place, about a dozen years ago in the foothills of a small town near the base of an active volcano. It was there that the country and the young Hugo were first introduced to the "*brujo* of the blue waters."

Ricardo and I had often discussed the unconventional character of our President, but we had never seen it written down anywhere in comprehensive form. So I began making some notes from snippets in the press and common knowledge. What I came up with was a bizarre sketch that, in retrospect, must have cast a dubious shadow on the international image of all the military regimes in this region.

General Martínez was not the imposing stereotypical figure of a military leader. Physically he was of medium height, thin with stooped shoulders, dark-skinned and with small, slanted, droopy eyes. For the most part, he was a soft-spoken vegetarian who subscribed to naturalness, such as only drinking water purified by the sun, what he referred to as "blue waters."

He was austere, abstaining from liquor, cigarettes, or other vices. He taught himself to read and speak English. He was also self-taught in the occult, and believed in reincarnation, astrology, Taoism, karma, and the medicinal power of meditation and herbs. This fascination with brewing his own cures earned him the label of *brujo*, witchdoctor or shaman.

That such a person ran our country for a dozen years cannot say much about us as a people. In self-defense, however, I can only say that at the time I was one of those that just did not care about politics or politicians as long as our interests were being taken care of and there was no public unrest. Not flattering perhaps, but honest. And this feeling can only be understood against the backdrop of what we had been put through at the beginning of the previous decade.

Today, it is his tyrannical use of political power for which he is renowned—that, and his brutal handling of the peasant revolt in 1932. But one has to remember that Martínez was 49 years old and a mere month into the presidency when he faced this national crisis. Today he is being blamed for quickly seizing the moment and thereby emphatically defining the character his regime would take.

But to understand the man, we must understand the moment. And in order to do that, we need to go back one more decade, to the uncertain highs and lows of that period. Upon such study, even an amateur's analysis concludes incontrovertibly that the insurrection of '32 was inevitable.

By the end of 1920, the country was at an all-time low, both economically and socially. There was widespread unemployment and hunger, especially in the *campo*. For several years *campesinos* had been moving into the cities frantically searching for relief. The situation was bleak and the prognosis poor. There was fear and desperation and a longing for the days of the legendary pacifist President of the early 1920s, *Don* Pío Romero Bosque.

Some national reformers looked for answers in the socialist basket. International communists were more than eager to take advantage of yet another socio-economic struggle in the Americas. To the desperate poor, the socialist propaganda provided the salve of hope since expectations for significant change under the traditional military governments were not many. Fraudulent elections had further eliminated any expectation of a political transformation through valid means.

This was not new to communist strategists. They knew that the road to communism passed through dismal days before igniting the civil revolt of the proletariat. They were patient, only occasionally flexing political muscle at public rallies. President Arujo's effort in the late '20s to disarm the communist opposition by giving them a voice in the constitutional process backfired after the global economic crash of '29. Businessmen nervously saw communist leaders grow bolder and stronger. When coffee prices plummeted in '31, Arujo's days were numbered. He was toppled by a military *coup* in December 1931, and his Vice President, *Generál Maximiliano Hernández Martínez*, ascended to power.

Personally, I did not know the historical and political details at the time, only the fear of revolution. There is no question that my father and his peers were desperate and made their feelings known through their financial influence. I now know that the communist intent in '32 was clearly the proletarian overthrow of the oligarchs, as advocated by Lenin and Marx during the Russian revolution. The Salvadoran rich and bourgeoisie understood this and totally supported an aggressive defense against a similar insurrection. Martínez was their shield and sword and he wielded the latter effectively. It was only later, after the total defeat of the rebels, that it became clear that he would be loath to set it down.

But at the time, only those who followed world affairs recognized the similarities to the fanatical nationalism that was taking place in other countries around the world. Global despair, it seemed, was breeding despots everywhere.

In retelling the story of the peasant's revolt, I had to rely on interviews with relatives and some church people I trusted. It was a dark period in our history and there was no national historian brave enough to document the events. Meanwhile, the writings of foreign correspondents were suspect. But whether from relatives of correspondents, their information tended to corroborate the details I was receiving from Hugo. I believe, therefore, that the following events are accurate.

Being confronted with the threat of insurrection, and feeling he had the full mandate of the industrialists, Martínez reacted quickly. On New Year's Day, 1932, the onslaught against communists began.

He used the finding of large amounts of arms and explosives in the capital city of San Salvador to declare martial law and abolished the free press. Then, so there was no doubt about his steadfastness, on January 18, 1932, he dramatically arrested a principal communist leader, Agustín Farabundo Martí, and several university organizers, including Alfonso Luna and Mario Zapata. As a consequence, he wittingly or unwittingly forced the communists to react, and the battle cry of rebellion was sounded.

Plans for a peasant revolt had been in motion for weeks. And so, on the 20th of January, with the eruption of the volcano Izalco as backlight, thousands of *campesinos* marched on a dozen towns. But since many of their key organizers had been arrested, the hurriedly planned attacks had few leaders at the vanguard. Disorganization quickly set in.

Furthermore, they had underestimated Martínez' swift defensive actions. The first rebel attacks were planned against military, police, and communication installations. But when their *machetes* and few rifles proved no match against reinforced fortresses, the rebel frenzy turned into riots. Sparked by liquor seized from looted stores, the rebels turned on anyone considered part of the establishment. Without guidance, rioters slaughtered many innocent people and destroyed any nobility their cause might have initially possessed.

Martínez' reaction was swift and brutal against a peasant army that was inexperienced and ill-equipped for a sustained effort. With their communications severed, the insurgents lost their momentum and spirit.

A few barely held on. Makeshift warriors like the student Abel Cuenca, who led the 1,500 *campesinos* who took Tacuba, were immediately faced with massive logistical problems, such as feeding the rebel army and the population. Without organization, the inexperienced Cuenca was unable to stop the riotous behavior or establish any provisional government. Neither could he mount a defense against counterattacks that now included a new terrorizing weapon—aerial bombardment. Within days, main towns had been retaken and the rebels were fleeing. Their rout was total.

As I say, the foregoing account of the *campesino* revolt and Martinez' fierce reaction is well accepted by the people I spoke to and other sources. The following parts, however, came to me in bits and pieces and I had to put them together as best I could. I am sure the events occurred as stated here, because subsequent events verified the names and places. The exact chronology, however, is uncertain. In the final analysis, this latter point is unimportant. What is important is that they are relevant to the mysticism that was to follow them.

After the capitulation, retaken towns and villages were scheduled for disciplinary action. In Izalco, in front of the church of the Asuncion, Jose Feliciano Ama, the *cacique* and leader of the numerous *campesino* workers in the area, was scheduled to be hanged by the victorious government forces. A young military officer was assigned to question the very humble worker-mayor, who had a strong following and was known to be a pacifist.

After a lengthy session, *Teniente* Valentín Aurelio Magaña reported to his commander, *Coronel* Jose Porfilio Mojano, that in his opinion the man might have better use as an informant than a martyr. For his enterprise, the lieutenant was reprimanded and ordered to hang Feliciano in the plaza immediately.

Tired and weary of overseeing the killing and burial of hundreds of *campesinos* and rebel sympathizers during the past three days, the angry lieutenant himself rebelled. He ignored the order and tried to desert. He was caught by perimeter guards and brought before the commander who callously ordered him beaten and executed with the next line of rebels in the morning.

During the night, the lieutenant escaped, wounding two of his guards in the process. Disillusioned and crazed, he made his way to where the commander was housed and summarily cut his throat. As he was leaving, the lieutenant noticed a young teen-aged girl sitting silently in a dark corner of the room. She was a villager whom the commander had earlier taken to his bed by force. The officer rescued her and returned her to her parents.

Afterward, the family helped the officer escape the zone on the condition that he take the young woman, Marta Ixtol, and another fugitive, a rebel leader named Miguel Mármol, with him. The latter had been severely wounded by a firing squad and left for dead. After several weeks of making their way from village to village, the trio finally reached Guatemala City. There, they learned of the vengeful murder of their respective families while they had been in hiding.

Later, Magaña and Mármol made their way separately to Europe. Both had adopted the zeal of converts, forever and fervently anti-fascist. In the years to come, one would fight against fascist governments in Spain and Italy, the other would opt to live and study in communist Europe. Like most exiles, both would long to return and effect respective changes in their native country. But, what they left behind that January of '32 in the Salvadoran *campo* was devastation and despair.

In his fervor to stamp out any potential for reoccurrence, Martínez ordered the total annihilation of the peasant army. To systematically carry out this purge, lists were compiled. During previous elections, voters had been required to register their political affiliation. With the names of those registered PCS, *Partido Communista Salvadoreño*, the "communists" were easily identified and rounded up. In groups of six to twelve, they were summarily executed by firing squads.

Eight to twenty thousand were put to death. No one would know the exact number, but as much as ten percent of the males in the provinces where uprisings took place were eliminated. In Izalco, the entire indigenous population was wiped out, along with their native language of Náhuat.

The killings continued unremittingly. Martí, Luna, and Zapata were executed in San Salvador. When international appeals for peace went unheeded, foreign governments threatened intervention. The U.S. and Canada even sent warships and troops along the coast as a strong sign of disapproval.

But the Salvadoran government, backed by influential industrialists and coffee exporters, proclaimed the matter under internal control. As a show of support, Salvadoran bankers and businessmen donated thousands of *colones* to support the troops. The *Guardia Civil*, made up of thousands of middle-class professionals and businessmen, offered to relieve some of the troops and police. Internally, and for the moment, the communal victory for Martínez was total. He also now had a red flag to wave whenever his authority was criticized or challenged in the future.

The reaction of the *martinistas* after the rebellion provided insight into their tyrannical nature, but few critics raised their voices. Over the years, however, *campesinos* and intellectuals alike began condemning the general's methodical extermination of thousands of non-combatants. The criticism was not lost on the *martinistas*, who began taking note of dissenters, and the repression continued. Leftists began disappearing or were found tortured and murdered on the side of the road, and those sympathizers with the means to do so began leaving the country. The concept of secret government-condoned "death squads" was born.

The *martinistas* continued to inculcate paranoia about other communist plots, some of it based on the "legacy of *El Negro*." Before his execution, the communist Martí, who was called "*El Negro*" because of his dark complexion, had reportedly disclosed that there were thousands of explosives and arms hidden all around El Salvador ready to be used in a greater rebellion. Marti took to his grave either their exact whereabouts or the real facts of his story. But this alone justified the government's repression in the eyes of some.

The events of '32 set in stone the type of government the oligarchs required to rebuild the economy and, in tandem, what Martínez required to remain in power. It would take years to bring prosperity back to the country. The decade became known as the "decade of iron," because of the select use of this metal and steel to build key edifices and bridges. For the oppressed, the reference to "iron" had a different meaning.

Now, twelve years later, Martínez was still enforcing this outdated suppression. From experience, Hugo knew that the populace would only stand repression for so long. He had seen it in Europe. He began recruiting the best academics and journalists to write anonymous articles for his underground press. He also started a network of creditable informants who could provide select information useful to his exposés. Hugo knew that to be anti-government did not necessarily mean you were pro-Communist. That was *martinista* propaganda, and while it might be enough to scare capitalists, it could be easily countered.

Hugo believed that to overthrow Martínez was only a matter of patience and having the right support. The oligarchs would not intervene and might even help the movement if Martínez became a liability. Hugo knew his country. The lieutenant had returned a general, and the titanic clash was on.

Interestingly enough, I did not receive any insight about Hugo's personal life from the communiqués I continued to receive anonymously. This could have been for security reasons, or it might say something about the man. The latter I find irresistible, given my profession, and because I have tried to look beyond the mounting evidence of his megalomania. But when I venture into that arena, I find instead indications of acute idealism, as in the case of Ricardo. Sociology, however, is not my discipline and I feel less comfortable with analyses of group behavior. Suffice it to say that there is an intersection in the psychology of these two men and the groups they led. Their motivations were not self-serving.

Hugo admitted little about his personal background to anyone. Instead, rumors circulated frenziedly among his followers. He was supposedly born in a small village near San Marcos to peasants who had managed to save enough money to send him to school in the capital. He spent most of his youth living in the suburb of Santa Tecla with a family who provided room and board in exchange for chores around the house. After primary school, he aspired to be a military officer and studied to that end.

Not much is said about the next years, but supposedly, while still in his early 20s, he lived in Puerto Barrios on the Guatemalan coast. He was reported to have worked in cheap bars and brothels cleaning up after drunks before saving enough to bribe his way onto a freighter bound for European ports. Stronger rumors claimed he was the same military officer who had killed a superior after the peasant rebellion in '32, and that was the reason he had to leave the continent.

While in Spain and later Italy, he was said to have enrolled as a student and lecturer at various universities, until authorities began to take notice of his impassioned anti-fascist discourses. When war broke out in earnest, he worked with the resistance for a year before secretly returning to El Salvador under the name Jorge Villareal.

What is certain is that he was auditing courses at the university under that name when he began organizing the insurrectionist groups. I began hearing the name Hugo while taking graduate courses at the university, but I paid little attention. Liberal groups, however, were enthusiastic audiences for his stories about events in Europe, because he would compare the totalitarian decrees there to what was occurring in Central America, pointing out the same racist and anti-intellectual practices.

"In this country, you cannot count on the citizens to bring about change," Hugo would say to them. "They are poor and have been beaten down into apathetic stupor. The majority of them will swallow the false patriotic claims of despots if only to satisfy a thirst for peace. Before they know it, it is too late. In Germany, even as towns fall around them, people are still asleep to the truth. It is always up to a few informed people to expose despotism and force change. The Americans know this from their history. That is why they do not remain neutral in wars."

From the temper of the notes I received, one thing is clear, Hugo always felt the Americans were key to his plans. So as soon as he could, he opened a "diplomatic" channel to the American legation in Guatemala, which was interested in his regional reporting. Hugo provided reports on the clandestine activities of Salvadoran activists, always mindful that these reports did not reflect any activity that threatened American interests. He also reported a litany of government abuses of power. So far, it had been a one-way street with the Americans; he had asked for nothing in return. He was patiently accruing leverage. To fight a bully, you must befriend a bigger bully.

During this time, Hugo initiated several proactive tactics. He encouraged his followers, for example, to share any encounter with police authorities or reports of police activity. He would collate and analyze these events, searching for trends and patterns in *martinista* thinking, part of what he called "strategic planning." Meanwhile, he would systematically publish pamphlets with news and editorials on the corrupt and abusive practices of the military. The subjects varied, but the theme was the same—the government is unresponsive to the interests of the country.

This information group was touted to be the "voice of the people," claiming to disseminate information that newspapers were reluctant to print. Hugo relentlessly attacked the unholy relationship between the military leaders and their patrons, the biased rich. He was careful to distinguish between the military establishment and conscripts, who he felt were as exploited as the poor. Most young men in the military were drafted by force and could not even read or write.

In 1942, a one-page exposé stirred up a popular chant of indignation that reverberated all the way up to the Presidential Palace.

The pamphlet read:

SOLDIERS, REMEMBER YOUR ROOTS

The rich, through their government lackeys, believe that they are the only ones qualified to make decisions on behalf of all citizens. Those who disagree are labeled dissidents and subject to the heavy-handed tactics of this fascist government. They want us to think reformists are communists, violent rebels bent on overturning "the logical order of things." But it is THEIR logic and THEIR order.

But do the rich even have *Pipil* blood in their veins? Do they have the right to speak for you?

Witness the writings of the privileged coffee grower from Coatepeque, *Doña* Gloria Cardona. This is what she writes in her letter to Chancellor-for-life Martínez:

"Dear Mr. President: I support you in your efforts to protect the people of this country. *Campesinos* are poor peasant workers who unfortunately have no ambition to better themselves. They want and need to be taken care of and that is our responsibility. At times they complain, as we all do, but they are just venting frustration about life's daily trials. Any talk of revolt is primarily the work of foreign troublemakers who do not understand the Salvadoran *campesino* as we do. These foreigners pose a threat to our internal security and you are right in using every measure at your disposal to deal with their menace. *Campesinos* deserve to live in peace like the rest of us. They do not want a complicated life; most waive their rights to education and other benefits. We provide them with a worry-free existence, shelter, a steady supply of their preferred food, and a day off a week to rest and respect the God that made them. That is the way they want it and we should respect their wish. It is our obligation to do so. The work your government is doing affords us all the opportunity to live together in peace. We all have the civic duty to support you.

"Respectfully, Gloria Escobar de Cardona."

My brothers, King Martínez has distributed this letter throughout the military as a commendation for a job well done. He and other officers seem to have forgotten that they themselves are descendents of peasants as are all the soldiers in the army. Instead, he enforces what he calls "constitutional laws" on behalf of the rich with the false ardor of a patriot. He thus claims to preserve the peace and the "natural order," but only for the select few.

Soldiers, you should not forget your roots and the roots of your fathers and mothers. Martínez does not speak for you. Nor will he ever suppress the **Voice of the People**.

The brochure had been secretly inserted into daily newspapers distributed throughout the Republic. When I got my copy, I thought it was another clandestine delivery of Hugo's information. It was, but not just for me. When I realized that everyone I knew had gotten the same leaflet in their newspaper, I realized that it had been a major *coup* for the underground because of its implication: It could not have been done without the collaboration of newspaper workers who handled the circulation.

Government reaction to the pamphlet was chaotic, to say the least. Meetings were hurriedly called and the President ordered retaliation. He tried to ameliorate internal damage by issuing a memorandum to mollify the worrisome young officer corps. In a feeble retort, he dramatically proclaimed that *campesino* blood ran in his veins as well. It was a lame attempt, and Hugo managed to get a copy of the communication. Excerpts from it were the subject of yet another of his editorials.

In another piece, Hugo criticized Martínez' agreement to provide protection to the Cardona plantations while their owners went off "on a hurriedly planned vacation" to Brazil. And still another piece reported the mysterious disappearance of several editors of *La Prensa* and the head of the circulation department. Martínez was now faced with the fact that Hugo's sources were well placed.

As the audience for these scandalous leaflets grew, so did the resolve of the authorities to squash them. Efforts focused on finding out who was funding them, so the police expanded their lists to include non-students and former student sympathizers. A special group was created in the *Guardia Nacional* to collect information against suspects and react with impunity. Universities and other student social meeting places were watched closely. The government would force regents to close down the main campuses at any hint of political activism.

With the universities closed, authorities could proclaim any student meeting place a haunt for subversive activity. Thus, in a land where academia was the only environment for intellectual contest, advocates were left without a safe setting for debate. During this time, students also began to systematically disappear.

In all my research, I never found an incident where Hugo took a defensive position. It was no different here. He responded by exposing duplicity across all institutions. Even the Catholic Church, the spiritual leader of ninety-nine percent of Salvadorans, was not spared. Brochures asked why the Church did not categorically condemn abuses of power. The poignant question hung over the populace like an ominous cloud, since it implied that any reform or government practice was void of ethical or moral guidance from a higher order. The Church remained steadfastly mute on the issue, not even offering the lame argument about the separation of church and state.

Hugo also declared war on government tactics. He was particularly obdurate about the government's use of informants. Hugo explained in one editorial how informants take on many forms and usually work for ignoble motives. And while they served a valid purpose when used judiciously, the *martinistas* were neither qualified nor prudent. Often, unscrupulous informants were savvier than the police and had private agendas, such as eliminating a competitor or just plain revenge. Government informants were the scum of the earth, he concluded, and were not to be tolerated. In this regard, Hugo was capitalizing that people already had an inherent distaste for this type of social treachery.

Hugo hit the *martinista* inefficiency and lack of representative-ness hard. He ended one of his editorials with this comment on the principle of governance under the current administration:

"...The people fear their constitutional protectors and question the rule of law. For one thing, there is no process of appeal under the *martinista* government. Without appeal, there is no justice. Without justice, there is no peace. Who has not been affected by what this government calls justice? Who has not witnessed the unclaimed bodies lying along roadsides or riverbanks? Poignant reminders that, in this predominantly Catholic country, catholicity does not extend to governance."

In time, those inside and outside the movement began acknowledging that Hugo was the motivator and the glue that bonded them and, as a result, the government considered him the most dangerous subversive alive.

Chapter 11

I cannot personally attest to the following information, but I know it came from a good source—Hugo himself. You see, he had spies everywhere. And because of this fact, and certain events that unfolded later, I believe the story's accuracy.

At about the time I was attending to Teco and Ricardo was making his way to Carlitos' *finca*, events were taking place inside the *Guardia Nacional's* headquarters that were to effect both our families directly and very soon.

Sitting behind a massive desk, General Marcos Aurelio Chulio-Lopez glared at the nervous officer who was reporting on the day's events. The general's hands were in a prayer-like position in front of his face, and only his dark unblinking eyes and short graying hair were clearly visible to the others in the room. Six officers ranging from the rank of captain to colonel sat stiffly alongside of the director's desk.

The briefing officer, a major in the *Guardia,* stood in front of them reading from a notebook. The air was formal and the tension high. The general had interrupted the major at least a dozen times in the past half-hour with questions and comments. This interaction was expected and always painful.

General Chulio was an intolerant man who was never satisfied with staff reports. Depending on the topic, he could react erratically on what he considered either too much or not enough information. And when it came to the subject of subversive activities, he was fanatical. No detail was superfluous. He knew more about this topic than his advisors, and no one left a briefing unscathed.

"In summary," the officer said, "of the 23 suspects targeted, 20 have been apprehended. Fourteen have confessed to their involvement in subversive activities, four are still being interrogated, and two were killed while trying to escape. We have the names of 20 more subversives and are searching for them now. No weapons were found and no one claimed to know anything about them. It was a successful first day of the mission and the *Guardia* acted bravely and with honor, *mí generál.*"

Chulio kept his scowl and his silence. The perspiration continued its capillary action on the major's collar.

He ventured, "That concludes my briefing, *mí generál.* Will there be anything else?"

Chulio did not answer immediately. Then, he said softly, "You believe that the mission was successful?"

The major was unsure if the question was rhetorical, so he waited a moment. When Chulio just stared at him, he began, "*Si, mí generál.* The *Guardia…*"

"And just what was the mission, major?" Chulio's voice was now sarcastic.

"To arrest an identified number of subversives, obtain the location of any weapons, and seize them, *mi generál.* We…we are still questioning some and will question others we have identified. I am confident that we…" He stopped when Chulio raised his hand.

"How many knew the whereabouts of any weapons?"

"None, *mi generál.*"

"You are convinced of that?"

"*Si, mi generál,* the interrogators are very efficient and they are confident…"

"You were there?"

"*Si, mi generál.*"

"How many of those questioned are students?"

"All are either current or former students. Of the 23 targeted, 16 are registered at the university on a full-time basis. Of the 20 other names we obtained, all but one are permanent students."

"And how many are foreigners?"

"None, *mi generál.* But we are told that of the 20 others identified, two are Nicaraguan."

"And what of Hugo?"

"All have met him, none know his whereabouts. Frankly, *mi generál,* we know more about Hugo's background than these subversives," said the major confidently.

"Really," said Chulio smirking. Then he suddenly slammed an open hand on his desk. "Then why the devil is the *hijo de puta* not in custody?"

All recoiled. Chulio walked around the desk to where the officer was standing at attention. He walked past him and faced the others. The major just waited, facing straight ahead.

Chulio began speaking slowly, "Gentlemen, in case you have forgotten, we are at war with a recurring plague that is contaminating the youth of this nation. There is no quarreling with, or cure for, this cancer. It must be completely cut out and buried for good, and it must be done swiftly. We did it in '32 and we will have to do it again today. The only difference between then and now is that these communists are more clever. They do not charge machine guns with *machetes.* They strike in the night and hide during the day.

"At least the communists in '32 were brave—stupid, but brave. These are cowards, but just as deadly. We have to fight them intelligently. Major Carrillo reports that these subversives belong to small groups and that they do not know each other's activities. I disagree. In this small country, everyone knows everyone else's business.

"These subversives are not confessing because they are zealots and have a higher threshold for pain. The major also reports that they only confessed to writing and distributing anti-government literature. That offense is inconsequential when compared to their true crimes. They are traitors!"

He walked in front of the officers and made I contact with each. The officials sat with stiff backs and face forward. Only their eyes followed him and there was the occasional nod.

"We have them and we will not allow their kind to continue to spread their poison," Chulio said. "If we turn them over to the corrupt courts, their families can easily buy their freedom. No, they must be made to confess everything they know about the weapons, about Hugo and about the other leaders. Who murdered the guards at the Armory? What are their plans? Everything! Then, when we are through with them, we will eliminate any trace of them."

A colonel offered cautiously, "I am sure that *mi generál* has thought about the implications of having these subversives disappear while in our custody. The raids were not secret; we will be expected to turn our prisoners over to the police for prosecution in the courts or release them. There will be questions, and some of these students come from prominent families."

Chulio shot him a glance, then in a tempered voice said, "*Por supuesto, coronel,* but the solution is not that complicated. When the questions begin, we merely say that the suspects were picked up, questioned, and released. We do not know what happened to them after that. If they developed a pang of conscience and fled the country without telling anyone, that is not our problem. We have done this before. There are just more of them this time."

The other officers looked at each other approvingly and agreed that this was the right tack.

"As I said," Chulio continued, "these *hijos de puta* know more than they are saying." Then he spoke to the back of the major's head, "Who is heading the interrogation?"

"*Sargento Miguel Angel Acuña, mi generál.*"

"I know him. Send him to me. He has spent too much time with the Guatemalans. They are soft over there, not at all like their ancestors. I will speak to him personally."

"Immediately, *mi generál,*" said the major.

"And Hugo," barked Chulio, "*ese hijo de puta*, must be found. And I want him alive. He is a coward and a traitor. He still has a debt to pay for what he did in '32. I will personally cut out his heart."

He let the comment sink in, then said firmly, "I want more informants sent to mingle with the students, with no other purpose than to find him. Now, tell me about the names on the other list, the sympathizers. How many names have been implicated through the interrogations?"

"Only one, *mí generál*, Jose Pablo Escudes, an attorney. He is the head of a group that writes and distributes subversive material. Our informant had reported that he was also heading a group that was responsible for obtaining weapons. The interrogations so far have not confirmed this. He was to be picked up this morning, but was warned and fled.

"We are also adding the name of Ricardo Cruz Carranza, a dentist, to that list of sympathizers. His name came up during the interrogations as a partisan, but they did not know him to be part of any group. Our informant had said that there was a dentist named Ricardo who was also a member of the weapons group with Escudes. We think this is the same person. We sent someone who knows him to his home to pick him up, but he did not show up. He may have been warned and fled as well."

"Is this the informant Dominguez?"

"*Si, mí generál.*"

"I never liked him," Chulio said annoyed. "Had he done a better job, we would have them all by now. He is weak, and if he betrayed them, he will betray again. He is useless to us. Take care of him, but I do not want his body found. I would not want the traitors to think we did them a favor."

"*A la orden, mí generál.*"

"I do not believe in coincidences, *caballeros*," said Chulio. "Put Cruz on the priority list to be picked up with Escudes. Watch both their families. Call Gonzales at the telephone company. Tell him that if he needs more listeners, you will send him some."

"*Si, mí generál.* We have already done so. I would be remise, *mí generál*, if I did not point out here yet another coincidence," added the major. "One which *mí generál* might find interesting."

The general walked around to face him.

Still looking straight ahead, the major continued, "When we began picking up the suspects, we expected to receive a large number of inquiries from family and friends, even some calls from influential people. And we did. Our response was simply that we would look into the matter. However, we received two telephone calls on behalf of people who were not arrested."

The major's voice was still formal, but had taken on a tantalizing tone. "The first was from Paco Poveda, the aviator who does favors for some of the officers. He has also done some training and flying for the new Air Corps. *Mí generál* has met him at official functions."

"Yes, I know him. The favors he does usually have to do with women. The flying he seems to do well enough. Go on," said Chulio in a harsh voice.

"Poveda called friends at the Air Corps to inquire about Escudes. He said that he had heard that Escudes was being accused of something and that he was sure it was a mistake. He said he had known Escudes since childhood and could vouch for him."

The major paused, but Chulio did not seem excited about the information, so he continued quickly, "The second telephone call was from retired Colonel Guillermo Gutierrez Ruiz."

He paused again for effect. This time Chulio's eyes narrowed and a hint of a smile was evident. The major knew this piece of information had reached him.

"Continue, Major," he said in a friendly voice.

"*Mí Colonél Gutierrez* called the *Estado Mayor* to complain about soldiers being posted at the home of the dentist Cruz. He said they were to be removed immediately because the family was beyond reproach. As a courtesy to *mí colonél*, we moved the soldiers from the premises but kept them in the neighborhood watching for Cruz. He has not come home." The major stopped there.

The general was clearly smiling now, and he began nodding his head as he spoke to no one in particular. "Well, well, *mi querido* Memo. 'Beyond reproach,' you say, your personal assurance. Just where have I heard that before?" Again to no one. "You poor stupid son of a bitch. Finally, your ill-placed sympathies and self-righteousness have betrayed you!"

He caught himself quickly and said to the major, "Well done, major. I want a memorandum prepared from me to the President. For his eyes-only...no, wait. I want that memorandum from you, major, to me. Secret. I will take it personally to the President."

"*Mí generál*!" The major clicked his heels. He was beaming. He knew such compliments were rare.

"Now find Cruz," the general said. "I want him and his confession. He is a priority now. I want to know everything about his background and his family. Where would he go? Put surveillance on Poveda. If we find his friend Escudes we will find Cruz and the weapons. I want daily reports. Understood?"

"*A la orden, mí generál.*"

"Dismissed."

The major turned and moved with alacrity to the door. The briefing was over and the general was smiling.

In many ways, the legend of Chulio is not unlike the folk stories of Martínez and Hugo. Authoritative figures are always the brunt of rumors, exaggerations, and fables. Not always creditable references to be sure, but understandable, and certainly a common and accepted practice in my country. But where much is recorded about Martínez and Hugo, Chulio remains an enigma.

Hugo certainly attributes most of the malice in the government's administration of justice to him. And this may be. Interestingly enough, in the few writings I uncovered, it seems that Chulio's preoccupation with Hugo is equally exaggerated. And it is not as simple as a variation on the eternal struggle between good and evil. It is more of a question that drifts between the moral and the legal, and I have come to recognize that these concepts are not automatically related.

In the context of our day-to-day life, the political side you favor depends largely on your socio-economic status. We, the growers and industrialists, had not yet fully recuperated from that onslaught of disorder caused by the economic crash of '29 and the rebellion of '32. No matter how justified Hugo might wish war to be, in the case of the so-called peasant's revolt, a group of usually humble peasants unmercifully murdered their patrons and were, in turn, unmercifully murdered themselves.

You might argue that that is a form of justice, albeit bestial. Even as a psychiatrist, I can make no sense of such unbridled violence in otherwise reasonable people. So the question remains, at what price order? It is that question, or rather his unique answer to that question, that frames the legacy of Chulio and all the Chulios of the world, who may only be guilty of loving war too much. Depending on where you sit, "Chulios" are either the devil incarnate or necessary evils. About *our* Chulio, I can only draw a caricature, as I have done for Hugo. Purists will have to argue if the term "patriot" better fits one or the other.

General Marcos Aurelio Chulio-Lopez's physical figure, much as was the case with his President, was not as imposing as his reputation. He was a short, thin man, now in his early fifties, but as fit as a recruit just out of basic training. He had discovered physical exercise early as a way of making up for other physical and social shortcomings. All of his life he had been known as the loner with the celebrated temper.

He came from a family of merchants who lived and worked in the small border town of San Francisco Gotera, near the border with southern Honduras. They traded in a variety of goods, but mostly staples for villagers and ranchers. The family was not wealthy, but more economically stable than most families in rural communities.

All eleven children worked in the business. All, that is, except Marcos, who was rebellious by nature and jealous of his older brothers. They, in turn, delighted in taking advantage of the "runt" of the family. On its surface, the rivalry did not seem any worse than in other similar households, but Marcos' reaction was definitely more violent.

Marcos did not recognize or display any inherent affection for his kin. His troubled parents did not understand the cause of the boy's anguish and, as a result, he endured considerable physical discipline for his sheer defiant spirit. When Marcos reached his teen years, his desperate and frustrated parents managed to bribe a local military commander to use his influence and get the angry and precocious lad into the military school of the day, the *Instituto Politécnico Salvadoreño*. His parents thought that perhaps the strict and controlled life of the military might harness Marcos' strong emotions. Friends thought they were merely throwing gasoline onto a fire.

To his parent's surprise and gratification, Marcos took to military regimentation immediately. Unfortunately, this was not for the honor and glory of serving his country, but because he was excited by the prospect of using the office to dispense and demand discipline from others. Even more attractive to Chulio's dark side was the prospect of being able to intimidate officially. With this sudden injection of purpose and confidence, he quickly set out to prove himself the better of his peers.

In the physical stamina department, he had no equal. Exercise being more determination than perspiration, he excelled in that regimen and it became his mantra. Staying in physical shape and demanding the same from those under his charge became an obsession. Whatever resentment toward rivals he harbored, however, did not dissipate with this newfound energy. The reason for his anger would remain unclear, but no one argued that he was good at it.

Upon being commissioned, he was assigned to the border outpost at San Ines near his hometown. Occasional raids by Honduran outlaws on village businesses required policing. The young lieutenant led a platoon that guarded what was no more than a horse trail used by merchants to cross the border from one village to another. However, the mere military presence failed to deter the night burglaries.

As a solution, the young lieutenant adopted an aggressive preemptive raid strategy; he would strike out indiscriminately against mere suspects. Very quickly the young officer learned the efficiency of intimidation through violence. The raids quickly stopped, order was restored, and he was highly commended by his superiors.

His achievements also revealed an unexpected personal trait. When he first ordered captives to be tortured for information or summarily dispatched if he thought them guilty, he also discovered himself. *I am acting under a legal banner of authority*, he thought, *I am respected and feared.* Hence, protecting his country by ruthlessly ridding it of its enemies became his life's resolve. That his vicious approach also gave him perverse pleasure was an added bonus.

On one raid onto Honduran soil, the platoon came upon a campsite. Hidden behind heavy foliage, the soldiers spied four men dressed in peasant clothing sitting around the fire. The soldiers could see three or four live chickens with their legs bound and sacks with the tops and bottoms tied to a leather *mecate* that the *campesinos* strapped across their foreheads to carry heavy loads.

Chulio motioned his men with his revolver to split up and flank the group. As the soldiers were moving to each side, they were overheard and the *campesinos* immediately went for their *machetes*. Chulio ordered a charge, and shot two of the men himself with his pistol. A bayonet from one of the soldiers wounded another. But the fourth man had mounted his own rush and it had surprised two of the soldiers on the right flank.

The man had already wounded a soldier with a slash to an arm and was in the process of attacking the other when a third soldier struck him from behind with the butt end of his rifle. The man fell face down over the wounded soldier. When he was pulled off and was about to be run through with a bayonet, Chulio ordered them to wait.

The unconscious man lay on his side and Chulio approached and rolled him over with his foot. He was young, perhaps in his late teens or early twenties. His complexion was dark and his hair was long and matted. Unfocused eyes were partially closed, but he was stirring. Chulio squatted down to examine the man closer. He turned his head to one side to inspect the wound that was bleeding from the back of his head. It looked superficial, but the swelling was already noticeable. Without taking his eyes off the man, Chulio told two of the soldiers to finish off the other three men; they would work on this one.

As usual the soldiers used their bayonets to conserve bullets. One of the wounded men was making screeching noises and was silenced first. Chulio was about to order the unconscious man's hands bound behind him, when the man suddenly focused and lunged. Chulio fell backwards as two of the soldiers began grappling with him. He was not large, but the two soldiers were clearly no physical match, and two more soldiers jumped into the fray. The man held his own with all four.

It took six soldiers to stop the man's arms and legs from striking out. He had hit two of them with enough force to knock them down. All the men were breathing hard, except for the Indian, who was still lashing out with his head and torso. Chulio was fascinated, approached where his men had their prisoner stretched out on the ground, and bent over him.

"*Calmate*," he told the man. "I just want to..."

But the man spit squarely into Chulio's face. The assault was so unexpected that Chulio jumped back, shocked and immediately embarrassed. He angrily kicked at the man and connected hard between his legs. There was a grunt and a grimace, and the man stopped his struggle.

When his eyes closed, Chulio approached again. As he got close, the man's eyes opened and he spat at him again. Chulio kicked him once more, this time harder. The pain had to be excruciating, but the man made no sound and he continued to spit.

One of the soldiers grabbed a handful of dirt and tried to force it into the man's mouth. The man bit his hand. The soldier screamed when the man would not let go. Another soldier hit him on the side of his face with the butt of his rifle and they heard the jaw break. Only then could the soldier extract his hand from the man's mouth and limp away, holding his torn hand. Dirt and blood spewed from the man's mouth.

Then, Chulio saw the man's eyes and was spellbound. He had seen that look before, but never in a human. It had been in the Petén jungles of Guatemala, where he had been bivouacked for a week near some Mayan ruins with other cadets as part of an exchange program. For sport, several of them had hunted javelin and jaguar in the dense rain forest.

They had set traps and, on the second day, they had followed a trail of blood from where the trap had locked on the paw of a big cat. The jaguar had managed to free itself at the expense of leaving part of its foot behind. The trail led them to a small area where the cat had to be; the bloodstains were fresh. They heard a low growl and readied their nets and rifles.

They moved in slowly and saw the hind part of the cat behind a rock. It was on its side and they heard faint breathing—the cat was dying. They threw the large net and the jaguar reacted, but too late. The men watched the entangled creature as it struggled to free itself. After some time, it stopped and lay back on its side.

Thinking it dead, one of the men approached too close, and the jaguar struck out catching him in the chest with its claws and opening up a good-sized wound. The man screamed.

The cat just stared at them, it's ears back, leaning on its bloodied stump, its hind legs poised. That was when Chulio saw through the weave of the net the wild, crazed frenetic gape of hate—not fear, but pure revulsion. The vicious animal was going to die, but it was going to defy its killers to the end. *I am better than you,* the eyes said, *because I am not afraid. I have won. I am fiercer and braver and will live forever!* It took several shots to the head to erase any trace of life from those eyes. It was a look Chulio would not forget.

He thought of the cat as he looked into the Indian's eyes. They were two black dots surrounded by strings of red veins that seemed to pulsate. The jaguar's eyes! They blazed with hate...*I am fiercer, braver.* Chulio felt a chill of fear and paused to savor it. The man was an animal, he thought, a wild animal that could not be tamed. He unholstered his revolver and pointed it at the front of the man's thrashing head. No reaction. Despite the broken jaw and a barrel of inevitable death pointed at him, his eyes were spitting venom.

Chulio pulled the trigger. The violent thrashing was replaced by uncontrollable body jerks as the mind and the body began their disconnection. Chulio stared at the eyes. They were unfocused, but still glowed. He put the gun to the man's right temple and fired again. The head jerked away. Chulio approached close and turned the face back towards him. The eyes had bulged from the impact.

The soldiers had moved away after the first shot and watched the ritual in stunned silence. Chulio could smell the burnt hair and he had one of the men bring him a torch. He illuminated the face and stared into the eyes until he saw it—the haze, like a fog drifting in, the opaque cloud that finally covered the iris. The man's eyes were now just like those of every other dead animal, not fierce or brave, only empty.

From that day on, Chulio was mindful of the blazing eyes of the cornered jaguar and looked for them in every opponent he encountered. Those who possessed that crazed tenacity, he thought, were the most dangerous of all adversaries. They were immune to intimidation by physical or mental agony. Of the hundreds he had extra-judicially sent to their deaths during the next 15 years, only a handful had been so possessed. But he had always wondered how many others were out there.

During the years he was assigned to police the provinces, he would experiment on those he suspected had this blind tenacity. He wanted to know the depth of their hate. *Could they be ultimately broken?* He would use drugs and mental torment. At times he would order the torture and murder of a wife or child in their presence to probe the limits of their rage. But it was always the same; their demented fury was beyond logic. And he was in awe of its wickedness. If an army were to possess such ferocity, he thought, it could not be defeated.

But in the end, these experiments yielded no insight and he stopped assessing. From then on, any person believed to be so demented he ordered immediately destroyed, as he would have any rabid animal. But he would do it in a humiliating way and made sure the results were shown to other prisoners. And always the *verdugo* was instructed to report directly to him that he had personally witnessed the hazing over the eyes.

When he took over the *Guardia,* he wondered if a similar characteristic could be indoctrinated into a select group. He started looking for certain traits in young recruits. He instructed his field commanders to look for precocious boys in villages to be sent to a youth camp near the *cuartels* where they could be further observed. While the boys matured, Chulio began handpicking those to be sent for "special" training.

There they had to endure violent indoctrination that included beatings and exhaustive workouts in hazardous and stressful conditions. He would preside over the sessions and personally probe and test the men's mettle. He selected the smartest and toughest and gave some of them scholarships to the military school. Others were taught theory and practiced techniques at special classes within the *Guardia,* where they were also taught to spy.

Those who passed the arduous training and scrutiny formed the nucleus of an elite corps that was clever, fearless, ruthless and, above all, loyal to him. He started with a twelve-man platoon that soon grew to company-size. He called the unit *Los Jaguares.* Their immediate mission: Eliminate subversives.

Chapter 12

"*Ola, Teco,* how are you feeling?" my Cora asked when she and I came to the house the next morning.

"I am all right," said Teco, who was in the rocking chair trying to nurse Ana Maria. "I did sleep last night, but as soon as I awoke, I felt cold and scared at what might have happened during the night."

"Ricardo is in Guatemala by now and out of danger," I said. "We now have to see about you and the children."

Over the next two hours, the three of us planned. We would take care of their house and their belongings. We agreed that the best thing was to rent the house furnished; Cora and I would take care of that. Choco was Ricardo's partner and could take of the clinic and clientele. We also agreed that Teco and the children would leave right away for her aunt's home in Santa Ana, and from there travel by land across the border to Guatemala. We were sure that Ricardo was staying at the home of Miguel Angel Alcaíne, who was a close friend of the family.

Miguel Angel was an influential banker who had relocated to Guatemala in '32 after the government had unjustifiably blamed him for failing to predict the fall of coffee prices. Once safely settled in Guatemala, I pointed out, he could help Ricardo and Teco work out long-term plans.

"Teco, Ricardo is sure that this will be over soon," I said. "You should not worry. Things will be taken care of here until you return."

"I know, Chepe. And I am prepared to follow Ricardo wherever this situation takes us. It is the children that I worry about. Ricardo León will be confused, and *la niña* is so frail. The doctor does not know why she is not gaining weight and is so listless. My milk is not good, but she does not seem interested in any other food."

"Teco," I shot out, "with all due respect, I know that Vito is Ricardo's friend, but frankly there are more…well, more modern pediatricians. Let another doctor see Ana Maria before you leave."

"*Si,* Teco," my Cora insisted, "it has been months and the baby is not better. Forcing cow's milk and vitamins may not be the best thing. I know a fine doctor who specializes in the nutrition of babies and I want you to let me take you and Ana Maria to him."

Cora and I could see that Teco was desperate. She had already confided in Victor Quejada, who had been the family physician for Ricardo's aunts, that they might have to leave the country if Ricardo continued his involvement in politics. Vito had shaken his head and said that Ana Maria would never survive the stress of a long journey. Some older doctors are conservative to a fault. Now, fraught with the responsibility of a decision to follow Ricardo and jeopardize the life of her daughter, Teco started to break down.

"Cora, if anything happens to my baby, I will die."

"Nothing will happen to her," my Cora said sternly. "I want you to come with me right now. We are going to take *la niña* to our friend. Doctor Miguel Cayazzo doctored in Canada and has been working here for the last few years. He was highly recommended when I had some problems with Jose Carlos, whom you remember was always a fretting child. Doctor Cayazzo strongly believes in the child getting the full and natural benefits of mother's milk. I did not mention it to you, but that is when I stopped offering to nurse Ricardo León. Now, come on, get the baby ready, we are going." Then to me she said, "Have the chauffeur take you to the clinic and return for us. I will help her get ready."

"*Por supuesto, cariño,*" I said.

I kissed Cora and Teco good-bye and left. The chauffeur dropped me off and returned to take them to a small clinic in the barrio of San Miguelito, which is in a less affluent section of town. Cora later told me that Teco had been circumspect about the credentials of a doctor who would set up practice in such a place. She was even more apprehensive when she saw how young he was. But that quickly changed.

He was our age, of average build, with light hair and dark eyes. When he met with the two women, he was wearing small wire glasses and an almost white examining smock. Teco recognized his exterior and was immediately trusting. She volunteered at the *Hospital Rosales* and had met the devoted nuns and aides who specialized in caring for the incurable and the dying. The doctor had the same tired but satisfied countenance. It was obvious to the informed that he took great pleasure from his work and benefited beyond superficial rewards. I have always admired the peace in such people, and Teco recognized it right away.

"Miguel," said Cora, "I want you to meet my dearest friend, Teresa de Cruz. Her baby has a special problem and we need your help."

"That is why I am here, Cora. By the way, it is nice to see you again." Then turning to Teco, "*Señora Cruz, con mucho gusto,* how can I help you?"

"Doctor," began Teco, who was holding a quiet and expressionless Ana Maria in her arms, "it is my baby. She is almost a year old and is frail and lacking in energy. She does not eat and seems to be getting weaker every day. *Doctór* Victor Quejada has been seeing her since birth and tells me that she will get better in time, but has warned me against traveling with her. Now...now I have to travel and I am afraid."

"Miguelito," broke in Cora bluntly. "Teco's husband is in exile and she has to join him in Guatemala right away. There are reasons that I will not go into, but it must be done. There is no question the baby is weak, but it is not knowing the cause that preoccupies us."

"Are you leaving, too?" He did not hide his concern.

"No Miguel. Chepe, the children, and I will remain to tend our restless sheep. I was born here and I will die here."

The two exchanged a personal smile. Miguel turned to Teco and said, "I will see the child in just a moment. If you could wait in my office." He motioned to a small room past the waiting mothers and children.

When they were alone in the austere space, Teco turned to Cora. "And what is that all about?" she asked in a girlish voice.

"Nothing," said Cora smugly avoiding Teco's eyes. Then, looking at her, she said, "All right, so he is smitten with me. I do not encourage it and he knows it is not reciprocal. Chepe and I donate money to his work. He is a brilliant doctor. Very promising, according to Chepe, and not politically motivated. That alone is refreshing. That is all, Teco, and do not give me that look. It was a hundred years ago that we flirted and talked about other men. Chepe and Ricardo changed all of that, remember?"

"*Mira,* Gringa…" Teco started to say with a smile, but was interrupted when Miguel knocked on the door and walked in.

"*Bueno*…let us have a look at this beautiful baby. What is her name?"

"Ana Maria."

"Well, Ana Maria, are you crawling around and getting into everything yet?"

Ana Maria just stared at him with her large round brown eyes. Teco answered for her. "Yes, doctor, but lately, she does less and less of it."

The baby started to cry as soon as she was set on the makeshift examining table. Miguel paid no mind as he listened to her heart, her breathing, then weighed her on a scale. While he examined her, he asked, "Are you still breast feeding?"

"Not really, doctor. I try, but my milk has all but stopped. I have been giving her milk from the store with some additives."

"Have you noticed any blood in her stool?"

"Well, sometimes her stool is dark and I believe that occasionally…well, yes. *Doctór* Quejada says that it is normal with babies on cow's milk."

"Yes, that is true. Was she a full term baby?"

"Yes, doctor, almost. But she only weighed five and a half pounds. That was small compared to her brother, who weighed over ten pounds."

"Has her doctor drawn much blood for laboratory tests?"

"Yes, I take her once, sometimes twice a month lately and he has taken blood a few times."

"And were you worried about something during the pregnancy?"

That question was unexpected. Teco paused, then said, "Yes...I believe so. Apprehensive, nothing like now, but something was there. Maybe more subconscious."

"Does she eat solid foods?"

"Yes, but not much. Fruit, beans and rice."

Miguel finished his probing of the baby and the questions. He motioned for Teco to pick up and dress the crying baby.

He said, "*Señora*, I will give you my opinion. You may check with *Doctór* Quejada and I think you should. I think your baby is suffering from what we call iron deficiency anemia. You see, a baby gets most of its iron from the mother early on and from solid foods later. Babies triple the amount of blood in their body during the first year. So when blood is drawn frequently for laboratory exams, iron content is lessened. Add to that the blood lost in the gastrointestinal tract from being fed almost exclusively unmodified cow's milk and some babies often become anemic. Tell *Doctór* Quejada to check the laboratory results for the level of mean serum ferritin and corpuscular volume. Here, I will write it down for you. If I am right, they will be low."

He scribbled some notes on a pad of paper and handed her a small sheet from it.

He continued, "I must tell you that not all my colleagues agree with me on this, but I do not think cow's milk should be given to children who are not old enough to eat a good quantity of solid foods. The intestine will not take it. But for now, you need to fortify what you are giving her with commercial iron drops that have ferrous sulfate, a source for iron. I will write that down, too."

He took the paper back from her, wrote on it again, and handed it back.

He smiled at Teco. "Your child does not have a rare disease, *señora*, she is a normal child. In this country, the quality of food needs to be prepared better for infants, that is all. Nature has taken care of that by providing mother's milk for that period of time when they are developing their ability to process food themselves. Weaning is not complicated. In this case you ran out of milk and she is having trouble adjusting; that is all. Talk to *Doctór* Quejada. I know of him and he is a fine man. We may disagree on clinical things, but not about helping the children."

"*Gracias, doctór.*"

"No need to thank me. Thank you for coming. I know it is not usual for downtown ladies to come to the *barrio*. But there is an equalizer out here that they do not teach in medical school. When people are ill, it does not matter who they are, their apprehension and reactions are the same and treatment should not discriminate. It seems I do as much teaching as treating.

"Most of the children you see in the waiting room are ill because of the ignorance of the parents. Ignorance about cleanliness, eating habits, treatments. Many parents have ingrained fears and superstitions from their parents and they pass these on to their children. Remember the *siguanava* that your mother said would get you if you did not drink your milk? I teach them about effective habits and they get better. Life is tough enough; it is harder when you do not know the basics."

"God bless you, *doctór*. Here, I want to pay you for your time." Teco reached into her purse.

"I do not have set fees here, *señora*."

"Then you will let me contribute to your work. Something for the clinic, perhaps? Books for the children to read while they wait. I have many at home that I will send to your office." Teco took out ten *colones* and handed it to him.

"You are most generous, *señora.*"

He walked out with the two mothers and child to the waiting car. "Please give my best to Chepe, Cora."

"*Por supuesto,* Miguelito. And you take care of yourself. We will see you soon. And, thank you."

"*Por nada.* You are welcome. *Hasta luego. Vaya con Díos.*"

That night, Cora told me about their successful visit to Miguel's clinic. She did not leave out Teco's quick assessment about Miguel's obvious attraction to her. I was not unaware of this infatuation; my Cora is quite beautiful and draws men's attention wherever she goes. Nor was I unaware of Teco's keen powers of perception. I guess I have led a sheltered life and pay little mind to these nuances, but I have noted that some people possess an ability to see more than others do, certainly more than I. Teco is one of these people. She was a survivor, and I was sure that she would prevail in this latest test as well.

"Report," Chulio barked without looking up from some papers he was reading at his desk.

Major Carrillo had arrived promptly at six that evening for the day's report. Only the general's aide, Romano, a small nervous man of dubious background was in the office.

The shifty Romano was not liked by the other officers and had been christened *Tapesquintla*, the name of a large rodent that inhabited the jungles of Central America, because of his rat-like features and actions. No one knew why Chulio kept Romano around but suspected that he was the equivalent of having the proverbial dog to kick when the mood suited. When Carrillo walked in, Romano was busily involved in sorting some papers on the top of the general's desk.

"*Mí generál*," began the major at attention. "I begin by reporting that we have brought in twelve new suspects for questioning. Additionally, of the twenty possible suspects mentioned in yesterday's briefing, ten have been picked up. In turn, we expect that these subversives will provide the names of others. The questioning..."

Chulio raised his hand to halt the briefing. The major waited. Without looking up, Chulio asked, "Are these twelve new suspects you picked up from the list of names we already had yesterday or from a new list gathered from subversives who have confessed?"

"*Mí generál*, these are suspects from a new list of sympathizers that..."

"What about the rest from the original list?"

"All have fled, *mí generál*. We have distributed their names to the other authorities, along with backgrounds and photographs..."

"All!" Chulio bellowed looking up.

Carrillo braced for a violent reaction. Romano began to move his chores away from the general's desk.

Instead of attacking him, Chulio glared for a moment at the major, then asked, "What about Cruz and Escudes?"

"Fled as well, *mí generál*. Neither returned home last night."

"I want details, Major."

"*Si, mí generál*. There was no activity at the Escudes house all day. A *Doctór* Jose Molina, a psychiatrist, and his wife Coralia Roca de Molina visited the Cruz house at 9:05 this morning. They stayed for about two hours.

"At 10:15, their chauffeur drove Molina to his clinic. The chauffeur, Jose Luis Arevalo, no prior record, returned to the Cruz house at 10:38, picked up the two women and a baby, and took them to *el barrio* San Miguelito.

"At 11:22, they were seen to enter a house at Urbanizacíon #43 owned by Maribel Rodriguez, who is on record with us as a landlord of several houses in that *barrio*, as well as houses in other *barrios*. Several suspected subversives have rented from her in the past according to our records, none currently that we know of.

"Renting the house at #43 is a *Doctór* Miguel Cayazzo, a national who has done pediatrics research in Canada and is now mainly treating people of the *barrio*. We have no record on Cayazzo other than that he graduated from the University of El Salvador in '37.

"At 11:45 A.M., the women and child left #43 and were driven back to the Cruz residence. Molina's wife stayed until 1:00 in the afternoon and then returned to her home.

"About 2:30 the maid went to the *mercado* two blocks away and bought some items at different stands, mainly food and one item at the pharmacy. A young man approached her at one of the stores, but we could not identify the individual. It was a brief conversation and he left right away. There was only one man watching her and he stayed with the servant. She returned to the house at 3:00.

"We have seen no more activity at the Cruz house since then. The listeners at the Telephone Company recorded all the calls to both the Cruz and Escudes house; nothing suspicious that we could tell. I have transcripts of their notes attached to my report, *mí generál*."

"Let me see them." Chulio held out his hand.

The major fumbled quickly through the papers and handed two separate reports to Chulio, who went through them slowly until he found what he wanted.

"Clever," he said audibly to himself. Then to the major, "It says here that at 4:00 in the afternoon a call was made to the Cruz house and the *señora* was asked for. The male voice said that he wanted to confirm that she got the message that the plumber would not make it to her house to take care of the problem her husband had called about yesterday. She responds that she got the message and that it had been taken care of. The Telephone Company does not say where the call came from?"

"*Mí generál*, they can only trace the caller if we ask them to do so ahead of time."

"I want to know who is calling that house!" Chulio snapped. "I would have hoped you would notice the significance of this call, Major. Frankly, I am disappointed. The caller said that Cruz made arrangements for a plumber yesterday. Yesterday I would think Cruz was too busy running from us to be thinking about a plumber. The caller asked his wife if she got the message. What message? Did the young man at the *mercado* slip the maid a note for the *señora*? Then she says she got the message and the problem has been taken care of. What problem did she take care of? I would think having stolen weapons in the house would be a big problem, would you not?"

"Of course, *mí generál*."

"Search the house immediately."

"At once, *mí generál*."

"If you find anything incriminating, arrest the wife. If not, continue the surveillance. Eventually, she will lead us to him. Now, Major, about this visit to a doctor in San Miguelito…"

113

The major started slowly, *"Mí generál,* we thought it suspicious."

Chulio ignored him while he thought out loud. "Yes. Let's analyze this. The wife of a subversive who has just fled picks this time to visit an unconventional doctor in an unconventional neighborhood full of other subversives." Then he snapped at the major, "Yes, 'suspicious' is an understatement, Major. Pick him up. He is a link. At the very least he is a sympathizer working with children. At worst, he is contributing to their cause by aiding and treating their injured. I want to know everything that they talked about, and what other aid this doctor gives in this *barrio."*

"Sí, mí generál."

"And what about this landlady who rents to subversives in San Miguelito?" Chulio asked rhetorically. "You are too young to remember, Major, but it was in that very *barrio* that I had the pleasure of arresting Marti, Luna and Zapata in '32. Those communist *hijos de puta*s had made that location their headquarters. If you remember your history, Luna and Zapata were communist student leaders."

"Por supuesto, of course, *mí generál.* Along with *El Negro* Marti they were preparing the urban phase of the insurrection when you arrested them."

"Yes…" Chulio mused. "Well it seems that *barrio* is at it again. This time we will destroy their home base before they can get started. Have the landlady picked up as well. Seize her properties and petition the courts to begin forfeiting the houses to us. Anyone who interferes or tries to use their *cuello* to help her could also be a supporter or suspect. Make that clear."

"Sí, mí generál."

"Now tell me about Hugo."

"Mí generál, we have sent numerous informants into the student community. I am handling the inquiry personally. As you know, his family was executed years ago for treason. We are searching for a possible adopted family, close friends, sweethearts, or habitats he may have collected or frequented in the years he has been back. So far, nothing is traceable to him, but it is only a matter of time."

"We do not have time, Major. His misinformation and propaganda are taking their toll. Because of his lies, many people do not believe what the President has declared about his plans to give up the presidency next year. Now some of his enemies have petitioned the Supreme Court to declare illegal the Executive Order on elections. Hugo has stirred up rumors that the election delegates will vote the President in for a fourth term and even declare him king. His missives are too informed, too timely. Someone is helping him on the inside. We have to find out who. What *tanda* was he?"

"The first, *mí generál."*

"Ah yes, the famous 43 from the first *tanda* in 1930. Get me the alumnae information from that class. We may want to start watching some of them. You are still watching Colonel Gutierrez?"

"*Si, mí generál.*"

"You are only using *Jaguares?* You cannot be too careful about this. We do not want to put the President in a vulnerable position with the officers loyal to him. Remember, he respects Gutierrez, despite the memorandum you wrote me about his support for Cruz."

"*Por supuesto, mí generál.*"

"I have arranged it with the President's personal secretary to provide me with a list of people the President feels are his most ardent adversaries. We will watch them as well. There are many influential people on that list, and any contemplated action will require my personal approval. Is that understood?"

"*A la orden, mí generál.*"

Chulio made a wincing contemplative face. He was thinking. "Something is gnawing at me about Hugo. Something you said."

"*Mí generál*...about the *tanda*...it was..."

"No, before that."

"*Mí generál*...I reported that we were searching for a possible adopted family, close friends, sweethearts, habitats..."

"Yes," interrupted Chulio. "Sweethearts. That was it. Hugo's file. Do you have a copy of it?"

"*Si, mí generál.*"

"I recall that when Hugo, the former *Teniente* Valentín Aurelio Magaña," he said the name contemptuously, "fled from Izalco, the coward was aided by a family."

"*Si, mí generál*, the family of an Indian woman. We have her full name on file, the infamous Marta. Her family was also executed for treason, but she was not found. It was rumored that she fled with Lieutenant...I mean Magaña after he murdered *mí Coronel Mojano.*"

"Yes," said Chulio, "bring me the file, but you go through it first. Project her age and start asking about her. Hugo is a man, and men have needs. He is also a romantic who would try to look up the person who shared such a pivotal moment in his life. Yes, I think he would. It would not surprise me if they are lovers and she is his closest comrade. Find her."

"*Si, mí generál.*" The major waited. He could see Chulio was deep in thought.

After a moment, the general focused on him. "Well, you have much to do, Major. Get to it. I want a report at noon tomorrow. Dismissed." The major was starting out the door when Chulio said, "Oh, one last thing...what about Dominguez?"

The major turned quickly, but Chulio was once more reading the papers in front of him. The scurrying Romano was behind him again, his head buried in some filing cabinets. The major risked a smile and said, "Taken care of, *mí generál.*"

Chulio said nothing and kept reading. After a moment, a more confident major clicked his heals, about-faced, and left.

Chapter 13

Before Teco and Lucha sensed anything, the intruders were inside the house from the front and back. They were fast. So fast, that Balalaika had just jumped up from her resting position in front of the children's beds and was growling protectively when the door to the bedroom sprung open and two soldiers entered with carbines aimed at Teco and the dog.

"*No, Bal!*" Teco screamed as the dog was about to lunge. She had been resting in the rocking chair beside the sleeping children's cribs, and sprang up with the dog to stand between them and the soldiers protectively. She grabbed the dog's choke collar and repeated, "No!" The dog growled. The children stirred, but remained in their deep sleep.

"What do you want?" Teco hissed instinctively, her eyes poised to defend her children. Rage had replaced the instant of fear, and she was focused, too focused, in fact, to even hear the maid screaming, doorframes snapping and glass breaking. "What do you want?" she repeated. No answer.

Two more soldiers joined the first two and the four spread out, covering all sides. They were silent; their trained eyes probed for danger areas. A hand signal from one of the men kept one rifle aimed at Teco and another at the dog. The other two men moved to the closet, threw the doors open and darted to each side, one low, one high. With the ends of their rifles they shoved aside clothing and prodded the walls and ceiling. At another signal, the searching men moved systematically and probed places where someone might possibly hide.

An incensed Teco wanted to impulsively strike out at this violation. Were she alone, it would have been a reflexive move, but she was held back by another drive, that of mother-protector. If it appeared that the soldiers were going to shoot, she would unleash Bal and strike out herself. She would not go passively. At this distance, Bal was her only weapon. For now, all she could do was position herself so that any shots would strike her before the babies. Her naked arm moved in front of her as if it held an invisible shield.

In the deepest part of her mind, she thought she heard a shrill whistle. Two of the soldiers, the ones who were searching, seemed to relax, and started to move out of the room. The other two remained strained and poised. It was two against two now, she thought. Then another soldier walked into the room...taller, an officer. He said something to the men; one of the men said something back. The officer moved alongside the two men holding the short rifles.

To Teco he said, "If either you or the dog make a move, my men will kill you both. Then I will kill every living thing in this house." Teco did not move. "Did you hear what I said? It makes no difference to me." The voice was authoritative and at the same time calm. "Everything will die."

Teco started blinking. *Everything. Her babies. They had no plans to kill them. At least not yet.* She nodded.

One of the men motioned to the officer and pointed with two fingers to his own eyes while looking at her. The officer said to the soldier, "*Interesante.* No, never in a woman before." Then, with an arrogant smile, he said to her, "You have impressed my men with your motherly defense. I, however, am not impressed. I do have a passion for German shepherds, though, especially obedient and fierce ones. If I did not, the creature would already be dead."

He then changed his face and his tone. In a menacing voice he said, "Listen to me carefully. We are going to search every inch of this house. If you resist, you and everyone in this house will be killed immediately. If we find anything that incriminates you in treason, you will be taken and everyone in this house will be killed. You will be tortured until you tell me everything, then you will be killed."

He paused to let his threatening remarks register. Then he continued, "So, what I am about to say to you now is the only chance you will have to save your children. We are only bargaining for their lives, you understand, not yours. I will ask this question once and only once. Are you ready? Where are the guns hidden? Tell me now and I will spare them."

Teco was thinking, and she kept blinking to get the blur out of her eyes. It was like a bad dream. *Was she dreaming? No.* She did not think it would help, but she found a shaky voice to say, "I do not know who you are but my husband is *Doctór* Ricardo…"

But the officer quickly held up his hand and spat out, "I know who your husband is! He is a traitor who has abandoned his family! And when I find him I will take great pleasure in killing him. So do not waste my time with that; I do not care. Answer my question. This is your only chance. Where are the guns?"

He is not a traitor, she thought, *and he has not abandoned his family. You will not kill him.* She stopped blinking and defiantly stared back at the officer. Then she vehemently exclaimed, "There are no guns in this house!" He stared back at her for what seemed a minute, a year. No bullets came.

Then he said, "We shall see. You are either very brave or very stupid." To the two men he said, "Watch them. If they move, kill them."

The search seemed to take hours. The officer had been right; they were thorough. First they searched the bedroom she was in. Then they moved to the other rooms. As best she could determine, there were about a dozen men in the house. Walls, floors, ceilings were all probed, some dislodged. She could hear digging in the yard. Large furniture was turned upside down or slashed. Anywhere that might have hidden even a small revolver was examined. And so too was the outhouse.

She sat in the children's room tightly holding Bal, who would occasionally growl to confirm her understanding that something was wrong. Teco prayed that the children would remain asleep. She did not know what they had done with Lucha. Her screaming and whimpering had stopped after a while. She said a prayer for her.

Ricardo had been right to guard their conversation around Lucha. She had not seen him hiding the bundle in the outhouse, and there was virtually no true thing Lucha could say against them. Lucha knew about the note from Tomas, but Lucha could not read.

Luckily, Tomas had spotted the soldiers watching the house and had waited for an opportunity. The note contained the instructions that Ricardo had given him. Upon reading it, Teco had taken the sharpest knife she could find, locked herself in the outhouse, and cut the rope that was hidden to one side under the stool. The weight had taken the bundle and any trace of the rope down with it.

If she lived through this night, she thought, she would leave immediately for Santa Ana. Her aunt and her uncle were respected and powerful members of the coffee growing community. They would protect her.

But first, she had to survive the soldiers. These were not regular militia, she thought. She had never encountered soldiers like them before. She started to realize the terror that Ricardo claimed was facing the country. She had not believed it. She thought him dramatic when he had described the fiendish ways of those in power. But she was wrong, she now thought. These men are not like Rodolfo Maria de Jesus Mendez. These are the people who sent him. She remembered his words, *I have heard what they have done to others and it would not be right*.

This, then, was the enemy, she thought, and things started to become clearer. She began praying to Jesus Christ and his mother in gratitude for this enlightenment. She had been wrong to think harshly of Ricardo. It was right to love and trust him totally. She prayed that he was well.

The two soldiers guarding the open door that led into the hall had not taken their eyes off her and the dog for a second. Through it she could see occasional movement beyond, but she mostly heard the destruction.

Their actions were intimate, she thought, a desecration of all their possessions. Then, in one swooping realization, she cast aside any importance to these material things. *No me importa! They do not matter*. Personally, she owned no material thing of value except the few trinkets her mother had given her when she died. Except for the children and Ricardo; these were her only sacred possessions. Everything else was now soiled beyond importance. Her immediate interest was protecting the children, with her life if necessary. She glared at the two soldiers. She had no idea she could hate so much.

The noise abated and the same officer walked back into the room. She felt the anger reach a higher pitch. She and Bal tensed, and she turned her frown on the leader of the intruders. If only I were a man, she thought. Behind the officer she could see Lucha being held by a soldier. Lucha was crying; one hand covered her face and the other clutched the front of her torn dress.

"We are taking the woman with us," he said. "She will be questioned further. I am also taking some papers to be examined by experts. Meanwhile, we will be watching this house. Your husband is wanted for…"

This time it was Teco who put up her hand and spit out, "You have nothing to say to me. If you are going to kill or arrest me, do so. If not, leave. And leave my servant. She cannot help you find what you could not. It does not exist. You have made a grave error."

"It is your husband who has made the mistake. Our interest is…"

She interrupted him again, "Since you did not care before, I do not expect that you care now about what is right or decent. Nor am I interested in your explanations. I do not know what you are, but you are not gentlemen or soldiers. The military men I know do not wage war on women and children. What you have done is despicable and unforgivable. If I were a man, one of us would already be dead!"

The major stared back surprised. After a moment, he put a whistle up to his lips and blew. All the soldiers began to exit, except for the two centurions who were still watching her. The major stood silent for a moment, then pulled out an automatic pistol from his holster. Teco just stood her ground, impertinently awaiting the worst.

As before, her awareness was beyond reality. She was outside herself, someone else calmly observing the slow-moving portentous scene. She watched her arm-shield rise slowly once again in front of her, and her body positioned itself in front of the sleeping children. She noticed the detail of the officer's handgun—a German military piston, a Luger, the type Ricardo had showed her once, not a weapon of this army. It was supposed to have a very fast bullet, she recalled through the fog building around her unblinking eyes.

As if in a dream, she heard these thoughts, and she also heard the officer ask something about the dog's name. From outside herself, she saw that the woman did not answer, just stared back insolently, and prepared for the inevitable. A prayer came to mind and she and the woman started saying the words, *Padre nuestro, que estas en los cielos, santificado sea Tu nombre...*

The dog growled just as the officer pointed the weapon and fired. The sound of the blast broke the spell. Teco recoiled. Both children woke screaming. Lucha shrieked in the hallway. Blood sprayed her hand and the sudden dead weight of the animal sprained her wrist. The bullet had hit the top of the animal's skull. Bal was instantly lifeless.

It was logical, she thought quickly, the dog first, then me, and then...She was about to react when she saw that the officer was holstering the weapon. She froze. *Were she and the children safe?*

The officer said complacently, "It was for your own good. Where you are headed, the animal would only be a burden."

"*Canalla!*" she yelled, but he was walking away from her.

From the front door, he said over his shoulder, "Leave the *muchacha.*"

"The wife?" asked Chulio incredulously. "*No me digas?*"

"If she had been a man, *mí generál,* I would not have left her alive."

The two men were in the general's office and, despite the negative report concerning the search of Cruz' residence, Chulio's demeanor was not hostile. He had been intrigued by Carrillo's description of Teco's attitude.

"Interesting. It had not occurred to me," Chulio said in a rare display of personality. "So, it is not merely *machismo* that sets it off," Chulio said as if to himself. "Well, it stands to reason. A female animal will protect her young to the death. In fact, this rage may be more prevalent in females, now that I think about it. But would they hate as much if the threat was only to their person, not their children? If not, then it is only man who is that pathologically egotistical. Same eyes, you say. Interesting. I must meet *Señora* Cruz one day."

"I do not know *mí generál,* that one has grit. It would be interesting to be in the same room alone with her." The major was enjoying the informality.

"Where is she now?"

"On the road to her aunt's house in Santa Ana, *mí generál.* She called the Hinez house this morning and made the arrangements. She will no doubt make her way from there to Guatemala to meet Cruz. We have alerted the border to let them through. We have people in Guatemala standing by."

"Handle the instructions regarding the Guatemalan surveillance personally, Major. We do not want an incident there. *Los Chapines* are not always our friends in these matters. Work only with trusted people in their military. Their police includes too many civilians. I do not trust them. They are corrupt."

"*Si, mí generál.*"

"Nothing at the Cruz house, you say?"

"*No, mí generál.* I am certain of that. We have some address books and papers and the readers are going through them, but nothing so far. But he is guilty for sure. We will have information on his family and acquaintances later today."

"Good. Now, what about the doctor from San Miguelito?"

"*Mí generál*, the man was able to support considerable pain, but I believe what he finally said to us is the truth."

"Yes, yes, go on. What did he say?"

"First, *mí generál*, he told us about his relationship with the Molinas. They contribute to his clinic with donations of money; they have been very generous. He has treated their children and holds them in high esteem. He admitted to being in love with the Molina woman, but claims she does not know it. We did not spend too much time on that point, because the Molina family is not known to be active in politics. They are good friends and *compadres* with the Cruz'."

"*Compadres* with subversives," corrected Chulio sardonically. "Yes, I am sure they are fine people. All right, go on."

"According to the doctor, *mí generál*, Molina's wife brought Cruz' wife and daughter to him because the child was anemic and they were fearful of her reaction to a trip they were planning. Cruz' wife and children have plans to meet Cruz in Guatemala within the week. That is what the doctor was told. They also told him that Cruz had fled to Guatemala for political reasons. He claimed to know nothing more. He said he knew nothing about Cruz before yesterday and that this was the first time he had met Cruz' wife. On another point, he said that he has only treated children, not subversives.

"However, when pressed, he confessed that on occasion he has treated unknown men, who could not afford to pay, for different types of injuries. He does not know these men, and he never questioned them about their injuries or reported them to the police, even though some of them were wounds sustained in violent acts. He said they might have been criminals."

The major paused for a reaction. Chulio was listening patiently with his hands in front of his face, but did not comment.

"As far as the owner of the property, the doctor claimed to have heard rumors, but knew nothing about her renting to subversives. He claims he is not part of any political organization. He held firm on that point to the end." Again, a pause, then, "*Mí generál*, the doctor was picked up by our special group in an unmarked car. Since then, there have been numerous people from the *barrio* asking about him, including several priests and a monsignor. We have claimed to know nothing about him."

"Very well. Is that all you learned from him?"

"*Si, mí generál.*"

"The man has aided subversives and by so doing has condemned himself. Besides, we do not need another subversive sympathizer in San Miguelito. If you are sure he knows nothing more, have his throat cut and dump him on a side street in the *barrio*. It will be a clear message to those he has helped. What about the Rodriguez woman?"

"*Mí generál*, the woman was questioned and has confessed that she has rented in the past to political activists. She insisted that she was not a participant and had no knowledge that they were people engaged in any plans to overthrow the government. For now, we have deemed that confession sufficient reason to hold her. It is possible that under further questioning she may divulge more."

"Perhaps," said Chulio, "but for now let her arrest be a warning to the other property owners in the *barrios* that their properties are at risk. To most of them, that property is worth more than their lives. Let her live for now. What about the properties?"

"The properties she owns with her husband have all been bought by them one at a time from proceeds of the rent of others. They now own twelve cabins in several *barrios*. They total about two thousand *colones* in value. We have turned the houses over to the military auxiliary office for their use. The husband has not come forward with a claim. The woman says he is Honduran and will probably return there if she is not released quickly."

"She is not to be released until I clear it."

"*Si, mí generál.*"

"Now, Major, you have new orders."

"*Mí generál.*"

"After you dispose of the traitor doctor, you will not take any more action against the sympathizers and students on the remaining lists for the time being. The President wants to get through this Supreme Court matter and solidify his future plans. You can continue your work on Cruz and Hugo, but I will have to clear any action. Is that understood?"

"*Si, mí generál.*" The major paused to see if there were other instructions. When he was sure there were none, he said, "*Mí generál*, we think we have a lead on Marta, the woman who escaped with Hugo in '32. One of our informants went back to Izalco to check out a rumor. She is believed to be right here in the capital, in a *ranchito* on the outskirts of the *colonia* Linda Vista. He will be back tomorrow with more information."

Chulio's eyes narrowed. Then he said, "Very well, continue with that, Major, but let me emphasize a point in case it is not clear. This investigation is personal with me, and it should be personal with you and every officer in this Army. The officer corps needs to be vindicated for Magaña's treason. He has damaged our institution and our country more than anyone else I know. I want those who think he is a hero to see his cowardice, and those who think he is invincible to see him fall. I want the legend to die along with him. He must not cheat the *verdugo*."

"*Mí generál!*" The Major exalted him in a loud voice.

Chapter 14

After the assault on the house, Teco spent the rest of the night consoling Lucha and the children. They had abused the maid, but she was not in need of medical attention, at least not the physical kind. They buried the brave Balalaika in the backyard as soon as the children were soothed back to sleep.

At dawn, Teco gathered a few essentials and left for Santa Ana. Lucha refused to be left behind. Teco had enough presence to avoid calling Cora and me for fear of implicating us further. Instead, she called for a taxi. She was short of money, but the *taxista* took pity on her and chanced the two-hour drive on a promise that he would be rewarded at their destination.

All during the drive, she had a foreboding of being suddenly pulled over and all of them killed. She could see the dark green sedan behind them, but it kept its distance, even when they went through a roadblock outside of town.

It was late morning when they arrived at Luz Hinez's home in the center of Santa Ana. Teco's aunt was outraged by the account of their ordeal. And despite Teco's supplication, she bitterly complained to the commanding general of the fort at Santa Ana, a man about to retire and beholden to her husband.

Later that day, the general personally stopped by the house with more information. Teco would not see him. She, Lucha, and the children hid in a back room.

The general had politely counseled Luz Hinez against raising the matter formally in the capital. He was circumspect with the feisty wife of the most prominent *cafetalero* in the region, but did confide that the "investigation" was being handled by Chulio's *Jaguares*. He explained that although officially disavowed by the government, the *Jaguares* were often used to "solve" political tribulations, and their audacious exploits were legend. The general felt that the best thing was for Teco to leave El Salvador and join her husband in Guatemala as soon as possible. He would arrange an informal escort if that would help. Luz Hinez passed all this on to Teco after the general left.

It did not take long for Teco to decide. While she felt she would be safe with her aunt, she wanted to be away from El Salvador and with Ricardo as soon as possible. In addition, she could see that her aunt was uncomfortable. She would not stay there any longer.

Sensing Teco's apprehension, Luz Hinez had soothingly said, "Teco, the general would not dare betray us. What he owes Polo he can only repay with his life, and he knows it. Besides, there is a large plantation waiting for him next year when he retires. And you can guess who owns the property. Do not worry."

Still, Teco's mind was made up. After a while, her aunt acquiesced and arranged to accompany them to the border the next morning.

Teco felt more comfortable riding in the escorted sedan when they finally left the next day, but the anxiety did not leave her. She still felt intimidated by the mere presence of military men, even though they were in civilian clothes. Luz and Polo Hinez had no problems obtaining exit permits and Guatemalan visas for her, Lucha, and the children from the border officials. Teco found this surprising in light of the assault of the previous night, but attributed it to her aunt and uncle's *cuello*.

After a tearful moment with them, the four crossed the land border at Las Chiamas without incident. But Teco had been terrified every second of the trip from there to Guatemala City. Only the peaceful look on the children's faces when they were not fussing afforded her any comfort and distraction.

In Guatemala City, Teco's cunning instincts took over. She did not give the military drivers a specific address. Instead, she told them that she could only recall general directions to her friend's home. She remembered from a previous trip with her godfather, years before, that they had stayed at a *pensíon*, a small hotel, near the cathedral on the main square. She directed the drivers there. Once there, she declared that they had arrived and dismissed them. They left hesitatingly.

Inside the *pensíon*, she moved the children and Lucha to an eating area and ordered them pastries. She waited about an hour, then called for a taxi, and they traveled to the home of Miguel Angel Alcaíne.

I can only imagine the shocking reunion, although I later heard all three versions separately from Ricardo, Teco and Miguel Angel.

Teco arrived cradling a fretting Ana Maria while Lucha held Ricardo León by the hand. The long dusty trip, three sleepless nights, and the abuse and anguish evident on their faces following their violent encounters with the military must have painted a most distressful picture.

Miguel Angel's maid, who answered the door, left them waiting in the foyer while she went to announce them. Within seconds, Miguel Angel and Ricardo rushed in from the back rooms. Ricardo León broke into a wide-eyed grin and screamed "*Papi!*" when he saw his astounded father. Ricardo swept up the running boy and went to Teco, who maintained a parched smile as she collapsed in his arms.

They passionately held each other for a long while. No words were necessary. Ricardo instantly recognized the emergency and the exhausting strain of prolonged tension and fatigue…and something else.

During the next few hours, Ricardo pieced together from Teco's brief excerpts a detailed account of what had occurred after he fled El Salvador a mere two days before. Only her ailing condition was able to quell his fury and compulsion to immediately return to El Salvador and avenge the outrage. He did not know how or when, but he would find a way to confront the people responsible. *His wife, Ricardo León, Ana Maria!* He was livid; the cowards had assaulted his only purpose for living and he would make them pay.

After Teco rested a few days and Ricardo's shock, anger, and pain ran their course, they talked. Alone at night in their bedroom, she told him everything again, and this time included the poignant moment when she first truly understood the nature of the evil and how wrong she had been not to support him better. He listened quietly, and when she had finished, just held her tightly.

"Do not leave me again, *Negro*," she pleaded.

"Never, *mi amor*," he said and immediately recalled his pledge to avenge her terror. Instead, he said, "After a few days, we will see about trying to get our own place. We will start a new life here. Miguel Angel says that we can stay as long as we like, but he is being kind and we do not want to impose."

"*Esta bien, Negro*," she said.

Their embrace was reassuring, although a presentiment remained. There was no telling what the future held, but for now, they would just lean on each other a bit harder.

Ricardo learned much about himself during the next few days. He was not invincible, and had been foolish to think otherwise. He needed to fully accept responsibility as the head of his family and protect them at all cost. He was committed to supporting Hugo, at least for the time being, but he would be judicious and shrewd in how he handled that relationship. He had been given another chance. He and Teco had escaped the best Chulio could throw at them, but they could not expect to do that for long—not without extraordinary help. He made his decision; he would contact Hugo to arrange a meeting with the American.

I cannot adequately tell you because I cannot find enough words, even now, to describe the terror Cora and I felt during the days following Teco's abrupt departure and the murder of Miguelito. The two events had happened so fast and were so extraordinary that they left us literally in a state of shock. The fear that replaced that trauma was so intense that I had to place my Cora on medication. At the same time, I asked my family to make surreptitious inquiries on my behalf.

What they learned from some trusted sources was that the authorities had no intention of questioning me as part of their investigations. That had provided some relief, but the apprehension persisted. The worst fear was not knowing what was coming next, or when. As it was, we did not know at the time what had really happened to Teco, only second-hand bits and pieces from Ricardo's aunts, who had talked to Luz Hinez.

Then, there were the circumstances behind Miguelito's murder. Was it a street crime, or was it related to Teco's visit to him? The government's silence over that atrocity, despite pleadings from prominent church and civic officials, was deafening. I concluded that it had to be related, which meant that we were at least indirectly involved. My family was not without influence with the authorities, but I knew that it only shielded us up to a point. As I say, it was a horrifying period for us.

As the days passed without incident, my Cora and I began feeling more comfortable. We were just settling into a feeling of relative calm when, without warning, *El Choco* Mendez brought back all the anxiety.

I had been in periodic touch with Choco, who had been efficiently covering for Ricardo's patients during the past weeks. I would occasionally call or stop by to check on him. On this occasion, Choco called to invite me to lunch at the *Asociación Dental Salvadoreña*; he said he had a letter for me from Ricardo. I was uneasy, but agreed to meet him.

"Chepe," he said after we were seated. "Ricardo needs your help. But first, I must tell you something in confidence." He was never one to waste time with courtesies. He stated bluntly, "I also am involved with Hugo and his underground movement, and I have been for the past five years. It was I who urged Hugo to bring Ricardo into the struggle. I am telling you this because it is related to what I have to report on Ricardo."

I must tell you that when he told me this, after all I had been through, I was struck dumb. I looked at him incredulously, chilled and at the same time incensed. Frankly, I was inclined to turn my back on both of them.

"*Mira,* Choco," I said adamantly, shaking my head, "this cannot be; you have to understand my position. I would do anything for Ricardo that does not place my family in danger. He knows that. But why does he, or you for that matter, persist in this madness? Look what they did to Miguelito and to Teco. I tell you, if he insists on coming back..."

"He is not coming back," said Choco strongly. "But do you think Ricardo is safe in Guatemala? No. He needs to protect himself there as well."

"What does that have to do with me? What can I do under these circumstances?" I was still trying to recover from the shock of what he had just revealed to me.

"He is not looking to you for help, Chepe. He has always protected you. Hell, he would be furious if he knew I was even talking to you about this. I was only supposed to deliver this letter and I am sure there is nothing political in it. *I* am the one asking. Be his friend, Chepe, that is all. You are his *compadre* and also a psychiatrist; you know how therapeutic it is to vent. He would do it for you. He did it once for me."

I must admit that these words bit into me. He was right, of course. My nervousness was getting the better of me and I was being overly cautious.

"Choco, it is just that I do not understand these radical choices that you have made. What is wrong with being patient and letting change run its course?"

"Listen to you," he shot back. "You are the one always quoting Nietzsche. Do you recall what he said about rights? It is a form of power, he said, and to exercise it demands effort and courage."

I had never won an argument with Choco, certainly not on anything philosophical, and this time was no different. Actually, he was being gracious in paraphrasing the German philosopher, whom I did know and admire very much. I knew the entire passage by heart. It was from *The Wanderer and His Shadow*, written in 1880, and read:

"To exercise power costs effort and demands courage. That is why so many fail to assert rights to which they are perfectly entitled—because a right is a kind of power, but they are too lazy or too cowardly to exercise it. The virtues which cloak these faults are called patience and forbearance."

Choco continued sternly, "And I am going to tell you something else, Chepe, that will surprise you. You think that your family's *cuello* is protecting you from Chulio and his thugs? Well, it is not, *papasito*; it is Hugo." He stared at me and let the words sink in, then resumed, "Yes...Hugo has people within Chulio's organization, and they have convinced the general that there is no percentage in going after a loyal and established family like the Molinas."

"How do you know this?" I demanded. Choco had astonished me again and I could not think of a better question to ask.

"Because I believe Hugo. It is that simple. *Mira,* Chepe, Hugo is going to help Ricardo by giving him an assignment that will make him valuable to the Americans. All Hugo and I ask of you is that you continue to be yourself in this matter—the best friend Ricardo has. You do not have to discuss politics with Ricardo or get involved in anything more than being an objective listener."

Then, in a more temperate voice, he said, "The time will come for knowledgeable people to speak out without worrying about a pack of animals raiding your home in the middle of the night, and that time is not far away. Hugo will see that you get any background information you require. I can be the conduit for you. All you have to do is ask."

There, the hook had been set.

The request was not unreasonable. *Be a friend to Ricardo*? I could not be otherwise. *Do not talk politics*? I had no intention of doing so. *Stay informed*; that was not an irrational demand of an academic. I could not argue with his words. After a moment, I simply nodded my head slowly.

Then, almost illogically, I inquired dumbfounded, "You said Ricardo and the Americans?"

Choco nodded. We talked for quite a while during that *almuerzo*.

And so it was that, with Hugo's blessing, Paco Poveda, the aviator who had flown Ricardo and Carlitos to Guatemala, arranged for Ricardo to meet the American diplomat, Brodrick Foreman Anderson.

Hugo was delighted that Ricardo had been ready so soon, despite feeling uneasy when Ricardo asked for the name of the officer who led the aggression on his house. Personally, he could identify with Ricardo's eagerness for revenge, perhaps better than Ricardo knew, but Hugo also understood timing, and decided to procrastinate on that request. Personal vendettas would have to wait. He needed Ricardo's focus on the American.

The meeting was arranged at Ruby's, an unassuming Chinese restaurant near the center of Guatemala City. After introductions, several beers, and the characteristic Latin small talk, Paco found a reason to excuse himself.

Ricardo was left alone with the overweight middle-aged American, who seemed to enjoy talking insatiably about banalities. His face was square and wrinkled and his gray hair was thinning on top. He was also quite comfortable wearing a perpetual smile, even when he talked. He was in a business suit that was obviously unaccustomed to being dry-cleaned and ironed. The usually convivial Ricardo, meanwhile, was anxious to discuss *his* reason for wanting to meet. When the American finally paused to change subjects, Ricardo seized the moment.

"*Señor* Anderson," he interrupted, "if I may…I know Hugo wants us to get to know each other and I am totally at your disposal. But first, I must consult with you about something of great importance to me personally."

"Yes, of course," Anderson said pleasantly while hiding his surprise at the directness. He had purposely avoided a substantive conversation until he had enough time to better scrutinize the young man.

"My family and I will need your protection while we are in Guatemala," Ricardo said directly.

"Oh? And why is that, Doctor Cruz?"

"I left El Salvador two weeks ago because I was warned that my name was on a list of people believed to be conspiring to bring down the dictator Martínez," Ricardo blurted out. "People on their lists are being picked up for 'questioning' and systematically tortured and killed by villainous members of the military. After I fled, certain elements of the *Guardia* searched my home and threatened my wife. I have reason to believe that they know where we are staying here. I am sure you are aware that people have been known to disappear from here as well."

Ricardo purposely kept his description of events brief. After all, he thought, the bargaining was just beginning.

Meanwhile, Anderson noticed that Ricardo seemed to be blinking and fidgeting excessively. He decided to evade a direct response and observe Ricardo more.

"Doctor Cruz, let me explain something to you. Ours is an unusual liaison. Relationships with exiles, especially from friendly countries, are not something we encourage. In fact, we generally discourage it. Obviously in this case you are bringing us information that we need, so we are making an exception. Protection, however, is another matter. It is not something we can offer. In these complicated internal matters, we are not adjudicators, but observers. We cannot be seen to take sides."

"*Señor Anderson*, I am not a fugitive, nor am I a communist, a fascist, or a criminal. My family's background is well known. All I am saying is that I can best serve you if I am not considered or treated as a criminal while I am here."

Anderson saw that Ricardo had stopped squirming. He bought a little more time to confirm this assessment. He said slowly, "Well, that is a good point. But frankly, I do not know what I can do about it." Anderson was now looking down and toying with some insignificant item at the end of one of his fingers. "I would think that the Salvadoran government would have to decide that. Is there a reason why they might charge you with a crime?" His eyes slowly looked up into Ricardo's as he asked this.

Ricardo maintained the eye contact and said, "The reason that I am in Guatemala is because I know that that government of my country does whatever it wants to people like me, with or without proof. But to answer your question, they would have to fabricate evidence or coerce others into lying in order to officially charge me with anything. But then, that is nothing new for them. Once your name is on their list, you are guilty, proof or no proof. That is their law and their practice."

"Still," said Anderson, who had already seen what he wanted in Ricardo's eyes, "I understand that confessions are considered sufficient to convict someone under the Salvadoran criminal code."

"That is true, but not under yours," said a confident Ricardo quickly.

"That is also true," said an impressed Anderson. "But I still do not see what my government could do to prevent them from accusing you of anything. On the other hand, if what you say is true, I would think they have enough problems at home to worry about. No offence, but why would they be so interested in you? Now, if they were to charge you, well that would change things for us. In that case, well…"

Ricardo measured the older man and his bantering. He knew he was winning the debate and Anderson was stalling. He decided to lay down his conditions—put the "deal," as the Americans like to say, "on the table." He leaned forward and interrupted.

"*Señor* Anderson, if you will allow me. As I said, there is no evidence against me in El Salvador unless they invent it, which they can do if they choose. My immediate concern is not that. My concern is that they will contact some of their fanatical friends in the Guatemalan government and encourage them to make my life here miserable.

"Likewise, they could also send or contract people here to have me and my family killed. That would not be hard either; it has happened before. Or they may want to make an example of me; I do not know. I have no illusions about my importance, but many unimportant people have been victimized by this regime." He paused to drive home his point. "What I am requesting, *Señor* Anderson, or rather requiring, if we are going to work together, is that you make our association known to certain people in this government, people in your confidence. If you could advise them merely that you would not take it kindly if this law-abiding and respected resident or his family were gunned down or met with some unexplained accident. You know that what you say to this government carries much weight and will be respected. We call it *cuello* in my country."

He stopped. He had been polite but firm.

After a moment, the American began nodding his head slowly, "It is called that here too, Doctor Cruz. *Palanca,* they call it in Mexico, but it all means the same."

Anderson was stalling while he pondered something else. This was not your average foreign source of information; this one understood the realities of covert relationships, an unusual trait for someone so young. Anderson made his decision and started again, this time in a more official tone.

"Yes, Doctor, you are right, we have *cuello.* And I do not think that what you ask is unreasonable. If I were in your shoes I would demand the same." A slight pause, then he said unswervingly, "But we are very selective and selfish about how we use our *cuello*. Since you were straight with me, I will be as *derecho* with you.

"If we are to have a working relationship, it has to be based on mutual trust. I will require that you be truthful with me and I will be the same with you. Keep in mind that, to us, you are part of a group trying to overthrow a government that, for all its quirks, we consider friendly. The actions of your opposition group can have dire consequences on our interests. So I will want to know your plans *before* you act against that government."

His eyes locked with Ricardo's for a moment and held. "And should you be declared a criminal, whether you think it is warranted or not, our relationship is over. Also, if I have reason to think that you have held something back from me, our relationship will also end. Now, I cannot be any plainer than that. In exchange I will let it be known to a very select group of people here that we are working together. That will afford you some protection and, if what you say is true, it should be enough. Are we agreed?"

This is not the way Latins would have negotiated, thought Ricardo, but he had what he wanted. *"De acuerdo,"* he said fervently.

"Good," said Anderson, his broad smile returning. "Very, very good, Doctor Cruz."

Both men walked away believing that it that it had been a worthwhile meeting.

A week later, they met at a different restaurant in a less commercial part of Guatemala City. As they sat across from each other behind one of the crudely shaped tables of the outdoor café, the frumpy American was again prefacing their business talk with excessive triviality. Meanwhile, Ricardo was fidgeting with a packet of information that Paco had delivered to him from Hugo.

"...Y no siquiera conocer a este Hugo, Doctór Cruz," the smiling Anderson was saying in almost correct but broken Castillian. "It is bad enough that I have never even met him, but I know very little about him."

Anderson spoke sufficient Spanish to make himself reasonably clear, while Ricardo spoke no English except for the few American slang words that all Salvadorans bastardized. So Ricardo was considerate of the American's effort, while at the same time conscious of the seriousness of any miscommunication.

The diplomat was wearing the same business suit as when they had first met, a dark brown gabardine double-breasted piece that, although not old, was a rumpled inexpensive version of the more tailored European fashion preferred by Latins. The same wide necktie with an unsecured double

Windsor knot covered most of the heavily starched and yellowing white shirt.

Ricardo had not noticed before, but this time it struck him that the tie's pattern of colors seemed to generally match the suit. Refreshing, he thought. Since arriving two weeks earlier, he had been distracted by the mottled color combinations worn by newly westernized Guatemalan businessmen. He wondered if the American knew that his clothes gave him away.

"Well, *Señor* Anderson," Ricardo said somewhat guardedly, "all I can say is that Hugo is a patriot. He wants to improve the living conditions in our country, as we all do."

"Yes, well as I say, I have not personally met him, but he sure has our attention, and the attention of the *martinistas*, or so I have heard. His information is very valuable to us," said Anderson nodding appreciatively. "Yes, very useful, I assure you. Helps us understand the politics over there, the opposition view and all that. You seem to have many problems with the *martinistas*."

"Yes, we do. And I have something for you now." Ricardo said placing the large envelope on the table.

"Thank you. I look forward to reading it." Anderson said while sliding it over to his side. "You know, the last time we met, the conversation was...well...more on the serious side. Not that it is not a serious subject," he added quickly. "But if we are going to be seeing more of each other, then perhaps we could be less formal. Do you not agree, Ricardo? May I drop the title and call you Ricardo?" He did not wait for an answer. "You see, I also have a doctorate, from Brown University; that is in the State of Delaware. Anyway, I find formal labels boring, do you not agree?"

"Yes, of course," Ricardo said insincerely. He rather fancied the prefix and wore it as a badge, as did all of his medical colleagues. "What was your doctoral thesis?" Ricardo asked, already sure it was not medicine.

"'Economic Destabilization and the Austrian Influence in Latin America'," Anderson responded immediately, taking a sip of his beer. "Impressive, no?" he said, smiling with raised eyebrows indicating false crowing.

"Yes," Ricardo said, "it is. I would think that having an international economics background is very useful to a diplomat, especially in this region."

"Right. Actually, I specialized in economics and international affairs. During my post-graduate years, I followed the Austrian economist Ludwig von Mises around Mexico. He did some work for their government during the reconstruction period, after their revolution. Fascinating stuff. Several of his protégés have received Nobel prizes for their work in economics. Are you familiar with him?"

"No, I cannot say I am," said Ricardo politely.

"Actually, few outside the discipline are, although his premise affects all of us. It involves applying federalism to emerging democracies. We had our John Adams and Europe and Mexico had their Von Mises. *Aproposito*, Ricardo, that is where I learned most of my Spanish, or *Chingoles*, as some call it. They call it that because the Mexicans are always *chingando*," he said laughing heartily at his joke.

Ricardo laughed with him but noticed that Anderson's noisy mannerisms were attracting the attention of people sitting at nearby tables. Anderson was unmindful or insensitive to the infringement on the reticent personalities of Guatemalans, who frowned at coarse language, especially in public. Miguel Angel had warned Ricardo about this trait because of the proclivity of Salvadorans to use the vernacular as often as possible.

"And please," Anderson continued, "call me Rick. That is what my friends call me; it is short for Brodrick. Come to think of it, in English you are 'Rick' too. We can call each other 'Rick.' What do you think about that?" He laughed some more and Ricardo joined him, more enthusiastically this time.

Ricardo had liked the man's smile and casual demeanor from the beginning. He had always thought most Americans were arrogant and condescending, but this man was different. A bit loud perhaps, but that part was easily lost on the gregarious Ricardo. Plus the man was older, well traveled, and educated. Encouraged by the conviviality of the moment and no stranger to it, Ricardo tried his hand at wit.

"Rick, while we are on the subject, perhaps you can explain to me why some North Americans have confusing interchangeable names? You could just as easily be Anderson Brodrick Foreman or Foreman Anderson Brodrick."

Now Anderson was laughing in earnest. "Rick...oh, Rick, you have found us out. I do not know if we can divulge such a closely held secret. What if the Third Reich were to find out?" He leaned over conspiratorially and in a hushed voice said, "O.K., I will tell you because you are a friend. It was purposely started by a Presbyterian at Princeton." He snickered. "They are all Tories in New Jersey, and over the years it just rubbed off on the rest of us. In other words," he said, laughing loudly again, "we are snobs." He used a Spanish/English pronunciation, "*es-snob-es*."

Ricardo laughed heartily with him because the American's cackle was contagious. In truth, Ricardo had not understood a blessed word the American had said. So, he just offered, "O.K, Rick, *te llamare: Rick*."

"*De acuerdo, Ricky,*" the American said jovially, patting Ricardo on the back. Then, they both let the laughter subside. After a pause, Anderson said in a more serious tone, although he kept the smile, "If you will permit me, Rick, I would like to get your opinion on some things."

"I am at your service," said Ricardo formally.

"Hugo's reports are helpful, but we could use the opinion of someone like yourself on how a change of government at this time would affect the economic stability of the country. Ambassador Thurston believes he can talk Martínez into holding honest and free elections. With the war ending in Europe, the *cafetaleros* will need to find new markets. The U.S. government will no longer be able to help with the purchase of coffee and tobacco as it has been doing. And...if coffee prices fall, some will fear a return to the difficult years of the past. It is not in anyone's interest to give communism a foothold in the region again."

Ricardo sat back and thought. When he answered, he was very serious.

"Let me first say that I feel I am the wrong one to talk to about economic repercussions and the effects of global market changes. I am a dentist, not an economist like yourself," he prefaced his thoughts quietly.

Then his brow wrinkled and he frowned.

"But, Rick, let me say this. I read somewhere that fifty years ago in the United States only one citizen in ten could read or write. Today, you are one of the most literate countries in the world. In my country today, only one in a hundred can read and write, and the prospect of that improving is almost nonexistent.

"Socialism will not work in El Salvador because the working class cannot govern. Any such leader would have to resort to repressive measures to enforce that system. In the end, we would just be replacing one despot with another."

Ricardo was troubled and let it show on his face. Anderson listened patiently.

"And I will tell you something else," Ricardo continued. "Martínez will not give up power without a struggle. He will not hold open elections because he knows he will lose. He will continue to promote a general fear about the threat of communism and a recurrence of the events of 1932. You are familiar with that dark part of our history?" Ricardo asked casually.

"Yes, of course," said Anderson.

"Martínez knows," Ricardo continued, "that your only concern in the region is maintaining stability to protect your interests. Do not get me wrong; I do not quarrel with that position. It is natural for you to do so. But I am Salvadoran, and I know my tyrant."

Ricardo was looking intently into Anderson's eyes. Then he lowered his gaze and said in an almost apologetic tone, "And in case you do not know it, Rick, he is not your friend either. He tolerates you just as you tolerate him. If you want my opinion, I would say that instability is already here. As I said, I am not an economist or a politician, but I would advise your Ambassador to test Martínez. Have him ask *el brujo* for a sign of good faith, something that is within his power to do immediately if he wanted."

"Like what?" Anderson prompted.

"See how he reacts when you ask him to free the press, for example. If he were to do that, you would not need me to bring you these packets. You would see for yourself the level of discontent. I tell you there is an uprising brewing worse than in '32 and it does not involve communists. It may not be clear to you because Martínez has not allowed honest debate. You only hear it from people like me, the bitter exiles that he calls traitors."

"Rick," Anderson interjected seeing that Ricardo was starting to get emotional, "we are aware of the repressive campaign that Martínez uses to maintain control. We are in favor of change. We just want a peaceful and meaningful transition of government."

But Ricardo was undeterred. "Every day that you stand by and support Martínez means another group of dissidents and their families die or are disenfranchised. All I know is that if he were to resign tomorrow, there are groups of people, respected people, young professionals, military officers, educators, even union workers who are not communist, who would step in immediately to stabilize the situation and establish a true democracy."

"People like who? Can you get me names?"

Ricardo paused suspiciously, then said earnestly, "You have to understand, Rick, I can give you names of people like myself who are on the outside, but the names of people who are working within the government, and businessmen who are still there, that is a different matter. In my country those who disagree with Martínez find themselves dead. Such a list would be extremely dangerous."

"But we need a sign from you as well," Anderson suggested. "Something to convince our government that a *ccup* by esteemed leaders can succeed. Demonstrate to us how this change is in everyone's interest."

Ricardo thought, then said, "*Esta bien*, Rick. Read the latest news from Hugo. There are some useful facts on the type of people who support our cause. Meanwhile, I will pass on your message."

"Very well, Rick. And I will pass on your thoughts as well. They are very helpful and, I am sure, spoken sincerely. We will talk in a few days." He shifted to a friendlier voice, "Now tell me, how is your family?"

"Well, as you know, they made it here all right. I have noticed nothing suspicious since we last talked. I assume you passed along my concerns to the appropriate people?"

Anderson made a slight head gesture which Ricardo took as assent.

Then, Ricardo said in a firm voice, "I am hoping that my family and I are safer now from Chulio and other animals. We are staying with the Alcaíne family. As you know, Miguel Angel is another exile, the caliber of statesman that we need, but again, someone who will not return until Martínez is gone.

"But I do not mean to digress. My wife had a difficult time in the days after I fled the country. They destroyed our belongings, abused our servant, killed our dog, and threatened to do the same to her and the children." He paused as the anger began to bring tears to his eyes.

Anderson jumped in, "You mentioned something about it, but I did not know it was that bad."

"Yes, it was, and believe me, it will not stand. But that is personal and does not concern our business."

Anderson looked at him skeptically and started to say something, but decided against it.

Ricardo continued, "My wife is rested physically, but is still recovering from the shock. Our son is fine and our ailing daughter seems to be better with a prescription given by a young doctor who saw her just before they left. Incidentally, that doctor, the one who saw my daughter, is now dead because of it. The cowards tortured and killed him. What do you think of that?

"Do you know what his crime was? Helping the poor and my family. Our oldest friends are now terrified and guilt-ridden. They were the ones who recommended him. Not only did they lose a friend and colleague, but they are now panic-stricken that they might be tainted by the events.

"You see, this government has a vendetta against peasants and young professionals. It seems we are all communists in their eyes. I tell you, as a Salvadoran, I am ashamed. That is something that cannot be appreciated by anyone who has not lived under this type of oppression. Your country would not tolerate it. But what is happening here is not affecting your interests. No, they are very careful not to harm a hair on *Tio Sam's* head."

Anderson saw that the young man was working himself up again, but could not let the comments pass without rebuttal. The senior diplomat said smoothly, "Rick, there are some of us who understand. Remember, we are in the middle of a world war fighting tyranny. Many of us have already died. I would be there myself, if I were healthier and younger. But I am serving here. You are right, we would not tolerate such oppression at home, and we condemn it everywhere we encounter it around the world. Let's work together and try to bring about a change that will make things better."

But the impulsive Ricardo was still upset. "I do not mean to be rude, Rick, but we cannot wait. I will pass on your message, but do not be surprised if manifestations intensify and there are more people killed in the process."

"Very well, Rick," said Anderson exhaling slowly, resigned to the fact that further placating him was futile. Rising from the table, he said in a friendly tone, "Let's get together Friday night. But let us do it socially. I would like to meet *Licenciado* Alcaíne and your wives. Would you let me buy dinner, some *carne asadas* for all of us at the Ritz Hotel on Seventh Avenue, say around seven?"

Ricardo realized that the chivalrous Anderson was quickly disarming him. He rose as well.

"You are very gracious, Rick. Please forgive my outburst, I am still aggravated. My wife and I have been through much these past weeks and our future is still uncertain. Yes, of course we will join you. We would be honored. I will pass on your invitation to Miguel Angel. *Gracias.*"

"*Por nada, Ricky. Hasta luego.*"

Chapter 15

A few weeks after my contentious lunch with Choco, he delivered another note from Ricardo, this time inviting Cora and me to visit them in Guatemala. Ricardo said they had settled into an apartment and he was working at a dental clinic. His letter sounded quite encouraging. I knew that I would not be able to convince my Cora to travel, so I wrote a note back saying that we would try to be there soon. Choco said he would see that Ricardo got it, and took a moment to tell me about the positive comments he had heard from Hugo about Ricardo's work with the Americans.

I listened politely, but made a point of not showing too much interest. The perceptive Choco did not push me, but it was clear that our meetings were becoming less social.

I was still not convinced that I was not a subject in some government file. Rumors of lists were common, and students continued to disappear. Already two more of my close colleagues had fled the country. But during this time, I had attended several professional and intergovernmental functions and failed to sense any hostility or scrutiny of me. I may not be the most perceptive person, but my countrymen are not difficult to read.

Meanwhile, the overall apprehension had penetrated deeper into my family life. I perceived that Cora was clinging a bit too tightly to the children and espousing a more traditional and conservative life style.

Many of her friends were also showing signs of strain. It had not escaped me that the use of pharmaceuticals, especially barbiturates, was becoming a status symbol among many of the affluent *Doñas*. So far, it was not a concern to anyone, because the use was no greater than the way we men availed ourselves of whiskey. My Cora had never indulged before, but she was becoming more and more dependent on these tranquilizers.

In our quiet moments, I confided to Cora my increasing interest in the psychology of those involved in the social turmoil that was evolving around us. She would pat my cheek, as she was apt to do, and smile, not smugly or condescendingly, but lovingly. She knew that the times were changing and that examination was appropriate and, although she did not like it, preferred to reserve comment.

I told her about Ricardo and the Americans and about Hugo's plans to use their influence to bring about governmental changes. I told her of my surprise with this tactic because I had never heard any political commentary from the veteran Ambassador from the United States, Walter Thurston, not even at the Chamber of Commerce meeting, which I had attended recently. If there was any plan afoot, they were keeping it to themselves.

Meanwhile, there was a growing preoccupation among my brother coffee growers about Martínez. The naïveté of the Cordobas, who had sent that patronizing letter to him, the one that Hugo exposed, was the subject of discord at the Chamber, and some of the debates were quite heated.

Considering the serious consequences of this internal rift, the American diplomats did not appear to be overly interested in the issue. That is why I found it surprising to learn that Ricardo, in a neighboring country, was passing them information about the political situation here, while in this country they appeared wholly nonchalant.

I would eventually meet Anderson, and many of the machinations that were taking place behind the scenes came to be explained. Diplomacy, after all, is ninety percent hypocrisy. But at the time I was wholly confused by these maneuverings, and convinced that Hugo and Ricardo's efforts to include the Americans in their plans were more of their time wasted.

"I read your latest report, Rick," said Ambassador Long. "Walt will be very interested in this one. Looks like things are coming to a head. You really believe this group can bring down Martínez?"

"Yes, Mr. Ambassador," said Anderson as he took a seat.

After the last meeting with Ricardo, the U.S. Ambassador to Guatemala, Boaz Long, had called Anderson into the Chief of Mission's office for one of their *ad hoc* meetings.

"It seems that, just like here, it is a question of how much support they get from the young officer corps," Anderson said. "It always is in these cases. But the report from Hugo is impressive. He withheld specific names, but there is enough information to show that there is a significant plan in place."

"And who are they proposing to replace Martínez?" asked Long.

"That is the question, sir. There are several people whom the military would have no trouble supporting. There are also others with strong communist leanings that the military would adamantly reject. My best guess is that it will be a military person because no one can hold power in Salvador for long without military support."

"Replacing one general with another does not seem like much change. Don't they all belong to the same club?"

"To a certain extent that is true, sir, but in this case, this general has held the office for over twelve years and was never popular within the ranks. Perhaps what they fear is that he has become a bad king."

"Well, I'll leave that analysis to Walt and you experts," said Long. "But from what I hear, Walt thinks a *coup* could work against them and even make things worse. *My* concern is the effect actions over there might have on the military establishment in this country. After all, the general here has also been in power for over a dozen years. I know the Foreign Minister is nervous about it. And incidentally, he is very appreciative of the information you are providing them. Their embassy in Salvador tells them nothing of value."

"I don't know if we will be able to predict exactly when a *coup* will happen, but Hugo's information has allowed us to be ahead of the game for a change. Washington will be impressed with this latest batch," said Anderson.

"Well, keep up the good work," said Long. "But, Rick, there is something else I want to talk to you about. It concerns Cruz."

"Yes, sir?"

"Do you think it is wise to let the Guats know he is working with us?"

"Those were his conditions, sir. And I think his concern for his safety is justified. It would not be the first time that Chulio's long arm has reached out this far to eliminate a political 'irritation.' Cruz knows he is rolling the dice by using our relationship to protect him, but he and his family have been through a lot and he is scared. I have to admit I was impressed with his inside information. Not many know or surmise that we maintain an undeclared liaison with the Guats internal security people. It was through that channel that I funneled Cruz' name to them. Frankly, it is best for both of us. It allows us to be honest with the Guats about our activities and it affords Cruz some security."

"Yes, but that could just as easily backfire," said the Ambassador. "The Salvos could eliminate an 'irritation,' as you call it, while sending us a message not to meddle with their exiles."

"Agreed. No one knows for sure how the Guats will jump. Our sources tell us, however, that the Guats have their own list of Salvadoran communist exiles, and Cruz is not on it. I asked them. I think he is being straightforward. I was pretty clear in my warnings about that."

"Yes, and all of that is fine, Rick," said the Ambassador, "But the President mentioned to me just yesterday, at our monthly lunch, that he had been placed in an awkward position at the regional summit last month. Martínez mentioned to him that Guatemala was becoming a haven for political dissidents trying to overthrow his regime, and that our Embassy was helping some of them.

"The timing of President Ubico's complaint seems too pat. He said that he told Martínez he was shocked by the information and that he would look into it. I don't know what his plans are, but I guess my question to you is, is Cruz worth it?"

Anderson chose his words, then said, "Mr. Ambassador, Cruz provides tremendous insight into the feelings of the young professionals. He is also the conduit for Hugo's information. The short answer is yes, I believe he is worth it. He has introduced me to several exiles of note, not the least of which is Miguel Angel Alcaíne, whom you have met and like. Even the Guats respect Alcaíne. Cruz is of the same cloth.

"Frankly sir, I believe that President Ubico is just posturing. He and Martínez have been members of the same dictator's club for the past twelve years, but they don't trust each other. You said yourself that the Foreign Minister is pleased with the information we are giving them. How do they think we get this information? We are doing their work for them and they know it. I believe that Ubico will tell Martínez that he has talked to you about it and that will be the end of it. I don't think Ubico was making an official démarche. The Guats need to know what is happening over there."

"Well, if you think so, Rick. But do cover it with your contacts. I will sit on it for a few weeks and see if he mentions it again."

"Yes, sir."

As he left the Ambassador's office, Anderson was irritated. For one thing, he was not thrilled with the role he had inherited as the Embassy's political officer. He was an economics officer, or at least that was his "cone." He was accredited to three Central American countries plus the Court of St. James, the latter because of his mission in British Honduras, a British colony. He imagined that he was not the only Foreign Service officer doing double duty because of the war.

Then there was the matter of having to coddle the various envoys. Ambassador Long was a relatively new political appointee from New Mexico and this was his first foreign assignment. Anderson was a career Foreign Service officer, and biased against those who were not. He thought most political appointees came to Latin America for a two-year tour just to get the prestigious title and gather material for a book—*My Experiences on the "Cucaracha Circuit"*. Meanwhile, old hands like himself got passed over for selection to the higher ranks.

Anderson thought better of Ambassador Walter Thurston in El Salvador, who was a career officer. Thurston had been at that post for almost two years, and was well acquainted with the repressive antics of the *martinistas*. He was committed to seeing them relinquish power, but only through peaceful means.

In that regard, Anderson thought him too passive in dealing with the action-oriented *martinistas*. Anderson had grown up in New Jersey and understood the value of being "street-wise" when involved in a war of words. And Thurston did not think much of Hugo's information. During their bimonthly meetings, Thurston would politely listen to Anderson's reports but rarely commented. His staff, however, was more appreciative and so was Washington.

Anderson suspected that Thurston was privately offended by his unorthodox relationship with Hugo and the exiles, and therefore tended to undermine the intelligence. The envoy thought giving credence to the grousing of ex-patriots was questionable enough, but actually meeting with them was diplomatic folly. Thurston did not outwardly agree with the practice, but stopped short of prohibiting the liaison. As a careerist, Thurston believed in firm diplomatic exchanges.

Anderson felt this was a major flaw in their mission. Relying only on official diplomatic exchanges was awkward and inefficient. Meanwhile, there was no recognized opposition, the newspapers were censored, and obtaining information from dissidents in the country was impractical. Embassy officers were short on tradecraft, and Chulio's people seemed to be everywhere.

So Hugo's information was invaluable, despite Thurston's reservations. Although Anderson believed Thurston's stance was wrong, he respected the decision because at least it was based on precedent, unlike Long's knee-jerk reactions.

Back in his office, Anderson soothed his bad mood by dictating some notes to the new young secretary that he shared with the Labor Attaché. Her name was Dolores, from Atlanta, and she had a pleasing, soft Georgia accent, which, he had recently discovered, had a calming effect on his disposition. Her effervescent attitude, bright red layers of lipstick and adolescent quality were contagiously cheery. As she read back the transcript of his brief, Anderson closed his eyes and concentrated on each word while breathing in and out slowly in a technique he had learned at a crisis management course. Fifteen minutes of her narration "treatment" and he was reinvigorated.

"Thank you, Lola," Anderson said. "That was just...perfect."

"You're more than welcome, Mr. Anderson, any time, any time at all. I'll just be right down the hall."

His smile followed her full plump figure right out the door. *Just perfect*, he thought.

He looked down at the manuscript she had left for his review. He took a last slow deep breath, and focused on the latest information from Hugo.

It confirmed that those planning to overthrow Martínez by a *coup d'état* included members of a group that the previous year had filed suit with the Supreme Court to rescind Martínez' executive decree concerning suffrage and free elections. The *martinistas* had hoped to use the decree to establish "constitutional deputies," who could then circumvent popular elections through their regional representation. They could elect Martínez to an unprecedented fourth term—until 1949.

Not wanting to take sides, the Supreme Court had decided to uphold the shelved Constitutional Reform Act of 1939. That legislative action gave Martínez, among other things, the Presidency without popular elections until New Year's Day 1945. By upholding that reform, albeit three years late, the court left Martínez less than a year in office. The legislation had automatically gone into effect on February 29 of that year.

Hugo further reported that he was certain that Martínez had no intention of relinquishing anything. Prominent businessmen who had been part of the suit, and members of the Supreme Court, were being victimized. Some were merely threatened, some had disappeared, and others fled. Still, the passage of the new constitution was a *coup* for the opposition. A *coup* of sorts, Hugo had reported, but not real; Martínez was still in power.

Hugo said he was unleashing yet another barrage of propaganda attacking the *martinistas'* strategy to keep Martínez in power for another unprecedented term. He had attached a copy of the headline of a pamphlet he was circulating. It read:

"If Martínez can be declared President for another term by his Appointed regional representatives, what is to keep them from making him King?"

Hugo was also challenging the military, the oligarchs, the banks, and young businessmen to examine the progression of events. The power move by the *martinistas* could not be clearer, he argued.

Hugo included in his report considerable information on the opposition and how he had compiled the list. Without naming them, Hugo was able to provide sufficient details on the intellectual authors of the *coup*. He explained that they were sympathetic officers who had graduated from the "Generál Gerardo Barrios" military school in classes V through XII. From each *tanda,* he estimated that there were a dozen leaders who in turn had loyal followers.

From academia and the business community he presented a list of intellectuals and supporters who were committed to change. All told, over two hundred prominent Salvadoran leaders became part of this list—Hugo's list.

On a separate sheet, Hugo identified exiled luminaries who had offered to return and serve in public or community services under a new governor. There was also a list of those individuals from all the social classes known to have disappeared or been inexplicably murdered in the past twelve years. The lists were comprehensive and undeniably powerful.

Ricardo had told Anderson that Hugo had two other lists. One included the paid thugs who posed as government aides, but were in fact responsible for political extra-official "enforcement." There was also a list of those close to Martínez who would not oppose a change when the time came. The latter list included two colonels and a general. Ricardo would see about getting these for Anderson. Anderson paused here, he suspected there was more than mere interest on Ricardo's part in the list of "thugs."

Anderson was impressed and put his staff to work on analyzing the volume of information before them. Their goal was to be able to predict the effects of a *coup* on U.S. interests.

"Let's face it," Anderson told them, "a *coup* in El Salvador is inevitable."

"And accordingly," the Labor attaché added, "such an action will cause a similar reaction here."

"Agreed," said Anderson. "And both actions are positives; they will provide great opportunities for the U.S. to help shape the post war years in Central America." Heads nodded. "Let's see if we can articulate this position to Washington, and back up the argument with some of this latest information. Remember, we need to convince some skeptics out there, so keep thinking: How is all this in our best interest?"

After his meeting broke up, Anderson sat back and reflected on their rationale. Something did not sit right, like a noise that grates on one's nerves. He understood the "U.S. interests" part of their mission, but the rest he found frustratingly hypocritical. U.S. policy was to insure that these governments remained democratic and friendly. The "friendly" part, like the "U.S. interests" part, was inarguable, but the brand of "democracy" that was likely was more abstruse.

Democracy in these small countries reflected nothing of the variety espoused by the American founding fathers, who had emphasized the significance of private property and free enterprise. Under their rationale, private ownership encouraged citizens to enthusiastically do what was in the social interest, thereby minimizing the coercive power that one person or state could have over another.

Anderson believed in these principles. In the United States, government was limited and taxes had always been in single digits before the war. But it was not taxes that were excessive in these Latin countries; in fact, there were virtually none. That was a separate, albeit, related issue. These were economically poor and underdeveloped nations where the primary wealth was held privately, but it was concentrated in the hands of a few rich and selfish families; there was no significant middle class.

Thus, dispensing justice and maintaining law and order without having deep public pockets forced governance to be a form of "acceptable autocracy," and security forces ruled by intimidation rather than consensus. These were not free societies. "Democracy" was only a word U.S. regional policy makers liked to bandy about.

Experienced U.S. career diplomats understood that they operated on imprecise political terrain where "abuse of power" was a subjective term. As a result, condemnation of "oppressive practices" was a diplomatic weapon that could be wielded as individual situations dictated. Latin leaders also understood this hegemony. Decisions by U.S. ambassadors often had the power of life and death. That some "two-year-wonders" never appreciated these realities is what tired Anderson most.

The more he thought about it, the more he longed for a week in a *cabaña* on some isolated beach with nothing more engaging than Lola reading him the Newark telephone book.

Chapter 16

It was perhaps a month before I heard from Choco again. During that time, I had settled into the daily routine of my work, which at the time consisted of a growing number of patients needing help dealing with the uncertainty of life during these troubled times. Although I was keeping long hours, I did manage to find time, mainly late in the evenings, to jot down daily impressions of the effect these days were having on all of us.

Rumors proliferated about plots to kill Martínez, *coups*, and even another peasant revolt. I found that the mere writing down of these notes was a form of self-therapy. The weekends, however, I religiously guarded as time with my family, although my Cora and I often commented that the spirit of our heretofore idyllic life had been altered.

It was on a Thursday morning that Choco called my office and asked me to lunch with him at the club. He caught me in a distracted moment and I halfheartedly agreed. We had spoken on the telephone a few times and I had occasionally received some anonymous mail with anecdotal stories of government abuses, but we had not routinely sought each other out. But I recall thinking that perhaps it was time to better our relationship.

I remember the day he called, because our family was getting ready for *Semana Santa*, the Holy Week of Easter, a period we Salvadorans celebrate more festively than even the days surrounding Christ's birth. The days before Easter are also the last days of Lent, and that alone is enough reason to rejoice. Not that Cora and I felt festive, but some things are reactively performed merely out of habit.

Incidentally, I should mention here that although my Cora is a very devote Catholic, as most women in my country are, over the years my colleagues and I have drifted away from the guilt-plagued sermonizing of the Church. It has even driven some of the more aggressive of us into a form of agnostic militancy: "I do not know, and you do not know either. So let us drop the subject."

That bravado aside, we all go through the motions while tending to keep any real prayers private. Choco fit into the latter group, and so confidently approached me on that Holy Thursday without the least consideration for its significance.

His news concerned the *Jaguares'* relentless search for Hugo. He was sure that Chulio had planted undercover soldiers among the students. Choco wanted to warn me to disassociate myself from any contact with unknown persons probing for information. I assured him that he did not have anything to worry about in that regard. Choco also explained that the unrelenting hunt for Hugo was the reason I had not received the background material I had asked for.

I must confess something here that may sound hypocritical. Although I had no use for the man, I had become more and more curious about Hugo's psyche, and I had asked Choco some probing questions the last time we had met. In truth, no one seemed to know much about Hugo's personal life, and Choco had offered to get some answers directly from Hugo. I had played down the request and counseled that he should take care not to put himself in any danger.

On this day, I reminded him of the risk. There were rumors of *coup* plots, and reports of more students disappearing. But he assured me that Hugo had everything under control and that, in any event, *Semana Santa* was certainly not the time for aggressiveness. I had to agree with that point. There was a standing joke that even wars paused during Easter so soldiers could take their families and *queridas* to the *playa*. As sure as the sun rose and set each day, we knew that there were things that even the great Hugo could not control.

Choco and I parted amiably that day, neither of us surmising just how wrong our assessment was.

The cottage sat on a high ridge at the end of a steep dirt road, at the far end of a new development called Linda Vista, because of its generous view of the valleys and foothills around the capital city of San Salvador. Tall *aguacate* and *mango* trees provided the home a canopy of shade from the parching sun. To the sides of the chalet were well-tended vegetable gardens, rich with tomatoes, *calabaza*, potatoes, and other low-growing crops. Directly behind the house was a severe rocky drop, part of which had been tiered by neighbors to grow other crops.

Few motor vehicles traversed the roads of this upper region because of the steep inclines and lack of paving. Ox-drawn carts were more efficient, and animals could be seen corralled on the numerous plots of land that dotted the hillsides.

Inside the small house, Hugo lay next to the woman, her head resting on his bare chest. He had his arms behind his head and was staring out an eastern window at a sky already lined with the orange glow of dawn. They had just made love. In the distance, roosters were crowing and soon the first flocks of parrots would pass overhead on their prattling breakfast flight.

"We are very close now, Marta," Hugo said contemplatively. "Yesterday, twelve more officers agreed to recognize a new government if *Generál* Marroquín heads it. He has agreed to support Crescencio Castellanos and Doctor Arturo García, even though the two are not friends.

It seems Martínez' oppression has brought them together, and they each bring a large following."

She said nothing and he continued.

"I tell you, we have never been closer. Today we will get commitments from the different *cuarteles.* Martínez will be away from the capital for Holy Week, so it has to be this week."

"How many will die?" she finally asked in a soft murmur, her face still buried in his chest.

He began stroking her long, thick dark hair. "Some will die, *cariño*, that is true. But many more will live, and their lives will be brighter. We will no longer have to fear for our children. We will all live together. Here if you like, or we can return to your birthplace."

"No, I would like to live here," she said in a firm voice.

"*Muy bien*," he said patiently. "Here it will be."

They were quiet for a moment, then he said, "I must be going soon, *cariño*. It is going to be a long day. I will be back late tonight."

"*Va' pues*," she said in a resigned tone, but still did not stir.

These were their special moments. Just before dawn, they would wake each other and spend a period of slow lovemaking. Then for a time, he would lie there and greet the daylight by consciously emptying his mind of the congested thoughts that always preoccupied him. Afterward, he prepared his day's activities, deciding which of his secret locations he would randomly visit. He never told Marta where he was going, but he told her everything else. She listened mostly. It had been that way since they had been reunited four years before.

They never talked about the past, there was no need; both knew the scars ran deep. She had wanted children and he had conditionally agreed. For the time being, the children would live with a neighboring family, for everyone's security, he had explained. She had not complained and, when the time came, had made all the arrangements. She endured the unconventional lifestyle and the frequent separations by faithfully waiting for him, resigned to whatever morsel of normalcy the future brought, just as she had for all those years. Theirs was a deep but practical love, forever marked by the tragedy of having had their families violently wrenched from them during their most impressionable and idealistic years. They were true children of the unsettled times.

Suddenly, two of the glass bottles hanging on lines all around the property as a warning system banged against each other in the garden. Almost at the same time, but from another area, more bottles clanged together loudly.

Hugo and Marta were up instantly. Without words, they dressed in a minimum of clothes and slipped on sandals. Hugo quickly peered out one of the windows and saw what he feared, dark figures moving rapidly towards the house on all three sides. Their demeanor was clear; they were running low and carrying rifles. He figured twenty seconds before the first group would reach the house. Other bottles clanged. The intruders were making no effort now to conceal their approach.

Hugo motioned Marta to a rear window, then moved rapidly on his hands and knees to the front wall. He gave hard yanks to several cords that hung from the ledges of the three front transoms. Then he ran to the rear window and helped Marta to climb outside. As he straddled the sill, he reached over and removed a canvas carrying case from a hook next to the window and slung the straps over his head. Once outside, he crouched next to Marta along the back wall as the first grenade exploded.

By the time the second grenade detonated, Hugo and Marta were making their way down the ravine wall using a knotted rope that had been secured to a tree years before. A volley of rifle fire accompanied the explosion of the third grenade, but it was not directed at them; no one had been sent to cover the rear.

The shooting in front of the house continued for several minutes, then abruptly halted. Shortly afterward, there were more explosions. By this time, Hugo and Marta were several tiers below, and swinging themselves on other ropes into densely wooded patches of land on the other side of the ravine. The spreading light from the rising sun made them move faster, while they hoped that the commotion up the hill would keep people indoors.

Faster and faster they ran. The path in the woods led to an open space where squatters had assembled a group of shacks. Dogs were barking, but no one ventured outside. The couple ran down another path to a corral with several horses. Without hesitating, Hugo and Marta jumped on a horse each and made their way bareback, galloping towards the forested areas along the mountainside.

They did not slow until they had made their way to a flat area just beneath the rim of the volcano. They finally stopped in a secluded spot. Hugo helped Marta down and let the exhausted horses walk free. At the base of a large tree, they sat down heavily.

"Are you all right?" he asked anxiously.

"Yes," she replied between breaths.

After their heavy breathing subsided, he looked at her and asked with soft but narrowed eyes, "Who?"

"I do not know," she answered plainly. "Memo and Berta know about us, but they do not know who you are. I have not spoken to anyone about you or your work. Could you have been followed?"

Hugo shook his head slowly at the thought of being tracked. Then, after a moment, he bowed his head a little and said gently, "Then, there can only be one answer, *cariño…*" She looked at him perplexed and he said straight away, "They were not after me."

It took her a moment, and then it struck her. *"Ay, Dios mío!"* she exclaimed. *"Mí amor,* I have to go back."

"No!" he said. "We will get word to Memo to bring the *niñas* to a safe place."

"Mí amor, you know by now they have started questioning neighbors. How long before they find out about the girls and where they are?"

He thought about that and said, "I will go with you."

"No, Valentín," she said determinedly. She took his face in both her hands and looked closely at him. With great emotion she said, "It was understood when I asked you to have these babies that we would not interfere with your work, your life. Remember?"

"You are also part of my life," he said evenly, his soft eyes burning into hers.

She continued, undeterred. "Yes, but they are *my* responsibility. You still need to get rid of the evil people who kill the innocent. You have to do it…because you can. Remember who we are. A part of you and me died long ago. We vowed they would not do it to us again. Remember, *mí amor?* We believed it then, we must believe it now."

These were more words than she had ever said to him at one time. Tears were now rolling down her cheeks, but she was not wailing. With the back of his fingers, he started wiping them away.

She smiled and said wistfully, "I am content with the thought of us all living together soon. Now I must go…alone. We will not argue; we never have. You know I am right." She was nodding as she said these words and staring intently at him.

After a moment, he slowly nodded back and reached for her. They embraced for what seemed to him an instant and then he rose and walked slowly to get her horse. When he returned, she was tying a sash firmly around her waist. She mounted the horse expertly and smiled at him.

"We will be with you soon, *mí amor,*" she said.

"I will be with you always, *mí amores,*" he replied.

He looked at her for as long as she remained in sight and then for a moment longer. Downhearted, he reached forward and picked up the backpack. He tried to focus, but the pain was too severe. He was alone, again. Even the heavy canvas army bag seemed lighter.

The sweep of the rural neighborhood had begun in earnest. Major Eugenío Carrillo had been furious that the scouts had not detected the alarms and the rear escape route. It had taken months to get this far! he shouted at them. A man and a woman had escaped, he reminded them. Hugo had been in the house and they let him get away! Both of them had gotten away! Incredible! Instead of being heroes they were goats.

But the worst was coming, he thought, visions of that rodent Tapesquintla gloating over the report before giving it to Chulio. *Jaguares* did not fail! He had to salvage something before the day was over.

Neighbors of Linda Vista knew little about the woman in the cottage, whom they called *Doña* Margarita. They knew a man often stayed there, but they did not know his name or much about him. They would see him leave very early in the morning, but did not see him when he returned.

The woman had lived there for as long as they could remember. During the last years she had been pregnant twice, but they never saw children or heard babies around the house. They did not know if she kept them or gave them away. But every day she would leave the cottage and walk down the road and was gone for most of the day. They did not know where. Once a week an ox cart would bring provisions and take back vegetables that she grew in the garden. The neighbors knew little about her other habits except that she was quiet, friendly, and kept to herself. They had never spoken to the man. But from the descriptions they gave, the two were clearly Hugo and Marta.

It had taken several violent interrogations to convince Carrillo that what they were saying was probably all they knew. He ordered the questioning area widened. He was certain that someone in the area had to know more about the activities of a woman who had lived there so long alone.

It was noon before a sergeant brought Carrillo the news that they had found Marta's children. Ecstatic, Carrillo drove with the sergeant in his jeep the two kilometers back down the road, across a ravine, and down a footpath leading to a small house. In the front yard, there were several soldiers guarding four crying children ranging from three to ten years of age.

Carrillo entered the house and saw a woman near hysterics sitting on a chair in the main room guarded by two soldiers. In an adjacent room was a bound and gagged figure with a bloodied hand. The man was alive, but his face was distorted from the burning anguish. Carrillo could see that several fingers of the man's hand were bloody stumps.

"Well, where are the children?" asked Carrillo of the sergeant in charge.

"*Mayor*," began the sergeant, "these people have admitted that they are keeping the children of the woman who lives up the hill. They say the children are not here now, but we think they are among the children who are outside and claim to live here. We were just covering that point, when I thought I had better come to get you."

"Idiot!" said the disappointed Carrillo. "Neighbors told us Marta was pregnant twice during the last four years. Only one of those *cipotes* outside could possibly be hers. We are looking for an infant and another child no more than three years old."

The sergeant recoiled but said nothing. Carrillo walked back to where the woman was sitting in the chair, her head buried in her hands. He wrenched her head back by the hair. She screamed.

"Listen," he said, "I am only going to ask once. If you give me the wrong answer, I will kill your husband. Then I will kill each one of your children one by one in front of you. Then my men will take their turns with you and cut off your fingers and toes one by one until you bleed to death. Do you understand?"

The woman did not stop screaming.

"Do you understand? Stop screaming!" he yelled at her face.

She continued screeching and uttered no words.

"Speak, woman!" he yelled slapping her hard. She was seemingly hysterical, but he noticed that she was observing him with furtive glances. "All right, if that is your game," he said.

He pulled out his pistol, snapped the slide back with the other hand, and walked into the next room. So that she could see, he aimed it at the man and shot him in the face. She screamed louder.

"Now, bring one of the children in here, a boy," he commanded a soldier who went immediately outside.

The woman could not control her outbursts, but now began speaking, pleading with him not to hurt the children.

"You will tell me what I want to know?" he growled.

"Yes, yes!"

"Where are the children of the woman you call *Doña* Margarita?"

"I do not know, I do not know!" the woman screamed.

Without looking away from the woman's face, he said to a soldier who was holding a crying young boy near the front door, "Bring the boy in here."

"No!" the woman screamed.

"*Major*," interrupted one of the other soldiers in the room.

Carrillo looked up at him angrily. The soldier was motioning to a rear door of the house.

Silhouetted by the light of the open rear door stood a woman carrying an infant in one arm and holding the hand of a very small girl, which the woman kept pushing behind her to shield the child from the tormenting scene. Carrillo could not make out the woman's face clearly, only that she stood erect with her head thrown back.

"Leave these people alone," the woman said. "I am the one you are looking for. These people are innocent of any wrongdoing. They do not know anything."

"*Señora*," said the woman in a woeful sobbing voice. "Why did you come back? I would not have told them anything. *Ay, señora*."

Carrillo ignored the seated woman and began walking towards the back door. The woman turned with her children and slowly walked outside the house. Carrillo followed her. Once outside, two soldiers flanked her and barked out, "*Alto!*"

They were all standing in a small back yard.

"Turn around," ordered Carrillo.

She did. Her face was expressionless, her eyes defiant. Her shoulders were back, the way indigenous women stand proudly to make themselves seem taller. Long straight black hair swept her waist. She held the baby now with both hands, her right arm forming a cradle, the left resting under the baby for support. The small girl stood beside her mother, holding onto a side of her long skirt.

The soldiers were trying to explain to Carrillo how the woman had just come walking onto the property from a wooded area nearby. They thought she had been hiding and would have found her, but she just walked back to the house. Since she seemed to know where she was going they let her come, but followed very close behind. They thought the major would want to...

Carrillo held up his hands and silence them. He approached the woman.

"Yes, it is you," he said eyeing her up and down. "The notorious Marta, the traitor's whore. Yes, I can see what *mi Coronel* Mojano saw in you. I would have done the same." Then he looked at the children. "And these are the traitor's bastards. We are going to enjoy having all of you as our guests."

She said nothing, just stared blankly past him. Then, without comment and before he could say anything else, Marta slowly crouched down to the height of the small girl. She said to her, "Maria Carmen, *te quiero mucho, mucho*; I love you very much. *Tu tambien*; and you, Lourdes. *Mis niñas lindas*." She smiled glowingly at them. Maria Carmen threw her arms around Marta's neck and hugged her.

Carrillo eyed the scene with scorn. He started to speak, but was interrupted by a noise, one that was out of the ordinary, illogical to him. It was a muffled metallic tinny sound, like a spring releasing. It was familiar to him, but not in this setting, not from this maternal scene, not from somewhere under...He dove to the ground, almost too late.

The blasts sent shrapnel in every direction. Pieces of the grenades tore into the back of Carrillo's legs, buttocks, and back. His hands, which he had gripped together to protect his ears and the back of his head, deflected some of the shredded metal that would have no doubt bored into his skull and killed him outright.

155

The two soldiers, however, had not heard the releasing sound of the clips that had kept the grenades inert. The sight of the major suddenly pitching himself to the ground had initially stunned them. Before their training and instincts could tell them to do the same, the force of the blast decapitated them both.

The next day, Chulio had more important things on his mind than studying a report that Romero had brought him about the raid on Marta's house. The activity inside and out of Fort El Zapote was chaotic. Frenzied troops were bustling around the inside courtyard, moving hurriedly in all directions seemingly at the same time. Reports of air raids at the other *cuartels* and sporadic gunfire on the streets outside added to the turbulence. Chulio had already assembled the commanders of the *Jaguares* and given them instructions to defend the fort to the last man. Although he was positive he could count on his men, he was not sure about the others brigades.

Despite these activities, the events at Linda Vista haunted him. *So close*, he thought. He tried to dismiss the feelings as just more gloomy news. Still, he could have used Carrillo and his tenacity right now. *Imbécil!* To have let his guard down like that. And twice in one day! It served him right to be almost killed. How quickly events can turn, Chulio thought. He could have used Hugo's arrest and Carrillo's firm hand to block this attempted *coup*.

Instead, events were racing ahead of him. The infernal information was so inaccurate. Blasted rumors, he thought. The hardest thing to counter in this country was the effect of rumors. What he knew for sure was that some idiots had seized the radio station YSP and declared a national *golpe* against Martínez. The plotters were calling on the commanders of the *cuarteles* to seize control and oust the *martinistas.*

Chulio knew that maintaining the loyalty of the commanders of the various military forts was key to squashing any *coup* attempt. So far, information was imprecise; it was difficult to know who was supporting the President and who was against him. Vague reports had the First, Second and Fifth Infantry Regiments, the communications building, the artillery regiment, and the airport all in the hands of the plotters.

Chulio suspected that it was the new officers, Gutierrez's *tandas*, who were behind these actions. They had supported *coups* for the past ten years. He recalled that over 200 officers during the last decade had been arrested and exiled for insurrection. That was the root problem, he had deduced; these exiles were always promoting dissent. Without them, Hugo's power base would be greatly weakened. As far as he was concerned, they should all have been hunted down and eliminated long ago. But Martínez had refused to act on the mere suspicion; he had wanted proof.

Well, Chulio thought, if he wants proof, he will have it. He told Romero to countermand the order to assault the radio station. He would allow the traitors to continue to broadcast, but he would be documenting every word. Then he turned his attention back to his most pressing task—getting Martínez back from the coast in time to reverse the treasonous attempt.

Hugo had not ignited the start of this rebellion, at least not directly. His anti-Martínez propaganda, however, had kept the citizenry incensed for the past months. His detailed information on the corrupt practices of Martínez' administration had been devastating to *martinista* efforts to establish public trust. Dissent was everywhere. Militants had only needed a sign, a spark to set things in motion.

It had been mere happenstance that while the private and public sectors, including Martínez, were vacationing for *Semana Santa*, a group of drunken plotters decided the moment had come. The audacious band of young professionals and businessmen marched from the bar of the Casino Salvadoreño to the national radio station. They seized control by force and publicly announced a call to arms.

During the previous weeks, Hugo had secretly met with several *coup* organizers to discuss the precise moment the action would start. They had agreed it would be soon, but a decision had not been made. From Hugo's call to join forces, most of the organizers had known that the moment of truth was close. So the seizing of the radio station was a signal to some of the conspirators that the *coup* was in progress.

Right after he left Marta, he learned of the false alarm and it had been too late. Unable to stop it, Hugo had moved from group to group, rallying them and forcing momentum. Even later, after he learned of Marta's death, he forced himself to press forward. Only now, a greater force possessed him.

Blindly, the more intrepid of the conspirators pressed into action. In this regard, Hugo's compartmentalization worked against them. Fearful of being excluded, some military officers launched fragmented attacks on loyalist positions. The attacks were met with heavy resistance. But for all the commotion and discharging of weapons, casualties were light. Members of the young officer corps were disinclined to vigorously battle comrades until the question of command was clearly established.

Young aviators, however, could not hold back their enthusiasm, and bombed the President's residence, police headquarters, and several garrisons, including the *Guardia's* Fort El Zapote, in the late afternoon. From the latter location, Chulio and his *jaguares* were forced to flee. They regrouped at the more centrally located National Police headquarters building.

Most lines of communications were severed and news from the other garrisons was mixed. The consensus of opinion among loyalist troops was that most military installations had been compromised and that the arrival of any reinforcements from the outlying forts would be the precursor for defeat.

Chulio had sent a runner to La Libertad to locate the President as soon as the assaults began at 1 P.M. The plotters had set up ambushes for Martínez, but he managed to slip through. Ironically, he had been guided by the radio station reports of which garrisons were still resisting and he bypassed them. It was not until just before 6 P.M. that the President arrived at police headquarters, alone and driving a private vehicle he had borrowed from a friend.

Once he was there, Chulio briefed him on the seriousness of the situation and Martínez immediately took charge, establishing a central command inside the police fortress. He ordered attacks to retake the garrisons around the capital. Given his presence and leadership, military officers in charge of the various forts were quickly brought back under his authority.

Some resisted, preferring to fight it out to the death, but most of the organizers of the military *coup* either surrendered or fled. The few holdouts in minor garrisons gave up when reinforcements from the provincial commands in Ahuachapán and Santa Ana failed to arrive in time. By the time these troops made it to the capital the following day, Martínez had the situation under control.

The weeks following the attempted Easter *coup d'état* brought back to many of us images of the ruthlessness that followed the peasant revolt of 1932. Military plotters who did not die during the assaults on the forts were executed at the *Cementario Generál*, reminiscent of the executions of Martí, Luna, and Zapata twelve years before, except that these victims were military officers. Twelve of them were sent to the firing squads. Other plotters managed to escape into neighboring countries.

The failure to oust Martínez was a devastating blow to the underground movement, and especially to those in exile. Many blamed Hugo, and for the first time his influence and leadership came into question.

Chapter 17

I had heard something about the trouble in the capital while we were at our plantation in Zacatecoluca for *Semana Santa*, but nothing of the magnitude that was described to me when I returned. It was Choco who brought me up to date on the failed revolt and the fate of Hugo's family. This very personal side of the man none of us had known, and it somehow made him more…well, human. The whole series of events was surreal to me, but then Cora and I were still fighting our demons over Miguelito. What had not happened to Teco and her children had happened to Hugo's family, and the burden he was carrying must have been immeasurable.

"How is he holding on?" I asked sorrowfully. Choco and I had met for *almuerzo* at the *Club Salvadoreño Dental* and he had just finished describing the dire news.

"By a thread," said Choco sadly. "He does not want to talk about what happened to them, and continues to carry on business communiqués with many of us as before. But between you and me, Chepe, he needs to talk to someone in your profession."

"Yes, of course…but you are not suggesting…" I stammered.

"No, I am not suggesting you, nor would he allow it. It is just that he has never faced such tragedy. Well, I say that, but what he suffered in '32 was as bad. You knew about that?" he asked.

"About his parents, yes; I had heard the story."

"No story. He lost his entire family, parents, brothers and sisters, and now he has lost his new family."

"Inconceivable. And what does this do to the movement?" I asked cautiously.

"A good question, my friend. At this point, we do not know."

I just shook my head at the wretched turn of events.

None of us felt much like eating, and after some effort at light conversation, Choco said we should stay in contact because he was sure he would have some news from Hugo and Ricardo soon.

As I mentioned before, unwittingly I had adopted the role of *de facto* recorder of Hugo's exploits. And obtaining information about him did border on clandestine behavior. Mainly I had to rely on Choco and what little public information I could find. You see, at the time only the government-controlled newspapers were faithfully detailing news internally. And naturally they stressed the positive which, to be fair, was significant.

Martínez had done more than just maintain order. During his decade of rule, he had administered the building of new roads, bridges, railroads, banks, and communications networks. He had even enticed the New Zealander Lowell Yerex Pinney to headquarter his expanding TACA Airlines in San Salvador in 1938. This infrastructure growth was important to us, especially after the cataclysmic economic events of October 24, 1929.

Before that, during the time of *Don Pío*, historians such as Miguel Ángel García had mainly chronicled the hopeful optimism of the 1920s. But free speech was not to be the trademark of Martínez' regime. As a result, the idea of liberated editorials, biographies, or even the jotting down of family histories was not a practiced trait, and neither was the practice of giving or soliciting interviews. So how did one go about researching current events? It was a dilemma for sure.

I was also facing another, more personal challenge during this time. My profession can be described as being more preventative than reactive. And, clinically speaking, most of the protagonists of this rebellious drama, many close friends, were in need of some type of psychological therapy. But I was not in any position to offer my services for fear of being implicated with them. At a critical moment in our history, I felt totally irrelevant, relegated to the role of reporter. Clearly, the reactive nature of crises leaves no room for preemptive treatment, let alone psychotherapy.

I cannot describe the consternation I felt during this time. My best friend was gone, my Cora was on medication for paranoia, colleagues were fleeing, and I was powerless to do anything about it. Although the word is not in my clinician's dictionary, what came to mind while trying to form any semblance of reason during the final days of Martínez was "madness."

Guatemala City, Guatemala

"The report from Hugo is here, Rick," said a dejected Ricardo, handing over a package to Anderson.

"I heard things did not go as planned," said the American in an uncharacteristically serious tone. "Frankly, Ricardo, we did not expect any rebellious activity over Holy Week. Very atypical of you *Latinos*. What happened?"

"Someone got drunkenly brave and gave a false signal," said Ricardo. "And now, many of our friends have died because of it. Including Hugo's wife and daughters."

"What! How? Where?" asked an incredulous Anderson.

"I do not know the details. Just that Chulio's thugs killed them."

"My God!" said Anderson.

Ricardo was shaking his head. "Truthfully, Rick, I do not know how Hugo does it. I heard that even after he found out, he kept rallying the troops to wait for the other *cuartels* to join them, but it was hopeless. Once

Martínez showed up, everything fell apart. Hugo managed to escape with Lieutenants Castro Morán and Lemus Rivas, who had been plotting with him. Those two made it out of the country, but Hugo stayed. He will never give up."

"I did not know he had a family."

"I did not know, either," said Ricardo. "He never spoke of them. I guess he was being protective. Curious, how we all arrogantly feel we are being protective of those we love. At this point, it is inexplicable to me how he can go on. I could not do it."

"Maybe, it is all he has now," said Anderson.

"Perhaps," Ricardo said sensitively.

"Rick, I want you to arrange for me to see Hugo," said Anderson directly. "We need to talk face to face. This unanticipated *coup* attempt has strained our relationship. Ambassador Thurston is livid. He expected us to know beforehand. I know it was not your fault, because you did not know either, but Hugo did or should have. You should know that many of my colleagues do not approve of our arrangement. Please inform Hugo that we need to meet."

"I will pass this on, but it may have to be in El Salvador. He will not leave."

"Whatever the case, I have to see him."

"I will try," said Ricardo.

They spoke for a while without much enthusiasm or substance, then parted formally with the feigned smiles and verbal amenities of those expressing condolences.

Ricardo was wrong. As usual, Hugo surprised them by agreeing to meet Anderson near the Guatemalan coastal town of Retalhuleu later that week.

On the prearranged day, Paco flew him over early in the morning. Using the coastal village of Champerico north of the Guatemalan port of San Jose as a guide, the experienced pilot had turned inland. With the Mayan ruins of Abaj Takalik to his north, they landed in one of the growing number of airfields that rich coastal farmers were building for personal use. These uncontrolled fields were also becoming popular for clandestine activity along the Pacific coast. Since the start of World War II, the U.S. government had subsidized Guatemalan army garrisons at San Jose. Spotters were paid to watch the coast for unusual activity. A Salvadoran light plane, however, was not considered unusual, especially since Paco occasionally restocked the garrison's supply of cigarettes and liquor.

Paco dropped Hugo off at an out of the way airstrip and returned to El Salvador for another run. He had been ferrying rebel aviators to Guatemala and Honduras since Easter. Martínez had specifically singled out the rebel pilots for punishment, primarily because of the bombing raids on the Presidential Palace, the forts, and police headquarters; the latter had kept Chulio and his *Jaguares* jumping from one barricade to another. Only a few people knew how near these young adventurous airmen had come to winning the day for the rebels with one well-placed bomb.

After being dropped off, Hugo had made his way through the countryside to a small hotel on the outskirts of Retalhuleu. From a phone there, he called Ricardo. He instructed him to take Anderson to a café across from the hotel where he was staying. After he oriented himself with the area, Hugo rented a room and tried once again to sleep.

Meanwhile, Anderson and Ricardo took an embassy car and driver and made the five-hour trip early the next morning. The change of climate between the highlands, which surround the capital city and extend north, and the Guatemalan Pacific coastline, is quite dramatic. Extreme heat and humidity quickly replace the temperate northern weather as the terrain flattens to sea level. The air at this stage is usually muggy and without movement, which makes for uncomfortable travel along the tropical Pan American highway. The only moving air is self-produced, unless your limousine happens to be stuck behind the dust of a slow-moving truck.

By the time they arrived at Retalhuleu, Ricardo and Anderson were dusty, sweating and drained of energy. By 2 P.M., they had been waiting about an hour in the dingy hot café, and Anderson was getting irritable.

They did not even notice Hugo's entrance from the rear until he was suddenly standing alongside their table. "Sorry for my tardiness," he said.

"Hugo," Ricardo said, surprised. He stood quickly and the two men embraced. Then Ricardo turned to Anderson. "Rick...I want you to meet Hugo."

Anderson stood and the two men shook hands.

Hugo's appearance was haggard. He was unshaven and his eyes were red and irritated. His hair and clothes were soiled and disheveled. Except for the expensive snakeskin boots on his feet, the man looked like a homeless vagrant.

The three sat down and Ricardo ordered beers and a glass of milk. It was Hugo who spoke first. In a respectful tone, he said, "*Señor* Anderson, I am pleased to meet you at last. I apologize for my appearance, but I have not been in any one place long enough to make myself presentable."

"No need to apologize, Hugo, we know what you must be going through. My most sincere sympathy on your loss."

"You are most kind, *señor*," said Hugo meekly. "My wife and children were innocents, as I call them, pure and beautiful. It seems God put so many of them in this world ...untainted and vulnerable...many more than the evil ones. Yet they cannot seem to defend themselves against those vicious few. *Es una lastima*, very sad."

He stared off into space. No one said anything.

After a few seconds, he continued dispassionately, "Then there are those of us who are neither good nor evil. And we also number more and pretend we know how to care for the innocent, but we cannot seem to protect them, either."

Ricardo and Anderson only occasionally glanced up at the morose Hugo. To them, his spirit seemed broken, and it was not a pleasant sight. The three were respectfully silent for a moment.

Then Anderson began softly, "Hugo, I wanted to see you because we were disappointed at not being informed about the attempted *coup* before it happened. We had an arrangement. It also seems that lately there have been other delays and gaps in your information. These things make it difficult for us to continue supporting you. In these sensitive political situations, our government needs frequent reassurances. It is the nature of our business. You understand.

"These twelve officers who were executed died needlessly, and we were not in a position to condemn their execution, because technically they were traitors. That is the most upsetting thing of all to me, having to take sides with Martínez and Ubico in this matter."

If Hugo had taken note of Anderson's words, he did not show it, just continued to stare at his hands. Anderson was beginning to think that the man was through and that the trip had been a waste of time.

But he continued, "Ambassador Thurston is requiring that we inform you that if you continue to promote a takeover by force you will be condemned by our government. If you are successful through violent means, we will not recognize the new government, and sanctions will be imposed. Martínez has assured the ambassador that elections will be held and that in due course, the government will be turned over to a duly elected administration. Ambassador Thurston is holding Martínez to that with the same warning that he is making to you."

Hugo still said nothing. Anderson looked at Ricardo for help. Ricardo did not entirely agree with what Anderson was saying, but knew that Hugo had to speak for himself.

Instead he said, "Look Hugo, I am on your side on this and so are Carlitos, Miguel Angel, and all the other exiles. If we have to fight we will, but now we must regroup. We know that this is not the *golpe* that anyone had planned. I do not agree with Thurston that Martínez will give up power. That is pure shit. But we need to organize. Stay here with us and rest. Then we will talk. You are exhausted. I do not know how you have made it this far. I told Rick this. He is not holding you responsible; he is only doing his job. We now have some time to think."

Ricardo and Anderson waited.

Outside, along a road that was visible from the restaurant's window, a procession was passing by. The three serious men saw it at the same time from their table and allowed themselves the distraction. Several of the patrons in the restaurant removed their hats and crossed themselves.

A child was being buried. They could tell because the coffin was small and carried by several children, girls in white dresses. There was a boy and a young man walking behind the coffin and the boy had a protruding belly and carried a cross. Others, including several women hugging a young girl, also followed the coffin. Hugo, Ricardo and Anderson watched respectfully in silence until the marchers passed and the dust they had kicked up dissipated.

Hugo was silent for a few moments; then, as if speaking to no one, he said, "Do you know that when an *inocente* is killed as a result of a political decision, that person is oblivious as to the reason? They have no concept of evil. They are trusting and respectful of everyone. Can you imagine that there are people out there who are that pure?

"They acknowledge life by calmly accepting their daily sufferings. They esteem and help each other. Their pride is the only government they know or need. They are like children...no...more like angels. They are natural, like a beautiful meadow of flowers, part of a select group of humans whose mere existence gives glory to God."

Hugo was smiling as he said this, but his eyes were still focused out the window. Ricardo and Anderson were now uncomfortable and embarrassed. Then, without warning, Hugo turned his head and stared at Anderson.

In strong intonation, he said, "*Señor* Anderson."

Anderson was startled, and looked up attentively. Hugo leaned forward, apparently sobered from his reverie.

He said straightforwardly, "Let me apologize for my incoherent wandering. I did hear what you said and it deserves a response. But first, I want to make a point about the innocent people who are dying in these countries. Every time one of them is killed, many others lose their innocence and are forced to choose sides. As a result, the number of non-innocent people is growing rapidly.

"Soon there will only be non-innocents, people like us, neither good nor bad, constantly battling those who are inherently evil. I am not overly religious or superstitious, *Señor* Anderson, but I do believe in devils." He stared away for a moment, then narrowed his eyes and focused on Anderson again.

"What must be done cannot wait. Those of us who believe in the inviolability of these innocents will need to organize and launch a different kind of revolution, not like in '32 when more innocents died than at any other time in our history. They underestimated Martínez and, left alone now, they will underestimate him again as we just did. So they will need to fight again, not with *machetes*, but with something they are more familiar with, something the evil ones cannot defend against."

He was sitting taller now, and Ricardo recognized the confident cadence in his voice even though he did not completely understand Hugo's rambling. Anderson was even more confused, looking at one man and then the other as though he had lost something in the translation. *Los inocentes y los no inocentes?* Instead of asking for clarification, he tried to capitalize on Hugo's newfound attention to repeat his message.

"Yes, Hugo, many innocent people have died in this conflict and it would seem that a change is in order. But I want to say again that organizing a rebellion is something we oppose. And it will terminate our relationship. The immediate strategy is to support honest elections, and we will weigh in with those moderates who see it that way."

But Hugo was not listening to him. He was his condescending self again. With flashing eyes he said, "*Señor* Anderson, let me try to clarify. You are an economist, I am told. It is a fitting and important discipline. You will no doubt recall what H. L. Mencken said about elections: 'Government is a broker in pillage, and every election is a sort of advance auction sale of stolen goods.'

"In that case, he was talking about the abuse of taxation, but the inference about government corruption is the same. I have no illusion that this government or that one will be any better unless it as non-intrusive as possible. Martínez, *sotano, o mengano,* it makes no difference, they are all for sale to the highest bidder.

"In our poor country they are the lackeys of the wealthy few. Everyone knows that. That is the way it is, and it will be that way for the foreseeable future. Our cause is not about bringing in an 'honest' government, but rather a representative one, one that is not repressive and listens to the voice of the people. It is that voice that I am advocating now be heard.

"Please tell your ambassador that with all due respect he is wrong to believe the *martinistas*. In my heart I know it will take violent action to bring them down. But tell him that I stop promoting the violent overthrow of this government. If a *coup* occurs, it will not come from our campaign. I will continue, however, to see that the truth is known about this government's disregard for the people's right to be safe and free. Martínez cannot decree or make legal what is immoral. Nor can he continue to use coercion to govern. It is evil. The people do not deserve it, and as of today they will not stand for it. If we cannot do it through political means, we will do it with brutal submission—we will strike!"

Anderson was taken aback. "You can do this?"

"Yes," said Hugo confidently. "Now, let me ask you something. Do you still want to receive my information?"

"Well...yes, of course."

"Good. We will continue our arrangement as before. Ricardo will be our conduit." Then he turned to Ricardo, "I would have a word with you, Ricardo. If you will excuse us, *Señor* Anderson."

"Yes...certainly," he said hesitatingly, but he wanted to hear more.

Hugo noticed and said, "We will talk as long as you like after I have spoken with Ricardo."

"Very well," said an obviously irritated Anderson. In a way he was marveling at the enterprise of this man, but he could not help being put off. He was being dismissed. *Had Hugo planned it so?* Anderson just shook his head and said derisively, "I will go see if the driver has had his lunch."

After Anderson left, Hugo turned to Ricardo. But Ricardo, who had seen this before, spoke first. "Welcome back, *compa*," he said with a dry smile.

Hugo ignored the comment and said instead, "*Mira,* Ricardo, you have done a fine job with the Americans; they will be our *verdugo* with Martínez. I am sure that we can turn this failure to our advantage with the Americans' help. The publicity of the attempted *coup* has drawn the attention of the international community. It has signaled that things are not right here.

"The Americans will react to that. They consider this their backyard, although they are not the experts they think they are. As you know, diplomatically Martínez does not have a stellar reputation. The world war is almost over and there will be much posturing by all sides. The *martinistas* are thugs and that is their weakness. The Americans must be made to see this."

"How?" asked Ricardo. "Our credibility is not what one would call at the top these days."

"You are right about us, but not about the credibility of the innocents, the apolitical, the common people who just want peace. Their collective voice is still strong enough to penetrate the walls of embassies and presidential palaces."

"You have a plan, then?"

"Not a complete one, but yes, I have a plan. But I need to get back. You will keep Anderson informed. Agreed?"

"Of course," said Ricardo.

Then Hugo changed his tone, "Now, Ricardo, there is something personal I want to say to you; two things, actually. I consider you a friend, and someone who has a long life ahead with a loving and caring family. There is nothing more important than protecting them. Keep in mind that it may not be safe for you to return to El Salvador even after a change of government. Villains are difficult to kill; they have a way of resurfacing in similar positions over and over. And they have long memories.

"Think about a new life somewhere where your family will be safe. The work you are doing for Anderson is important to them and you should maintain that alliance. When the time comes, you must be in a position to ask them for a favor that they will consider reasonable. You understand?"

Ricardo nodded. The thought had occurred to him as well. He said, "Of course, you are right, and I have been thinking the same thing. But Hugo, let me ask you. Are you all right? We were never close personally, but I am worried for you."

"Ricardo, thank you for that, but I am fine. This meeting has been an epiphany. I know the steps that must be taken, and achieving the objective will brace me."

The two men nodded and exchanged a smile of brotherhood.

Then Hugo said more seriously, "There is another thing I want to say to you."

Ricardo waited.

"The man responsible for the raid on your house is the same person who caused the death of my wife and daughters. His name is Eugenío Carrillo, a major in the *Guardia*, a *Jaguar*. It was Chulio who ordered the raid on your home and mine, and it was Carrillo who carried it out. The two are evil personified."

Ricardo started to flush and took a long slow breath.

Hugo continued, "But he will not survive the wounds he received after the raid on my house." He looked at Ricardo and they shared a deep and serious warriors' moment. "I thought you should know."

"Who do I have to thank for saving me the pleasure?"

"Marta," Hugo quickly answered.

Ricardo was stunned. "Hugo, I do not know what to say."

"Say nothing. Make peace with yourself. Take care of your family. You have no idea how important they are."

"I think I do. A little more after your words, Hugo, but I honestly do."

Chapter 18

It was about a week after Ricardo, Hugo, and Anderson met in Retalhuleu that I had the opportunity to personally meet the American, Anderson. It happened because I decided to finally respond to one of Ricardo's pleas to visit him in Guatemala. I relented more out of curiosity than a sense of urgency. I had sensed an invigorated spirit in Ricardo's last letter, which was curious given the negative reports I had been receiving from Choco after the failed *coup*. This time, Ricardo said he wanted to discuss with us (although I am sure he meant me) some unexpected news. His tone was quite upbeat.

When I told Cora about his intriguing letter, she gave me a pleading look, but refrained from comment. It was her way of capitulating. She understood that Ricardo had never been out of my thoughts. I explained that my trip would coincide with a planning meeting for an upcoming Central American Psychiatric Conference, which the *Chapines* had scheduled for the fall. It was a legitimate diversion and it somewhat eased her apprehension, especially when I had no trouble getting the required exit visa from the Treasury Police. But when the day of my departure came, her anxiety was evident.

As I bid my goodbyes to her and the children, she asked that I give Ricardo and Teco an *abrazo* for her. She had written Teco a long letter explaining her need to stay behind with the children. Her lively demeanor was convincing as she and the children accompanied me out of the house to the waiting car. But as we pulled away for the eight-hour road trip to Guatemala City, I did not fail to notice she was choking back tears.

I had not realized how much my visit to Guatemala would mean to all our exiled colleagues. It turned out to be quite a festive reunion. Because my family is considered a member of the so-called establishment of wealthy landowners, my presence was a particularly encouraging sign to them. Frankly, I would have preferred that less be made of it, but when I saw their joyous expressions, I was deeply moved. These were serious patriotic young men whom I had known all my life. They were not the stereotypical subversives described by the *martinistas*, and I was saddened by their predicament. We met at Miguel Angel's home.

I must tell you that as much pleasure as it gave me just to see Ricardo and Teco well, it gave me greater pleasure to see him in high spirits, just like the old days. I had been harboring the memory of his morose pained impression at the *pupuseria* when we had last met. That is the picture that had been breaking my heart all these days, and the real reason I came to see for myself that he had rebounded.

And then, there was Teco, the survivor. Oh, she was emotional, especially when we embraced, each of us no doubt recalling the details of *our* last meeting. But now there was a peaceful continence on her face, a confident air that prevailed and appeared sincere.

The three of us exchanged family stories and light gossip. It was evident that any talk of politics and the outrageous events we had all experienced was to be reserved for later. To me, just seeing the expressions on their faces and knowing that Ricardo was not involved in any more clandestine operations was enough to alleviate my deepest concerns. The physician in me was healing himself.

After the guests left, I used the pretext of performing my "godfather duties" and spent some time with the children. I was not surprised to see that Ricardo León was still his impish self, but Ana Maria's change in demeanor was just short of miraculous. There was a tense moment for all of us when Ricardo and Teco reported that the baby's newfound zest was a direct result of the iron enhancement treatment recommended by Miguelito. But not even that raw poignant moment, which admittedly brought tears to my eyes, was enough to dim our hopefulness and resolve in overcoming past misfortunes.

As it got late, Teco excused herself, and Ricardo, Miguel Angel and I automatically retired to the living room, where we uncharacteristically faded into wistful silence for a few moments, as though we were remembering the fallen. It was customary following periods of revelry to engage in outlandish liquor-induced braggadocios. Instead, we reverentially spent the next few hours sharing stories such as the remarkable meeting between Hugo and Anderson in Retalhuleu. Ricardo spoke about the American diplomat's support for their cause and of Hugo's wise counsel to him about using the liaison to help them resettle in the United States. I assumed that this was the news he had alluded to in his letter. I listened in relative silence, already missing him.

The next day, at noon, the American came to Miguel Angel's home for *almuerzo*. He and Miguel Angel, both being economists, enjoyed each other's company and had started this weekly ritual. It was also a convenient place for Anderson to meet with Ricardo.

First impressions being everything to me, I did try to be objective. But I must confess that the American's informal deportment was distracting. I am not a prude by any means, but there is a time and place for jollity. I cannot speak for substance, because as I keep saying, I do not seek, nor enjoy the topic of politics, but his disregard for formal social practices seemed insensitive, especially for a diplomat.

He was too loud and used the familiar tense with people like myself whom he was meeting for the first time. Since my visit was short, I feared there would not be sufficient time to see a different side of him. After all, Ricardo and Miguel Angel thought highly of him and I did not want to be rude.

When we found ourselves alone on the veranda after the meal, I must admit I was uncomfortable and tried to avoid conversation. But, predictably, he broke the silence.

"Chepe, I'm told you have a coffee plantation in Zacatecoluca."

"Yes," I said, "It is a small family *finca*."

"How many *campesinos* would you say that you employ?"

"Many families have been born and raised there. I would have no exact figures, but I would say several hundred families." The preoccupation with numbers is definitely an American trait.

He kept nodding his head at my answers as though what I was saying was very important. There was an uncomfortable pause, and he smiled even more animatedly and continued to nod his head. It was very distracting. As I now analyze that moment, my discomfort had more to do with knowing that he was in league with Hugo and Ricardo. He must have been warned about my political sentiments, because he seemed to be avoiding controversial subjects.

But then he asked, "Do you think the *campesinos* are happy laborers?"

Well, that did hit a nerve with me, because we have always been proud of the way we treat and care for our workers. They are like family to us. That is why the revolt of '32 was so painful and still vivid in our minds. And here now was this foreign political economist asking a most sensitive and intrusive question.

"*Señor* Anderson," I said irritably, "I am not sure how much you know about our people, but I can attest that the *campesino* leads a very peaceful and carefree existence. They love their children, they work hard, and are very religious in their own way. What is most important to them is being able to obtain their *frijolitos* and *tortillas* every day, to have a place to live and some spending money for weekends when they can buy their necessities, and perhaps some Tic Tac *guaro* to celebrate their Sunday holidays. They do not seek or aspire to any more than that. Our responsibility is to see that we meet their requirements so that they can live in harmony. Any discord that you may hear about the *campo* does *not* originate internally."

I said these words sternly and passionately and let him draw his own inference. I was unsure that I made my point, however, because he just laughed at the reference to the *agua ardiente*, Tic Tac, the sugar-cane liquor that the *campesinos* seem to enjoy so much. But he also changed the subject.

He said softly, "Ricardo tells me you are his oldest and dearest friend, Chepe. He thinks the world of you."

"You have no idea, *Señor* Anderson, how much our lives, my wife's and mine, have been disrupted by all of this. What hurts most is that at a time when we should be there for each other, we are pulled apart. El Salvador is our land, our heritage, and there can be no substitute. I hope, *Señor Anderson*, that you are aware of what all this means to our people, and that you will be able to help him when the time comes, because I cannot."

We held eye contact, and even though he maintained that constant grin, I knew we had communicated. He continued to nod and promised to write and keep me informed, which he eventually did or I would not have been able to report the next accounts in such detail.

But on that day, my meaning to him was clear: You, *Señor* Anderson, will leave one day, but this is our life.

San Salvador, El Salvador

"A strike?" asked an incredulous Thurston. "What kind of strike? The military will not strike."

"I don't think he was referring to a military strike, Mr. Ambassador. Hugo spoke of a citizen's strike, working people, students, young professionals."

It had taken Anderson two weeks to get in to see Ambassador Thurston and brief him on Hugo's plans. Meanwhile, Hugo had continued to send weekly reports through Ricardo about his progress in organizing the students to intensify their propaganda against the *martinistas*. Although their influence had diminished after the failed *coup*, their pamphlets were still the only way for many to receive balanced information, because the newspapers were still censored. The braver of the students had begun using the balconies of old buildings in the center of the city to attract workers to sermons about the government's repression of its people. Predictably, this activity was aggravating the military authorities, and students continued to sporadically tangle with police.

"Well good luck," said Thurston sarcastically. "Look, Rick, there are a couple of things you need to keep in mind. I have impressed upon Martínez that another massacre of his citizens is unacceptable. He has a leadership problem and he will have to fix it if he hopes to continue as President. I believe that I am finally getting through to him. Besides scheduling elections, he has agreed to several social and institutional reforms, including the police. Of course, we'll have to wait and see, but this time I think he means it."

"Well, those are sound words, Mr. Ambassador. Like you, I am anxious to see what the details are."

"I know about one for sure…He mentioned dissolving the *Jaguares*."

"Wow," said Anderson, impressed. "No question, that is a step in the right direction. You obviously have been successful in appealing to a side of Martínez that few have seen, Mr. Ambassador. How soon?"

"He plans to announce the initial steps during next Thursday's radio broadcast. I believe he will not specifically mention Chulio by name, but the inference will be there. He will also announce a fixed date for the election. These two items alone should be enough to postpone any further discussions on trade sanctions. You should send off a cable with my recommendation to that effect today. I will continue to press him for elections this year."

Anderson jotted the task in his notebook. As he was writing, he said, "That will be well received, sir. Of course, the students will have a field day with these promises in the wake of the executions of so many popular military officers. Their refusal to attend classes and urge others to do the same is having some result."

At this comment, the Ambassador rose from behind his desk, walked around to where Anderson was sitting and took a chair next to him. In a concerned voice, he said, "Look, Rick, I know you disagree, but I am instructing you to advise Hugo and his students not to provoke this government. Tell him to let us do our job. I am serious about this. It is in everyone's interest."

"Sir, you have seen their pamphlets; they have a new tone to them. They are not advocating violence. On the contrary, they seem to be condemning all types of violence. They urge citizens to make their voice heard in the only way it can be when newspapers are censored and people are prosecuted for any public criticism. They are merely refusing to participate as members of a society that does not recognize them as human beings."

"Oh, please!" the ambassador said. "Next you will be urging me to endorse Hugo for the Nobel Peace Prize. I'm not buying it, Rick. He is provoking the *martinistas*, and if that results in violence, they will share the guilt. Make sure he knows that."

"Of course, sir." Anderson made a few more notes and stood. "Anything else, sir?"

"No, that should do for now, and thank you, Rick. Let's get that cable out and then come back and brief me about this so-called strike. Whether I like it or not, I guess I need to know more."

"Mr. Ambassador."

"I do not care what the President's directive says," Chulio barked at the colonel, "You will follow my orders."

"*Si, mí generál*," said the colonel nervously.

During the past two weeks, Chulio had seen the striking students take to the streets and openly distribute dissenting literature. Now it was becoming a daily ritual. Behind the locked gates and docrs of the aged downtown building that once housed the former University of El Salvador, activists had taken to terraces to preach their anti-government rhetoric. It was galling, and Chulio had no patience with this disorder.

In his opinion, this anarchy was an extension of the revolt and it would continue to escalate until it was exterminated. But Chulio was losing faith in Martínez' resolve. No doubt pressured by the Americans, he thought, Martínez had relaxed his strong support for weeding out student dissidents. The attempted *coup* and subsequent execution of fellow officers had taken its toll, and Martínez seemed to be questioning his mandate.

Chulio, on the other hand, saw the peril of displaying remorse. Just this week he had read a report indicating a substantial increase in the number of demonstrators. Some stores were looted and skirmishes with the police were also mounting. If the crowds were getting larger, that meant more people were not at work. Reports were now coming in that several government offices were being shut down because civilian workers had simply not shown up. *No*, Chulio thought, *I am not going to wait. I do not care what the directive said; we need to bring order to this situation.*

"You have your orders, Colonel. Do you want me to repeat them?"

"*No, mí generál.*"

"Then get your group together. I will talk with them personally."

"*Si, mí generál.*"

Chulio knew that what he was asking them to do was contrary to the oath that every soldier had been forced to sign after the *coup* attempt. The loyalty oath to the President meant unconditional adherence to his directives and command. Now, Chulio was asking his *Jaguares* to go against an order not to engage in unauthorized actions against the citizenry. Chulio knew that Martínez would be reticent to authorize covert operations against the student strikers. But Operation Zero was exactly that.

Later that day, Anderson was summoned to Ambassador Thurston's residence to follow up on their earlier conversation. After they finished refreshments in the living room, the Ambassador stood and motioned for

Anderson to join him on the patio. Anderson took his *marañon* fruit drink with him. When they were alone, Thurston offered Anderson a cigarette, a conventional gesture to put the subordinate at ease.

"Rick, I'm scheduled to see the President later tonight at a function at the Foreign Ministry," Thurston said lighting their cigarettes. "So if it wouldn't be too much trouble, it might be a good time for you to provide me with some background on this latest threat by the underground. I'm not quite sure I want to get into a discussion of this so-called strike with Martínez, but I do want to be prepared just in case."

"You know most of it already, sir, but I'll get you some talking points right away. I can take the morning flight back to Guatemala."

The Ambassador nodded his appreciation. Then, he said, "Rick, I know that this back and forth to Guatemala has been hectic for you these past weeks. I just want you to know that I appreciate your effort. After this is over, I'll see to it that Boaz and the Department know how hard you have worked."

"Thank you, sir; just part of the job."

The Ambassador smiled at him, then casually added, "By the way, how is that new TACA Trimotor aircraft working out?"

"Fine, sir. Seats a couple of dozen people and is quite fast. The flights save me a lot of time. I hear TACA is expanding their service to Balboa and Havana via Belize."

"Yes," Thurston said, "Lowell Yerex confirmed that. I had dinner with him last week. He is another one that is worried about this strike business. Mechanics and planes sitting around would eventually force him to move out, and that would be a significant blow to the region's development. You know that he is looking to expand his business to Brazil; last year he bought Aerovias del Brazil in Rio."

"Yes, I heard. He seems to be doing fine, sir. Recently just the exodus of dissidents and the back and forth of their families and friends is keeping his flights full."

"Well, that's a sobering thought. Speaking of exiles, how is the Guatemala bunch doing?"

"Still depressed and anxious. There are some genuinely fine people just waiting for the chance to return. I've met most of them. You've no doubt heard Ambassador Long mention Miguel Angel Alcaíne. Great banking mind. He would make an outstanding Minister of Economy under the right leadership. Detests Martínez, however.

"Then there are several groups of young officers and professionals who got caught up in the movement through no other sin than voicing their opposition; one day they signed a petition, the next day they were fleeing for their lives. Others might have gone a bit too far, more than just signing a petition, that is. But most of them are honest and patriotic to a fault. Frankly, Mr. Ambassador, I can't help feeling sorry for them, outside the fence so to speak, just watching and waiting for a chance to return to their native land and pick up the pieces."

"Really?" said the Ambassador in a condescending voice. "I have heard that Guatemala is very alluring. Climate, culture, working conditions. Much more modern than here."

"True, but to the exiles their native country possesses every single frame of reference; it makes them who they are. Come to think of it, I imagine that is probably a sentiment shared by all the exiles of this world war."

"Perhaps, Rick, but if yearning to return is such a passion among them, I would imagine the same would hold true for those in the U.S. Hell, we are a nation of immigrants, yet you don't see a wave of them returning after acclimating to our life style."

"True, but in our case, geography does play a role. These Salvadoran immigrants are right next door. And frankly, Guatemala is not the U.S. No, this group is obsessed with returning home. And I'll bet that it is true for most first-generation immigrants everywhere. I have not studied it, but my guess is that geography and economics aside, if the situation that drove them out in the first place improved, even U.S. immigrants would happily return to their roots. I believe we sometimes overlook this dynamic. Because we live in such a rich, free country, we ethnocentrically assume everyone else is craving to immigrate there.

"I recall attending a hilarious presentation at our Foreign Service Institute, by a Brit of all things, about the 'un-Americans'. 'What Americans fail to recognize,' the fellow would say, 'is that '95 percent of the world's population is *not* American."

"Interesting," said Thurston, smiling politely, "And perhaps you are right. I can't think of anything that could make me permanently leave Arizona, let alone the U.S. To give up my residence, friends, relatives, would indeed be traumatic."

Anderson said, "There is one thing, sir—fear for your life or that of your family. I don't think just improving the quality of life is enough to make someone do it, not permanently."

The Ambassador pursed his lips and nodded. "So, Rick, are you suggesting that we maintain a liaison with and permanent files on exiles around the world? If I follow your logic, we will always have an opposition group outside a country fancying to get back in and set things straight and all that. Do we need an exile intelligence unit at State?"

"Mr. Ambassador," Rick said with a chuckle, "in this region, I am State's 'exile intelligence unit.' And yes, I believe that in these unstable countries, we will always need a political officer engaged with them, for reporting purposes, if nothing else. It would even be helpful to develop a level of reciprocity between our legations. Frankly, until there is some type of central intelligence reporting center on such information, we are it."

"Rick, you are not advocating an intelligence or police attaché, are you? Good Lord! Don't say anything to Boaz but, frankly, having political appointees is bad enough. I, for one, think that limiting the number of non-Foreign Service officer attachés is critical, and they should never be put in the position of conducting foreign relations. Can you imagine having a U.S. policeman doing your job?"

They both laughed.

Then Anderson said, "Well, all I know is that we wear many hats overseas and a policeman's is not one I cherish."

"And we thank you for that, Rick," said the Ambassador, moving back into the main house, a signal that the visit was officially over. "I have enjoyed our chat. Very informative. And not to worry, your 'exile police' role will hopefully end soon. I believe you have earned a civilized assignment. There will be great demand for your talents when this war in Europe winds down, with some of our allies perhaps. You will have my total support. And, joking aside, I am very interested in your idea of reciprocal exile reporting. Give me a concept paper on that, I'll see that it gets to the right people."

"Thank you, Mr. Ambassador."

Later that evening, the Ambassador did have an occasion to meet individually with President Martínez and resolutely delivered the U.S. government's position *vis-à-vis* this latest political crisis. He used Anderson's points to deliver a clear message. Martínez should reach out for the opposition groups and establish a dialogue to ensure a peaceful transition during the election. Thurston underlined that such a move would go a long way to defuse the escalating strike situation. While not a formal démarche, the words carried enough firmness to impress the now weary Martínez that he would have to do something proactive. It was not too late, Thurston said. Martínez had listened and said he would take it under advisement.

But the following day, Martínez did act. The press reported a series of impromptu visits by him with striking government workers, hospital employees, and lower working-class people. He promised social reform, although he gave few specifics. There had been little dialogue or substance, but the unorthodox gesture by the notorious dictator had an effect. During the following days, the impetus of the work shutdown strategy began to lose momentum.

Chapter 19

San Salvador, El Salvador

The twelve *Jaguares* selected for the operation were young men with modern styled hair and dress, indistinguishable from regular university students. They were also more literate that the average soldier and skilled in the argot of the young. Their mission was to infiltrate the student movement, identify activists, and find their bases of operation. To accomplish this they were to disperse themselves surreptitiously among the free-flowing activity around the cathedral where the students were passing out pamphlets and organizing daily speakers for the demonstrations. Within a few days, the undercover agents would be able to identify the principle dissidents and the locations where subversive literature was being prepared.

Their orders did not include enforcement actions; it was to be an intelligence operation only. Chulio had informed the men and the colonels that they had the approval of the "highest authority." But because the operation was covert, Martínez must be in a position to disavow knowledge of Operation Zero should it become necessary in the future.

After the *Jaguares* had been deployed, Chulio sat in his office, still fuming over the latest directive from the President. Romero skulked in the background, arranging paperwork, but always cognizant that at any moment he could be struck by misdirected rage.

Chulio suddenly threw the official paper at Romero in disgust. Martínez had ordered Chulio specifically not to try to break up the strikers by force. And to all his commanders, the President had written:

"I will not be intimidated nor provoked by striking dissidents into taking enforcement action unless specific laws are broken or public order is threatened. In such cases, the police will deal with it. An unarmed public does not constitute a military objective."

To Chulio, this directive did not prohibit the gathering of intelligence. By the time he completed Operation Zero, he was sure the escalating situation being stirred up by Hugo would be so volatile and threatening that Martínez would be forced to take action. He would have the evidence and information he needed, just as he had during the last attempted *coup*. Then he would make a final sweep of these traitors and wipe them out once and for all. Chulio was sure the President would approve his plan then, because it would save the nation from being overrun by these communists. And when Hugo surfaced in some last ditch effort, Chulio thought, he would have him.

The night's rain had left the morning humid and overcast. The usually congested streets around the center of San Salvador had taken on an eerie look as the drying precipitation on the cobblestones created a steamy cloud along the ground.

These days, few cars and pedestrians used these avenues except for demonstrations, which centered on the side streets around the cathedral. The daily activities did not start until a parade of protesters made its way from the Hospital Rosales down Primera Calle to the cathedral.

Before setting out on the march, organizers distributed banners and cardboard signs scrawled with dissenting slogans. When they moved forward, students with bullhorns led the rhythmic anti-Martínez chanting. The number of marchers usually swelled along the route as the group picked up stragglers. On this day, they numbered close to a thousand, and the first of them began arriving in front of the cathedral just before noon.

It was a diverse group that traveled to these daily rallies. They were mainly service workers and people of lesser means. But there was also a sprinkling of young professionals, educators, and other sympathizers. Among them was Rodrigo "*El Choco*" Mendez.

Hugo had been using Choco sparingly since the failed *coup*, mainly to funnel missives to Ricardo and me. But Choco*'s* passion for seeing this government overthrown had not tempered during these months. Despite Hugo's warnings to the contrary Choco, sensing a shift in the momentum, had insisted on being part of the public protests.

During this particular march, he had struck up a conversation with Armando Acevedo, a lawyer and professor at the university, who was also a former Liceo schoolmate of ours. It was Armando who later provided me with the details of that significant day.

It seems that Choco and Armando had walked most of the way to the cathedral together, mainly talking about how the remarkable Hugo had managed to rebound after the movement's crushing defeat and the loss of his family. A general worker's strike was a brilliant ploy, they had remarked, because it captured the sullen yet respectful mood of the people.

The press had called the action *La huelga de brazos caidos*, "the fallen-arms strike," referring to the fact that the only action being taken by the strikers was refusing to work, tantamount to keeping their arms passively fallen at their sides. They were not penitents, but a resolved people coping with a lost battle, not a lost war.

As they arrived at the cathedral, Armando and Choco noticed that the atmosphere was rather festive. Vendors of *masapan* candies, fried meat *pasteles*, green mango slices flavored with lime and salt and shaved ice with a variety of sugar flavorings, were already setting up their stands for the hot afternoon activities. People were greeting each other warmly, enthusiastic about their camaraderie, while smiling students were passing out information pamphlets and a schedule of the day's speakers.

As Choco and Armando passed a corner of the cathedral, a young man handed them some literature. Choco glanced at the young man and thanked him with a smile.

But the smile abruptly faded. Choco and the young man had made eye contact for only an instant, but in that instant they both recognized something untoward. Choco began feeling queasy as an old painful memory flashed before him. The young man was also uncertain, and instinctively turned his face and started to walk away.

A stunned Choco reacted slowly, but then began pointing at the departing figure and said to Armando, quietly at first, then loudly, "I know that person; he is not a student. He is a soldier. A Martínez spy!"

People around him stopped their conversation and looked at Choco. Foreheads frowned and the crowd started buzzing. *What did he say? A spy! Who's a spy?*

Choco started after the student, who glanced back one time, then started walking faster. The young man pushed some people who were in his way and they reacted with indignation.

Choco screamed, "Stop him! Stop him!"

Several demonstrators started reaching for the fleeing man and he started to react violently. His military training was now obvious as he punched and kicked several students, disabling one with a severe blow to the throat. By now Choco caught up and faced the young man, who was challenging others in a fighting stance. The man had a look of defiance that Choco immediately recognized in his fiery eyes. A crowd began forming around them.

"I know you," said Choco, squinting at him through his thick glasses.

"And I know you, *culero*," spat out the young man. "Come on, you want some more?"

Then, it all came back to Choco. There had been a very young person in the room on the night he was assaulted, while he had been training with the *Guardia Civil* many years ago. Choco had thought it was a boy at first, but later rationalized that it must have been his imagination. The small boy/man had been dressed in the same fatigues as the sergeant and other soldiers. This young man was that same boy. He must have been only ten or twelve years old at the time, but it was he!

How was that possible? thought Choco. *Why would anyone have subjected a boy to witness such a violent act? Who were these people?* For a moment he felt sorry for the lad. Choco looked around nervously. *He cannot be alone,* Choco thought; *there must be others.*

He spoke to the crowd. "Who knows this man?"

People started looking around. The crowd was growing now and several started cursing and threatening the soldier.

As Choco started to look around again, he caught movement in the corner of his eye and turned just in time to avoid a kick to the groin. He parried the blow with the side of his thigh and instinctively went into the soldier's body with punches. His glasses flew off his face.

His counter-strike was enough to force the soldier back and they faced off. This time, Choco mounted a boxers attack, jabbing and working his way into his attacker's body again and again, as eight years of frustration released itself and he heard ribs break. The soldier crumbled and Choco started to kick at him, but was pushed to the side as dozens of protesters also began venting their aggression on the fallen soldier. Someone handed Choco his broken glasses, and he noticed that the protesters were now chasing another person down the street. A poster was thrown into a store window and the riot was on.

After the crowd parted, a perplexed Choco looked at the bloody body on the sidewalk. The only discernible mark was the tattooed head of a jaguar on a bare shoulder. A block away, he heard police whistles, and several in the crowd began to run. Armando, who had caught up with Choco, told him it was better that they leave, and began pulling him away. In the distance they heard gunshots. Choco was still confused, but started to move with his friend.

He did not hear nor feel the shot that struck him in the temple. He died instantly and without knowing why. Armando later said that the shot had not come from the police but from somewhere in a nearby building. The bullet had struck swiftly and very accurately.

Guatemala City, Guatemala

A hundred and fifty miles away, Ricardo and Teco lay down for their *siesta* following their *almuerzo*. The children were sleeping, and Lucha had drawn the curtains and turned on a small light above their beds. Relaxed by the silence, Ricardo and Teco drew themselves close to each another.

It was a quiet time that they had come to relish since Miguel Angel had found them a furnished house to rent near his home. Ricardo routinely came home daily at noon and in the evening from his new job as a dental technician for a friend's clinic. It was not yet routine or anything close to a normal life, but they were adjusting. Meanwhile, their love had grown even deeper because of their reliance on each other.

"*Negra*," Ricardo said in a low loving voice, "there is something we need to talk about."

"What, *mí amor*?" said Teco as she nestled closer in his arms. She was smiling and felt warm and safe. Ricardo's attention to her and the children was nothing less than doting. She noticed he was more mature and focused in his role as a father and husband.

"Martínez is finished," he said. "Hugo has put together a skillful plan that even has the Americans shaking their heads in amazement. In two weeks he has turned the disconsolate spirit of the people around and they are making their point in a way that cannot be censored or condemned."

"*Gracias a Díos, cariño*," she said. "When this is over, I want to meet him. You admire him, no?"

"Without question. He and his lieutenants are making dramatic changes."

"And you, too," she added admiringly. "He could not have done it without your work with the Americans."

"I happened to be here, that is all. When I think of what brought me…us here, and how close I came to losing everything…well, I do not feel much like a hero."

"Sh-h-h," she said softly. "That is behind us. We must look forward. Things are going to be just as before. You will see. I have faith in you. When you put your mind to something, you do it. I have been praying to Our Lady, and she has always answered my petitions. We will be celebrating with our friends soon. Chepe, Cora, Choco, Nando. All of them. Ana Maria is getting better. Things are changing for us."

Ricardo was silent. Over the weeks he had told her everything, about Chulio, Carrillo, Marta. He even told her about what had happened to Choco in the *Guardia Civil* and about Gutierrez and his tormented form of exile. He had only left one part out. And now he must tell her.

"*Negra*," he started, "I spoke to Hugo the other day and he told me certain things. I confirmed them with Carlitos and some of the exiled military officers. It has to do with this code of theirs, the military I mean. Martínez violated that code when he publicly tried and executed his officers following the attempted *coup*. More than anything else, that action will not be forgiven or forgotten by the young officer corps. And when the pressure gets high enough, they will make it clear that he does not have their support and he will have to step down. Things are going to change; there is no doubt of that…but not quickly."

Through their embrace, Teco sensed the seriousness of the moment and tensed, unsure of the words that would follow.

181

"Like Martínez' action against his own officers," he continued, "anyone who has targeted the military will not be easily pardoned. The honor of the military institution must be upheld," he said mockingly. "I am convinced that it is their involvement in politics that has corrupted them and eroded their respect."

He paused, recognizing that he was starting to digress. "Sorry, *cariño*, I did not mean to sermonize. What I am trying to say is that those of us who were involved with the guns...well...people died in that effort. I mean, where does one get guns, anyway? You do not plan it that way, but it happens."

He stopped there. Teco was silent and felt a chill. She thought about his words. They had both aged years in the past few months, and still visited their *secret place*. There was nothing more he needed to say or that she wanted to know. She slowly looked up and kissed him deeply and passionately.

When they broke away, she said, "As long as I am with you, I am complete. Our love, like that of Hugo and Marta, is stronger than anything else, and it will carry over to our children and their children, no matter where we are." Then she said sarcastically, "I have seen the evil that has infiltrated their *miseráble* code. What they do is wrong, and if that situation is not going to change, I do not want to ever go back."

"I am not saying that we cannot go back," Ricardo said, "just not right away. We could take our children some place for the time being. Somewhere we do not have to worry about politics."

She smiled and asked teasingly, "Oh, and what place might that be?"

"Well...I do not know. Anderson says he can arrange resident visas for all of us if we want. A visit to the United States for a while could be just the thing."

She gave a knowing and playful laugh.

He smiled back. "Maybe you could write to your sisters in California and I will work on the other details."

"You mean you have not already?" she said raising an eyebrow.

"No," he said. "Well, not completely."

"Liar!"

He smiled and pulled her to him, then reached over her head and turned off the night-light.

Chapter 20

San Salvador, El Salvador

"I need information and I need it fast," said a furious Thurston over the phone to Anderson. "They've killed an American, God damn it!"

"What?" said Anderson, "What happened?" He was sitting in his office at the U.S. Embassy in Guatemala City when the emergency call was patched into his office.

"I'll tell you what I know; it's not much," said the agitated ambassador. "During today's demonstration at the cathedral, it seems that a protester uncovered a soldier posing as a student. A fight broke out and the crowd beat the soldier to death. Then a dentist named Rodrigo Mendez was shot and killed, but we don't know by whom."

Ricardo's business partner, thought Anderson.

"About the same time, several blocks away, the police saw fit to open fire on a crowd that they say was rioting. They hit several people, one of whom, an eighteen-year-old American named Jose Carlos Wright Alcaíne, was killed outright. He is the nephew of that Guatemala exile you know, Miguel Angel Alcaíne. The boy's father is a prominent Salvadoran landowner now living in the U.S."

"Jesus," said Anderson, incredulous about the series of coincidences. "Does Miguel Angel know?"

"I don't know," said the Ambassador curtly, seemingly irritated by the trivial point. "Staff is trying to get more details, but I need answers to a lot of questions, and fast. I don't even have a consular or security officer in town and I'm not getting diddly-squat from the Foreign Ministry. Damn it, Rick, it seems we just had this conversation. What I need right now is a cop, one of ours. They have drug us into their fight and, damn it, I won't stand for their lame excuses. I need you here."

"I'm on my way, sir."

After he absorbed the call from the ambassador and made reservations to leave that night for El Salvador, Anderson went to see Ricardo and Miguel Angel. He found them both at Miguel Angel's home. They had already heard about the Alcaine boy and Choco. A sorrowful Ricardo filled in Anderson about Choco's ordeal many years ago while they were serving in the *Guardia Civil*. Ricardo also offered his theory about how that incident might have been a factor in yesterday's events. Anderson took note, but maintained that his immediate focus had to be the facts surrounding the death of the American.

The astute Ricardo, however, thought there was a connection between the two crimes, and he saw something else, a political opportunity. He recognized a pattern in the violence and told Anderson that he would arrange for Hugo to contact him in San Salvador. After all, who would have better access to inside information than Hugo?

Anderson agreed. Ricardo also saw the immediate danger that these fast-moving events could cause me, since Choco was our interlocutor, and so he asked Anderson to keep me advised. Anderson said he would do that as well.

Then Anderson and Miguel Angel made arrangements to travel together that night on the flight to El Salvador. Miguel Angel was making his first trip back to El Salvador after fifteen years of self-imposed exile. He also sensed the significance of the moment, and chose to make his move. On the way, he briefed Anderson on the background of the Alcaíne family and the sheer injustice of killing such an innocent young schoolboy who was making his first visit to El Salvador.

Ricardo, God bless him, had been right about my situation. He had been through the agony of being uninformed during a crisis, and so could appreciate my reaction. I was, of course, totally distraught when Armando came to my office that day and told me about Choco. I now felt what Ricardo had felt months before when that student *coreo* had come to his clinic with a message to "go see his godfather." I felt the implication of his words in my bones. Choco had linked me with Ricardo and Hugo! I went home immediately, and my Cora and I sequestered ourselves, glued to the radio and telephone.

I was just contemplating a call to Ricardo when I received two astounding telephone calls, one right after the other. The moment I hung up the telephone after the second call, I knew. I knew for the first time and for certain that Ricardo and the others had been on the right side; this was *my* epiphany.

The first call was from the American, Anderson, who assured me that my family and I had nothing to fear. He did not explain how he knew this, but the announcement did offer some relief. The second caller remained anonymous, but I knew who it was, and his words will remain engraved in my heart forever.

I had never met or talked to Hugo, or even wanted to, for that matter. Just the thought of encountering him filled me with apprehension. But now, this "stranger" was taking the time to reach out…to me.

The voice merely said, "We do not know each other, Dr. Molina, but we have mutual friends. The purpose of my call is to assure you that you and your family should be at peace. You are good, patriotic and honest people with many years of joy ahead. *Felicitaciones.*"

And the line went dead. I replayed those words over and over until I could recite them by rote. The messenger could have been a priest or a soothsayer, but he was neither. I knew the meaning of his words, and the message deeply moved me. It also meant something tangential—I was part of their brotherhood. I did not know what I had done to merit this honor, except to be a friend to Ricardo and Choco and, lest it go unsaid, to be a secret sympathizer with their cause.

Apparently that was all it took. I had listened to their voices when they were in need and I had not denounced them. In point of fact, I believed in their cause, despite subliminal efforts to hide behind what was "safe."

I reasoned that while the *martinistas* were censoring public information and killing innocent doctors, Hugo was systematically informing and logically explaining things to us. He understood the essence of freedom of speech, and now many of us did too. Like most people, I also appreciated the priceless quality of sincerity. Because I believed him sincere, I trusted Hugo, and this trust was a bond stronger than faith. There was no doubt in my mind that he had masterfully co-opted me, but he had not lied or pressed while so doing. In the process, I had become a follower, and his words over the telephone that day had been my ordination.

The events of the next days happened very fast and very furiously. During the twenty-four hours following the deaths of Choco and the young Alcaine, Anderson was relentless in pursuing one interview after another. Facilitated by embassy and government assistants, he began taking affidavits from officials and other witnesses. Hugo wasted no time, either. He immediately assessed the significance of the events and made all his information and resources available to the American.

Like an opportunistic card shark in a game of poker, Hugo recognized the right moment and bet everything he had against the house. With Hugo's aid, Anderson took statements from dozens of inside sources. Other, much deeper sources, still fearful of disclosure, would only provide background information, but did provide supporting documents corroborating their data.

One individual in particular stunned Anderson. Hugo introduced him only as a staff sergeant with the pseudonym Tapesquintla. Anderson did not understand the meaning of the word, nor did he care, because what the small fidgety soldier with the mousy face delivered to him was pure gold—copies of Chulio's personal files including the operational plan for Operation Zero.

What Anderson ended up with was a comprehensive picture of official incompetence, overreaction, and blatant violations of the *Guardia's* own policies and directives; all of which contributed to the events of May 7th and caused the violent death of an American citizen. Armed with these findings, a furious Ambassador Thurston demanded and got an audience with Martínez the following day.

"Read the cable, Rick," said Thurston, leaning back in his chair. He had assembled the staff in his conference room at the American Embassy following his meeting with the President to make the formal announcement.

Anderson read, "Quote—'The Ambassador has been notified by President Maximiliano Hernández Martínez, who has served uninterrupted since December 1931, that effective immediately, he is resigning as President of the Republic. The announcement will be made tomorrow, 8 May 1944, during a national radio broadcast at 1900 hours. The National Legislative Assembly will meet within two days to accept his resignation and issue a decree to that effect. In the interim, General Andres Ignacio Menéndez, First Designate and Minister of War, Navy and Aviation, will assume the position of President. Ambassador has met with General Menéndez, who has promised complete cooperation with USG. General Menéndez, as First Designate to the Presidency, has been a strong USG supporter. He has had the complete confidence of President Martínez since assuming his former charge in 1934. He is highly respected within the military and by the private sector. A peaceful transition is expected'—end quote."

There were low whistles, a few "ahhs," and a couple of "wows" around the room. "Well done," someone said.

"Well gentlemen, that's it in a nutshell," said Thurston. "When you have substance, the message does not have to be long. I want this sent to the Secretary, via Flash and Eyes-Only. Meanwhile, the rest of you can start forwarding bios, reactions, and opinions separately. And don't forget opinions, gentlemen. I always found comments helpful when I was on the desk; they form the basis for dialogue. I'll take the heat if someone questions your enterprise."

"How did Martínez take the démarche?" asked the Deputy Chief of Mission. "I recall it was tantamount to an ultimatum."

"Frankly, it was not as difficult as I expected," said the Chargé. "I presented the démarche as approved by the Department this morning, with an attachment of Rick's fine investigative report. I explained that because the subject matter was so grave, I had requested to meet with him personally and bypass the Foreign Ministry. The Foreign Minister was present, by the way.

"The President glanced at the documents but did not read them. He said he would get to it in due course, but I was not going to let him off that easy. I summarized both documents for him. He, in turn, did not defend nor condemn Chulio. I kept looking for body language, but he was his stoic self throughout. His face did not project what he must have felt.

"On the matter of Alcaíne, he said he accepted total responsibility. He said overzealous officers had panicked and acted beyond their authority. There would be a thorough investigation. The police officers who had fired into the crowd had been arrested.

"He said the shooting of the dentist is a mystery to them, and I tend to believe him. Since Chulio had deployed *Jaguares* among the demonstrators without his authority, we can only assume that one of them did the deed. But that is their internal matter. Alcaíne, however, is ours.

"I was prepared to tell him that he must resign, but he preempted me. I could only comment that I felt it was the best thing. He felt he was leaving the Administration in good hands with Menéndez. Martínez is a proud man, but even he recognizes that he has stayed around too long."

The public information officer said, "Mr. Ambassador, there were reportedly thousands of people at the Alcaíne funeral today."

"I did not know the number, Charlie, but I knew it was large. The number of luminaries that attended would have been impressive at a state funeral. They seem to have used the event to also make a reverent political statement. Quite moving. I would have liked to have attended the other funeral as well, but they ran simultaneously, I understand."

"Yes, sir," said a haggard looking Anderson. "I went. Not as many as at the cathedral for Alcaíne, but the number was also notable. Some of the Guatemalan exiles asked that I pass on messages on their behalf to Dr. Mendez' family, which I did. I let them know of your sympathy as well, Mr. Ambassador."

"Thank you, Rick. And let me take this moment to commend Latin America's answer to J. Edgar Hoover for that timely and outstanding report. It brought down the 'mystical tyrant,' as some called him. I'm sure one of our more creative staff members can come up with an appropriate accolade for the occasion. It was 'above and beyond,' Rick."

"Thank you, sir, but there were more than enough people willing to come forward on this one. I just recorded what they said. Hugo set up interviews with his most secret sources within the military. They provided copies of Presidential Directives and other information, such as Chulio's unauthorized deployment known as Operation Zero.

"Cruz was able to explain how Mendez might have been able to recognize one of the *Jaguares* from many years before. Mendez had only confided to Cruz that he thought he had seen a young boy as a member of the group that attacked him. Only he knew that, but it explained several things, including the rumors that we had heard for years about youth camps similar to those run by the Nazis. You know, sir, Cruz said something to me when we first met that has proven true: They *do* know their tyrant. They knew that egregious violence was more apt to come from the *martinistas,* and that in the end it would be their undoing."

"Well done, Rick. But I think you are being too modest."

"Hear, hear," said the group, and everyone in the room burst into applause.

The old diplomat blushed. The fast pace of the unfolding events had congested his mind. *Los inocentes y los no inocentes*, he thought. *You were right*, Hugo. The unwitting actions of the innocents and the death of an innocent boy, who did die without knowing why, were enough to bring down their oppressor.

Outside the Embassy, horns were honking and people could be seen milling around the downtown streets trying to confirm the rumor. There were no secrets in this small country. Within hours, *El Diario de Hoy* carried a banner headline and sub-comment:

MARTÍNEZ RESIGNS
General Strike Successful

Chapter 21

The next day, a solemn Chulio visited a convalescing Carrillo at the El Salvador military hospital. The wounds to Carrillo's legs, back, and buttocks were healing well enough for him to sit up periodically, but they were still sore. Chulio used the pretext of the visit to hold a covert meeting of his commanders to discuss the political situation.

"Martínez' resignation," Chulio started, "means General Menéndez will take over immediately. He is a *Santaneco* and knows how to rule. Menéndez plans to reorganize the Cabinet and will honor some of the recommendations made by the followers of Dr. Arturo Romero. You no doubt recall that Romero led the largest opposition against Martínez and organized the *Partido de Unificacíon Democrática*."

Heads nodded and Carrillo started to say something, but was stopped by Chulio's glare.

"Menéndez will also announce that free elections will be held in January 1946," Chulio continued. "And he will rescind the order to censor the press. Recognizing the PUD and announcing elections will mollify the Americans. Releasing the press will disarm Altamirano, who recently founded another political party, *Frente Social Republicano.* Other political parties are also being organized." He shook his head, then shrugged.

"While all this seems threatening to public order, Menéndez has confidentially told me that there was logic to some of these concessions. Allowing various liberal parties will keep them divided and nipping at each other. Perhaps he is right; we will see.

"Meanwhile, it is imperative that the transition be seen as peaceful. Menéndez has promised this to the American Ambassador and it is important that the Americans not interfere with the real agenda, which is to insure a proper power transfer within the military. While I disagree with all this appeasement, maintaining our unity is vital. Unlike Menéndez, I do not trust the PUD on this point, and I made this clear to him."

"Everyone knows that Romero is a communist, *mí general*," said Carrillo dramatically, unable to control himself. "It was a miracle that we did not kill the coward last year when we shot him in the face trying to flee into Honduras. The 9 mm bullet was too fast at close range; a slower .45 caliber would have been better."

Chulio ignored the interruption. "What we need," he informed them, "is time to assess where loyalties lie and time to let the Americans fade away. I am not going to publicly oppose the order to dissolve the *Jaguares,* because it is not expedient to do so. But it is merely symbolic. I will continue as

Director of the *Guardia*. In due course, another change of leadership may be necessary."

He paused to let the seditious remark register. He narrowed his eyes and made eye contact with each man before continuing. Two of the officers exchanged a blank stare at each other, as if confirming that they both had heard the same thing.

"We will prepare for that moment," Chulio continued. "The fall of General Ubico in Guatemala is imminent. Already forces are organizing to replace him with Dr. Juan Jose Arevalo, an Argentine lector and another communist. With enough time, our prominent families, and even the Americans, will have empirical proof of communist plans to take over the region. At the right moment, we will step forward once again and be recognized as the true protectors of our Republic."

Then Chulio turned to Carrillo and said irritably, "I want you to take advantage of this self-indulgent public celebration to finish what you started."

"*A la orden, mi general.*"

"I sent the list of the Salvadoran exiles to the *Chapines*. Lieutenant Okler delivered my letter personally to General Castro-Niche; he is over there now offering assistance."

"*Mi general*, I will discharge myself immediately and will be in Guatemala tomorrow. You can count on me."

"Very well. Let Okler handle it, but you supervise it closely."

"*Si, mi general*"

The meeting lasted another half-hour, primarily reviewing administrative matters. By 10 P.M., Chulio and his staff left the hospital and went their separate ways. By then, final round inspections had been started by the night watch.

The wing Carrillo inhabited was reserved for officers and was located on the side furthest from the main road. Adjacent to his room was a grove of trees and thick vegetation that extended the length of the building and served as a barrier from the exercise field used by the recruits at the *Escuela Militar* next door. Throughout the day, the sounds from military drills were clearly audible and had served as a distraction for Carrillo.

During the *coup* attempt, he had listened irritably to the radio broadcasts from his bed. First there had been anti-Martínez broadcasts and a call to arms. Then, for what seemed like most of the day, Carrillo had heard the sounds of gunfire and bombs in the distance. And finally, he smugly listened to the evening radio announcement by Martínez that the attempted *coup* had failed.

Martínez had read off the names of the arrested military traitors, and Carrillo had not been surprised. His people had been watching most of them. The next day brought news of their summary executions of the traitor officers, and Carrillo gloated.

After a few days, however, his apprehension returned. There were rumors of a lobbying group encouraging citizens to join in a work strike. Then he listened to the daily reports of the faction gaining momentum. *A people's strike*, Carrillo had disgustedly pondered, *who would have thought. It had to be Hugo! Who else*?

And then, during a riot, Carrillo heard that they had killed Beto. Beto had been one of his favorites, a true *jaguar*; he had seen it in his eyes, Carrillo remembered, even as a child. He had heard that it had taken dozens to best him and that he had taken several of them with him, and without a weapon.

That part had not been reported in the press, Carrillo had noted contemptuously, only that the *maricón* Mendez had exposed him. Well, he thought, Mendez would not be exposing anyone again; Okler had seen to that. Carrillo was proud of all his men.

Lost in these thoughts, he barely heard the door open. He turned from his facedown position on the bed to see an orderly in a white smock carrying a tray. The orderly closed the door behind him and slowly approached Carrillo.

"What the devil do you want?" he barked.

"The doctor wants you to have a vitamin shot before you are discharged," said the orderly, and waited to see how Carrillo would react.

Carrillo eyed the man warily. "Well give it to me in the arm," said an irritated Carrillo as he rolled up a sleeve.

"As you wish, major," said the man.

Carrillo eyed him. He was older than the usual orderlies and light-skinned for a *cholero*, he thought. He had not seen him before, but something about him was familiar.

Carrillo watched him closely, but the orderly seemed to know what he was doing. He cleared the air in the syringe through the needle, and then swabbed the target portion of the upper right arm with a wet cotton ball before carefully inserting the needle through the skin and injecting the fluid. He then swabbed the exit with alcohol-soaked cotton. Still holding the needle, the orderly then took a step back.

Carrillo was about to ask him his name and rank when he was hit with a jolt of nausea and dizziness. His tongue felt swollen, and he could not make himself move quickly. When he tried to speak his larynx shuddered and the sounds were blocked by a wave of vomit that rose from his stomach and spewed out his mouth. He coughed and sputtered. The orderly just watched as the man continued to soil himself with the granular fluids that continued nonstop.

After a few minutes, the seizures became intermittent and the orderly said in a calm and quiet voice, "It will pass soon, Carrillo, then we will talk. It is difficult to know how much animal tranquilizer to give humans." As he said this, he sucked a capsule of air into the empty syringe. Carrillo continued to retch periodically.

The orderly leaned close to him and said, "Listen carefully: When we talk, you will not scream out or resist. You will speak and act calmly, all right?"

Carrillo could not speak, but made wincing eye contact. As he started to calm down, the orderly quickly turned Carrillo's head and expertly inserted the needle into the carotid artery on the side of his neck.

The man said, "I would not move too quickly, Carrillo, because my thumb on the end of this hypodermic might slip and then your brain will explode."

Carrillo was frozen with fear and panic. He did not even feel the prick of the needle, just the force on his neck.

"Now, let us talk," said the orderly, leaning over close, his mouth next to one ear. Calmly he continued, "Tell me, Carrillo, do you like to read...you know, books...say, anything by Dumas?"

The man was deranged, thought Carrillo. He tried to speak but when he did, he started to gag and had to swallow fast. His confused and terrified eyes were bulging and darting back and forth, but he resisted moving. He could still feel the firm pressure on his neck.

"I know it is hard to speak," said the understanding voice, "So you should try to answer by either nodding or shaking your head. But not too quickly now, you do not want to upset my grip. Now where were we? Ah yes...we were talking about Dumas. He writes so well about retribution, would you not agree? You remember Edmond Dantes and his quest for vengeance?"

Carrillo's eyes tried not to show fear by narrowing, but the orderly read his thoughts and said slowly, "No, I would not do that, and yes, I am mad. So, tell me, do you remember Dantes? Just move your head one way or the other."

After a moment, the man's head moved gradually from side to side.

"Oh...that is too bad. You see, if you did, you would better understand what I am going to propose. Are you a devote Catholic?"

Again a pause, then a slight nod.

"Good, that helps. You see, I know that you have killed many innocent people, and like many of Dumas' villains, you are not worthy of paradise in the afterlife. But vengeance really belongs to God, does it not? So, here is my proposition. For you to continue living in this world, you will have to

192

renounce God and forfeit any glory in the hereafter." The orderly paused to let the words sink in. "Do you understand?"

Again a slight nod.

"If you break this oath, He and I will know. Do you understand that?"

The suspicious eyes flickered; he understood better now. The orderly was not only deranged but also a religious fanatic; killing was a sin to them. This was a morbid and meaningless effort to seek revenge by some mystical ritual. *Pathetic!* Carrillo thought, as he gave a small nod.

"Good. So tell me on your mother's grave, on the oath of the *Jaguares*, that you renounce God."

The eyes stopped moving and a hint of mockery twinkled in them. His head slowly nodded.

"Try to say the words, Carrillo, 'I renounce God.'"

Carrillo focused and his mouth started to move slowly. He slurred, "Ah-h re-ou-ou-ce ou-oughd." He needed to cough, but just swallowed rapidly.

"You renounce God?" The orderly asked triumphantly.

Carrillo nodded, and to his horror, understood who the man was.

"Then, rot in hell," said the orderly disdainfully as his thumb pushed the plunger to the hilt and he stepped back.

Carrillo jerked uncontrollably. Soon, the violent jolts subsided and he lay still. His eyes were wide, bulging, and frozen in an expression of incredulity.

Unlike the one in the classic novel, this vengeful execution was successful. It would now be up to God, thought the man, to decide whether this unrepentant and miserable soul, or I for that matter, merit a place anywhere near *los inocentes* or, for that matter, anywhere near the spirit of a faithful dog.

At five in the morning, Chulio was awakened with the news that Carrillo had been found dead. The preliminary diagnosis was some type of convulsion that had occurred during the night. Chulio would hear none of that explanation; he would see to it personally.

By 5:30 A.M., he was dressed for his morning run. He never started a day without this five-kilometer ritual. Despite these setbacks, first Martínez, and now Carrillo, he was not going to lose focus. He had much planning to do, and the *Jaguares* were still a loyal and feared force.

He stepped out of his living quarters in the center of the *Campo Marte* garrison and spotted the two figures standing at attention by their parked motorcycles. The two *Jaguares* were in full battle gear, cradling their German MP 40 submachine guns. It was traditional for the guards to jog along behind him for the five kilometers around the grounds. It was an honor to accompany the Director during his exercise; volunteers lined up for the duty.

Chulio smiled and recited his mantra: *We are fiercer and braver and will live forever.* Chulio stretched his hamstrings, his calves, then stood erect and inhaled several gulps of the sweet morning air. Dawn had not yet broken, but the birds were already stirring noisily in their nests. Chulio took it all in before trotting down the path towards the waiting soldiers. As he passed them, he noted that these were new men and that would explain why they had not shut down the motors to their bikes. Neither had they started their jogging in place before he passed. He only went a few yards before deciding to turn and angrily reproach them.

The first rounds were low and hit the dirt pavement and his legs. But as they are prone to do when on full automatic, machineguns mechanically rise from the repeated and furious striking of the ejection bolts against the housing. The next volley struck Chulio in the chest and face. The two men continued to empty the rest of their 20 round clips into the twisting body.

Just before his confused mind totally disengaged from his body, Chulio saw that the uniforms did not have the unmistakable emblem of the spotted yellow and black cat.

Guatemala City, Guatemala

Lieutenant Pedro Okler had not heard about the deaths of Carrillo or Chulio. He had been patiently waiting with the other *Jaguar*, Lieutenant Ignacio Marr, outside Carlos Escudes' residence. It was 10 A.M. in the morning and they had been there most of the night. Yesterday, Okler had delivered Chulio's letter to General Castro-Niche of the Guatemalan *Hacienda* Military Police and waited for a response. Receiving none, he and his companion had implemented the alternative plan given to them by Chulio.

"If the *Chapines* do not request your services in eliminating the traitors, you will acknowledge your mission completed to the general and inform him of your plans to return here immediately. Before leaving, however, attempt to locate the people on this separate list."

Chulio had handed Okler another, thinner envelope. "These are Salvadoran traitors known to be responsible for the murder of our soldiers. If the opportunity presents itself, you are to act against them unilaterally. Am I clear?"

Okler had replied enthusiastically. It was the type of assignment he relished.

That same evening, Okler and Marr had located the home of the first person on the list, the attorney Carlos Escudes. They returned in the morning and waited most of the day parked in a *callejon*, an alley behind another house across from Escudes' home. So far, the two *Jaguares* had seen Escudes arrive at 4 P.M. and not leave. Another person on their list, the dentist Cruz, arrived at 5:15 P.M. Two other men, with faces resembling those on copies of passport pictures Okler and Marr carried, had entered a short time later. According to the dossiers, they were former Salvadoran students, Thomas Elkingson and Leo Guíen.

Their patience had paid off, thought Okler; four of them, a good catch. They would just wait a few more minutes until the daylight expired. If Escudes or Cruz exited before they were ready, they would take them on the street. But under the cover of darkness, there was a possibility that they could get all four inside the house. He and Marr had checked their Luger automatics several times. With the folding stock attachments and six-inch barrels, the 9 mm weapons were accurate within fifty meters. It would be the same type of shot that had killed the dentist Mendez, Okler mused.

Just then, the two *Jaguares* saw movement at the front door. One man was coming out and two more were standing by the door. One was Cruz. He was leaving. Okler motioned for Marr to follow him, and they noiselessly slipped out of the front doors of the dark sedan. They made their way along a hedge where they were partially hidden from the front of Escudes' house. They had a clear field of fire. Okler's hand motion indicated he would take Cruz, leaving Marr to take the man on the right. Two shots each, then they would focus on other targets of opportunity. It was standard procedure. The figures were more than adequately silhouetted against the house lights.

As they were bracing the shoulder stocks to steady their aim, the headlights of a car approaching from their right caused them to pause and crouch low. Okler quickly realized that it was not just one vehicle, but three, and they were stopping in front of Escudes' house. Okler glanced over the hedge and noted that the lead car was a large black Buick sedan with diplomatic markings, an American car. The other cars were camouflaged ten-year old Essex coupes, the type used by the *Hacienda* military.

Were the Chapines acting on the list? Okler wondered. But then, the diplomatic car did not make sense. He saw Cruz wave at a *norteamericano* who was exiting the diplomatic car. Then the two entered the house.

The befuddled *Jaguares* made their way back to their car. Before they could speak, Okler noted that another car was coming up behind them in the *callejon* with its headlights off. Without hesitation, Okler started his car and pulled out onto the main street. As he and Marr drove away from the neighborhood, he spied through his mirror that there were two camouflaged vehicles now following them.

Several days later, Carlitos invited Ricardo to meet him at a café near the miniature replica of the Eiffel Tower on the outskirts of Guatemala City. When he got there, Ricardo saw the man sitting alone in a corner of the café drinking milk and smoking a cigarette.

"Ricardo, my brother!" Hugo called, standing up.

Ricardo smiled and shook his head slowly. Carlitos had not said why, but from his voice, Ricardo had sensed it was more business than social. Instead, the unpredictable Hugo had surprised him yet again.

"I take it you are Carlitos today," said Ricardo.

"I did not want to disappoint you by failing to make a dramatic entrance," Hugo said.

He looked tired, older, and wore the beginnings of a beard, but was not disheveled as when they had last met. And he still wore his trademark gray and black cowboy boots.

After a firm *abrazo,* Ricardo said, "And what is this miracle, a trip all this way from El Salvador just to see me?"

"Oh, I will be seeing some other people, but mainly…yes. After all, it will be more difficult to get Paco to fly me all the way to California to see you," Hugo said, smiling.

"I will not be away for long, Hugo. I will be back."

"Of course you will. And how is your family?"

"Apprehensive, engaged in preparations, although we are not taking much with us. We will be totally dependent on the generosity of my wife's sisters, who have offered their home until we get settled. I will give you the address and we can write. It is on Missouri Street in San Francisco."

"Thank you, Ricardo, but I will not be writing much, and I do not want to carry your address around with me. But we can continue to use Carlitos or Miguel Angel."

"Yes, of course," said Ricardo. "It is just that a great deal has happened and…well…there is so much that I want to say. Besides, where else am I going to get my inside news?"

Hugo smiled back at him. "Oh, you will always find a way, I am sure. Actually, Ricardo, I need to go away myself, but there are some things I wanted to disclose to you personally."

"Ah yes, I heard about Chulio and the considerable manhunt for his killers. Do I dare ask what you know?" Ricardo asked seriously.

Hugo dismissed the question, as he was apt to do when diverted by other thoughts. It was a haughty side that had always annoyed Ricardo, but a trait he had learned to tolerate. In deference, he waited for Hugo to make his point.

"Ricardo," Hugo began deliberately, "first, I want you to know that my real name is Valentín Aurelio Magaña; my family was from San Marcos. I am 36 years old. In 1932, I was a lieutenant in the *Guardia*, a graduate of the first *tanda* in 1930. Memo Gutierrez was my professor.

"I was a loyal, even idealistic soldier until Martínez ordered the wanton killing of those innocent peasants in Izalco, and I was turned into a butcher. The commander, a Colonel Mojano, ordered me to expedite the executions. I refused and tried to desert, but was caught and he ordered me killed. I escaped but not before killing him."

Ricardo noted that Hugo's vice was disdainful, but rather penitent, a side he had not seen before.

"I did it," Hugo said painfully, "because he was a callous bloodthirsty coward who relished killing and had turned *me* into a killer. I fled the country and ended up battling similar fiends in Europe. After several years, I returned to fight them here. Now, as a result, the woman I loved and my two daughters are dead." He lowered his head for a moment, then continued sardonically, "But we did manage to overthrow the purported cause of all our grief."

He raised his head and looked intently at Ricardo as if waiting for a reaction. Most of this information Ricardo already knew, so he expected that there was a point to this affirmation, and just nodded and waited.

Hugo continued offhandedly, "You asked about Chulio. Well, there is an example of the mocking truth. Although our cause was noble and although we ousted the tyrant, the outcome may not have been as righteous as we expected. Our actions were at times as evil as those we condemned."

Ricardo was not following him. But he had seen this rambling before and continued to wait.

"Who killed Chulio, you ask?" Hugo sneered. "I wanted it to be me. But it was not. A sign was left next to his body. It read, 'Death to the Tormenter.' He had over thirty bullets in his body." He was shaking his head with a half smile.

"Quite a feat, no?" Hugo continued. "Someone diverted his escorts, got past all the security at the *cuartel*, boldly stood less than ten feet away from a man in better shape than most hardened recruits, and fearlessly executed him over and over. Oh, and then escaped undetected. And the imbeciles would have us believe the words on a stupid sign. Them continuing to think that we are so dim-witted is perhaps the saddest thing of all."

Hugo was on the brink of tears.

"Ricardo, I want to tell you that we have won the honorable fight, that some of us may have to leave for appearances' sake, but that we will all return in a short period to a better country. I want to tell you that, but I cannot. Changes here will take longer than we thought. Let us just leave it at that."

Hugo's words were distressing and flatly stated. Both men were much wiser than they had been a few months before, and both knew that there was more behind these sentiments. They had lost their innocence and their egocentrism. But the gained wisdom and deep respect and consideration for others had come at a great price.

Ricardo said, "Hugo—and incidentally, I think I will always call you that—I am convinced that what we have done here will make a difference. You are right, it will take time, but things will change. Do not despair. Look, come with us instead. We can wait out the political posturing in *El Norte.* I am sure Anderson can help you with a visa."

Hugo made a vain attempt at displaying amusement and said, "No, Ricardo, I could not do that." Then more seriously, he added, "I know where I must go and what I must do. There is nothing for me away from this country. But I promise we will see each other again."

Ricardo could not find the words to express in a manly way his feelings at that moment. He reached over, gripped Hugo's forearm, and nodded. Hugo was a warrior, had always been, and now the war was over. It was not clear to Ricardo what someone like Hugo would do now. Where would he focus his genius at organization and strategy? What cause would he undertake? Then Ricardo recalled their meeting in Retalhuleu and Hugo's "epiphany." *I know where I must go and what I must do,* he had said.

"Thank you, Hugo, for everything." Ricardo said soberly.

"Por nada, *mi hermano. Que Dios siempre te cuide.*"

"God watch over you, too, Hugo," Ricardo said in reply.

Outside the café, horns were honking, and the loudspeaker on a truck was blaring political slogans in favor of some candidate. A group of children—*patojos* the Guatemalans call them—were chasing alongside the van yelling back mockingly at the announcer. And on a nearby street corner, jeeps with soldiers inside keenly observed the scene, while sullen-faced pedestrians quickly moved along in silence.

And so, we are now back where I started this tale, on the tarmac of the Guatemalan International airport, La Aurora, where Ricardo, Teco, Ricardo León, and Ana Maria are in a queue waiting to board the bright silver and orange Aviateca DC-3.

On the other side of a chain-link fence, a sad group of well-wishers crowds together. Among them, my Cora and I, silently weeping, savor a last glimpse. As they approach the doorway of the airplane, the children are frightened by the loud sputtering and smoke from the engines as the propellers begin to turn. Ricardo and Teco are trying to distract them. We quietly watch, still hung over from the effects of that traumatic farewell scene in the lounge just a half-hour before.

I admit that, for a psychiatrist, I am hopelessly sentimental about those I love, and I love these people dearly. In the waiting area, I had dramatically told Ricardo and anyone else who would listen that it was unnatural for anyone to leave friends, family and country in this fashion. No one would ever understand the sacrifice involved in moving away from everything that is familiar. As the time drew near we embraced, and that was when I told him I would chronicle for him and his children what they... we...all of us, had just gone through. All he said was that we would see each other soon.

Interestingly enough, Teco had the greatest problem of all in her parting with Lucha. That scene was the most poignant to all there. It transcended social mores and customs. It was pure and unaffected. Teco shed all pretentiousness; Lucha did not have to. Their embrace said: *We are who we are born to be and yet, all essentially the same.*

Anderson, Carlitos, Ricardo and I had huddled briefly and discussed some last-minute news. The war was virtually over in Europe, and Japan could not hold out much longer. But we were just making perfunctory man-talk to pass the time. We did not speak of Hugo, the man and the cause that had brought us all together. As I said, no one had any information about him, although we did not believe he had been taken. Wherever he was, we knew it would not be far from Izalco.

Anderson did not tell Ricardo about Chulio's last order to his *Jaguares*, but he told me. I agreed that it had been a close call, and that no one on those lists would be safe if they stayed in the region. Anderson volunteered the information that it was only when General Castro-Niche learned of Chulio's death that he passed the information about Chulio's letter on to the Embassy. Anderson had immediately recognized the implications and acted; this was the danger that Ricardo had feared when they originally formed their alliance.

Anderson admitted that he had to embellish the information that Tapesquintla had given him to get Castro-Niche to act. He disclosed Chulio's secret plan to attack dissenters. Although Operation Zero had not been directed at the exiles, Anderson convinced the general that this action was part of that plan and could cause a major diplomatic crisis. The ruse had enough credence to satisfy the head of the Guatemalan Hacienda Police and he had placed several units at Anderson's disposal to rescue Ricardo and Carlitos.

Anderson did not know what had happened to the *Jaguares* who had been detained, but undoubtedly they were handled as political liabilities. Perhaps similar minds concoct similar diabolical solutions, I thought.

If asked, we merely say that we detained them, but they were released. If they developed a pang of conscience and fled the country, that is not our problem.

Besides, who was going to look for them in Guatemala, Anderson commented, if they were not supposed to be there in the first place?

Although Anderson explained these events in detail, the intrigues were far beyond my comprehension and only served to convince me that the conflict was nowhere near being over. And something else came to mind: The belligerency in these small countries will never be about the struggle between good and evil, but between those who perceive themselves to be on the "right" side, a case of good versus good.

This is a concept I have trouble with. Let me just say here that extremism, in any form, cannot benefit any majority. And if you will allow me an inappropriate aphorism for a psychiatrist, it is my opinion that *political* extremists are all *crazy* and well beyond cure. I will continue to treat the less malignant forms of psychic distress—the desperate, the anxious, and the doubters, but I will leave the political alone.

As we lingered inside the terminal, Anderson practiced his diplomatic skills in order to break up the solemn mood. Actually, I found his efforts quite *simpatico*, my reaction a far cry from the jealous sentiments I had felt when we first met. He told us about the large glass-framed copy of the front page of a Salvadoran newspaper given to him by Ambassador Thurston and the Salvadoran embassy staff after Martínez resigned. There were only two words covering the whole page: "*SE FUE*," referring to Martínez' flight from El Salvador to Honduras.

There had been a story on the inside pages that quoted from the former President's departing sermon. The excerpt read:

"I do not believe in history because history is written by mere men.—Generál Maximiliano H. Martínez."

Being one of the "mere men," I told Anderson of my promise to Ricardo about writing this account, and he genially offered to contribute what he knew.

I have come to believe that Anderson is truly a good man. I say this because of something he confided in me on the day we met. I paid little mind at the time, because I was still inclined to think him supercilious. It had to do with what had attracted him to his career many years ago. He said that if he was able to inject a farthing of reason during times of hostility and conflict, he was satisfied. Well, I think he certainly gave a good account of himself during this crisis.

As we were breaking up, Carlitos, Miguel Angel and some of the other exiles agreed to get together for drinks later at one of their homes to toast Ricardo. "With just a splash of soda," I had added, and the mood livened.

Just then, a loud rumbling noise outside distracted us and we all turned towards windows that faced the runway. As it roared past the airport, the bright orange and yellow Aviateca flight to Mexico City lifted off, and we kept it in sight as it slowly gained altitude over the city.

In the lull that followed, we distractedly looked at our watches—it was only an hour late. We exchanged wry smiles.

Vaya con Dios, Dr. Cruz.

Epilogue

As it turned out, Ricardo was the last member of the underground, or anyone I know for that matter, to see Hugo again. In the months that followed, I heard rumors that he had returned to live in Izalco under another name, but I do not know that for sure. It was logical, perhaps too logical for the unpredictable Hugo.

Ricardo, Teco and the children are in San Francisco, California and he is working for an American dental chain of offices called Painless Parker, of all things. We receive letters often. The children are healthy and my friend seems content. He tells me that several other exiles, including Carlitos, Armando, and Tomas ended up in San Francisco, and they have started community in an area called the Mission District. I sense the nostalgia in his words and I certainly miss him, but things have not improved enough politically for him to return. At least, not yet.

With the exception of the huge hole he left in my life, my Cora and I continue to enjoy our children and this land. We are wiser about politics, and aside from an occasional civic obligation, we keep to our personal routines, no different than before Martínez. We are tied to this land and will not stray far from it, not even to visit my oldest and dearest friend.

The only noteworthy event related to this story occurred several months after Ricardo left. Unexpectedly one day, I received a tattered copy of Friedrich Nietzsche's *Twilight of the Idols*, which the German thinker wrote in 1889. It came in the post and the source was anonymous. I thought maybe Choco's wife had sent it to me as a keepsake, because he and I were always debating the man's abstractedness. But I checked, and it was not from her.

I then surmised that it must have come from Hugo. It was like him, always choosing the unorthodox approach. After I browsed through it, I became more convinced that I was right. In the chapter, "Expeditions of an Untimely Man," which had to do with spirituality, a passage had been underlined. It read:

"The most spiritual human beings, assuming they are the most courageous, also experience by far the most painful tragedies: but it is precisely for this reason that they honor life, because it brings against them its most formidable weapons."

Was Hugo referring to his *inocentes* or to all of us? I guess I will never know for sure. As I say, I never saw him again to ask.

So why did I write the story? The short answer is: Because I could. I was Hugo's scribe, the one with the "inside" information. But that was not the only reason. I was aware that I was being manipulated. A more compelling *raison d'être*, perhaps, is Nietzsche's philosophical observation about man's fixation with what preceded him.

> "Man..." he wrote, "cannot learn to forget, but hangs on the past: however far or fast he runs, that chain runs with him."

To understand the reasons that your father brought you to live in a foreign land, you must understand your father and the value he places on his "moment"—his story. Again, Nietzsche:

> "Because men really respect only that which was founded of old and has developed slowly, he who wants to live on after his death must take care not only of his posterity but even more of his past."

In other words, Ricardo's plight, and the plight of all displaced Salvadorans of that period, needed to be recorded. And who else was going to do it? In my small country, it has never been wise to call attention to ourselves, let alone author anything historical.

Then there is the personal reason. I went through many changes of opinion and attitude because of this man, more than at any other time in my life. I am also recording these vicissitudes for my family, for my children and theirs. Too often men die without disclosing their innermost feelings and their reasons for doing the most outlandish of things. What I would give to be able to quiz my father, for example, about the events he witnessed personally, events that have now come to affect so many of us. Fathers tend to withhold the ugliness of the world from us, and that is fine for children, but as a man, I find the truth more beautiful and compelling.

And finally, there are the others—the displaced ones. Ricardo and Carlitos were but two of the thousands who moved their families away from everything that was holy to them because of fear or guilt. In turn, they will pull others to the new land because that is the nature of migration. And one day their children, like my godchildren, will want to know the truth, and the most they will get will be a theater of hearsay performed by actors with uncertain props.

Perhaps there are other reasons for this writing, subliminal ones that would tire me to search for, but these are the main ones, the ones that are important to remember.

Respectfully submitted, 4th of July 1948.

About the Author

Richard L. Cañas spent most of his 34-year government career with the U. S. Drug Enforcement Administration, serving in numerous domestic and foreign offices. He was also a member of the Senior Executive Service with the Department of Justice and served as Director of the National Drug Intelligence Center, Director for Counterterrorism and Counternarcotics at the National Security Council, and Special Assistant to the Directorate for Operations at the Central Intelligence Agency. During his tenure at the NSC he authored and vetted numerous national security policy documents.

Mr. Cañas is a graduate of the California State University at San Jose and received a Technical Teaching Credential from the University of California at Berkley. He has lectured extensively at numerous California colleges and Washington DC national security think tanks.

Mr. Cañas was born in El Salvador and immigrated to the U.S. in 1945. He is married to the former Elaine Betts Smith and they live with two of their five children, Frank and Sara, in Richmond, Virginia.

Decade of Iron is the author's second book. It is the prequel to *Jaguars—A tale of El* Salvador, which was also published by 1st Books Library.

www.ingramcontent.com/pod-product-compliance
Lightning Source LLC
Chambersburg PA
CBHW030313290526
45785CB00001B/334